"*Overarching Patterns* is not only a wor ........ on a complex subject—culture—but an .......... gated patterns globally. The flow of ideas, laid out in very succinct chapters, holds attention throughout and provokes incessant reflection. For anyone fascinated, intrigued, confused, or just inquisitive about patterns of culture in various global contexts, this is almost a mandatory read."

—**Prabir Jha**, Mumbai, India, President and Global Chief People Officer of Cipla

"Fascinating! The book deepened my understanding about how 'consciously incompetent' I am when it comes to understanding other cultures. . . . This book is an extremely helpful resource for anyone engaged in cross-cultural work. It will heighten awareness and understanding of cultural divides and lead to more effectiveness in getting things done with and through people from other cultures."

—**Stephen Anson**, Perth, Australia, Co-Founder and CEO of Vortala Digital

"We live in a world of architypes. All stories revolve around seven basic plots. Human personality falls into a limited number of predictable types. And culture, as the Strausses—father and son—so admirably show here, can be grouped into four overarching (though overlapping) patterns. This is the hitchhikers' guide to the universe of perceptions and behaviors, applicable immediately and everywhere, from your next trip to a Chinese restaurant to a venture into the old quarter of Hyderabad. The tale is told through stories and anecdotes, as captivating as a travelogue. Their globetrotting— eyes wide open, curiosity and humility at full tilt, a passion for observing, learning, and synthesis—has led to this fascinating guide. A triumph!"

—**Ken Strauss**, MD, Brussels, Belgium, Endocrinology Fellowship at Harvard Medical School, Global Medical Director of Becton Dickenson

"What the authors have done is to artfully translate the understandings and perspectives of an anthropologist to the practical insights and needs of students of culture. The foundational, fundamental, and practical frameworks come together to assure that readers are better prepared for their intercultural and interpersonal interaction across multiple cultures. The personal stories and examples they share are equally delightful and insightful."

—**Kenneth Cushner**, Emeritus Professor at Kent State University and Fellow with the International Academy for Intercultural Research

"The book is phenomenal. . . the father-son-scholars make cultural behaviors, values, patterns, and application of knowledge accessible to anyone wanting to deepen their understanding of cultural frameworks in a concise manner. With the publication of *Four Overarching Patterns of Culture*, Strauss and Strauss have given us a gift—a tangible strategy for building intercultural competency through triangulating observable behavior and patterns of culture with actionable insights."

—**Mary Kay Park**, Executive Managing Director, Far East Broadcasting Company-Korea in Los Angeles, and Adjunct Professor in Intercultural Studies at Biola University, Middlebury Institute of International Studies, and Gateway Seminary

"Countless introductory books on a topic are so general as to be impractical. *Overarching Patterns* is not one of them. Robert and Christopher Strauss give us one of the most concise yet comprehensive overviews of culture and worldview I've read. And somehow the book is full of concrete examples! Because they present various worldview patterns in a balanced way, this book also prepares people to appreciate cultural complexities with humility. What else could one ask for?"

—**Jackson Wu**, author of *One Gospel for All Nations* and *Saving God's Face*

"*Four Overarching Patterns of Culture* provides a practical framework for the critically needed but often underdeveloped and overlooked concept of worldview, as well as the cultural patterns of thinking and behaving that emerge from it. An integral part of culture, worldview is the powerful but invisible force that drives everything people think, say, and do. True competence and success in a global environment cannot be achieved without understanding predominant cultural patterns. On the cutting edge in the private and public sectors, this book explains four prominent patterns and outlines practical advice for applying that knowledge in real-world situations."

—**Elena Tartaglione**, Germany, Founder of Global Perspectives Consulting

"I have had the honor of working with Robert many years as a scholar, practitioner, and fellow learner. I have seen his work put to practical use both domestically and internationally. Now he has captured not only the four overarching patterns of culture but also stories and recommendations to improve our cultural interactions. This book is a useful resource for both the scholar and the businessperson looking to improve self-awareness, interpersonal understanding, and intercultural effectiveness."

—**Angela Edwards**, Coaching Practice Leader at the Center for Creative Leadership in Colorado Springs, Colorado, and Owner of AK Edwards Consulting

"This is a beautifully written book grounded in both theoretical rigor and practicality. The stories are vivid and varied, ranging from the Middle East and India to the Southern United States. Whether you are a student or educator of culture or a business traveler who desires insight before embarking to a new land, this is a great read."

—**Paige Graham**, Senior Faculty at the Center for Creative Leadership in Colorado Springs, Colorado, and President of Graham Consulting Group

"My reading of the manuscript was interrupted by a trip that involved helping a team analyze cultural material. Two days into the consultation, 'fear/power' leanings were suspected. Remembering one of Strauss' chapter headings, we read 'Harmony.' Lights came on. All around."

—**Mike Matthews**, Owner of Novel Approach Konsulting and author of *A Novel Approach: The Significance of Story in Interpreting and Communicating Reality*

"There are many books available that focus on cultural and intercultural issues. However, there are only a few that deal with these issues as comprehensively as *Four Overarching Patterns of Culture*. A study of culture is a study about the commonalities within communities of people, in terms of inward assumptions of reality and outward expressions of behavior. With intellectual expertise, out of a wealth of experience, Dr. Strauss and his son Christopher carry the reader first through a journey exploring the underpinnings of these community commonalities, then the construction of a framework to facilitate success when everything is common within the community but different to me. An abundance of diagrams and figures showing the nature and relationships of their observations provide clarity and understanding in the journey. Through the years, others have noted broad overarching patterns in culture. This book expands and deepens observations and connections within those patterns, providing the reader access to invaluable intercultural expertise to understand, live, and work comfortably within a variety of cultural contexts. The reader may simply desire to gain a greater understanding of why people from other cultures seem so different, and the discomfort felt by being the 'outsider.' Or the reader may be searching for insights to hone intercultural skills applicable for successful intercultural negotiation and navigation. Whatever the case, this book is a valuable must read."

—**John Cosby**, Latin America Consultant for Worldview Resource Group

"Robert and Christopher Strauss do a deep dive into the complexities of culture, supported by both research evidence and applicable stories that allow the reader to more fully understand underlying cultural differences even in the most mundane interactions. *Four Overarching Patterns of Culture* should be an integral part of employee training and onboarding for international and domestic organizations alike."

—**Katie Kellett**, Latin America Research Fellow at Love Justice International, and graduate student in the Masters of Nonprofit Management program of the Anderson College of Business at Regis University, Denver, Colorado

# Four Overarching
# Patterns of Culture

# Four Overarching Patterns of Culture

A Look at Common Behavior

### Robert Strauss

WITH
Christopher Strauss

WIPF & STOCK · Eugene, Oregon

FOUR OVERARCHING PATTERNS OF CULTURE
A Look at Common Behavior

Wipf & Stock
An Imprint of Wipf and Stock Publishers
199 W. 8th Ave., Suite 3
Eugene, OR 97401

www.wipfandstock.com

PAPERBACK ISBN: 978-1-5326-9318-2
HARDCOVER ISBN: 978-1-5326-9319-9
EBOOK ISBN: 978-1-5326-9320-5

Manufactured in the U.S.A.                                    08/16/19

# Contents

## Part Two: Building the Frameworks

## Part Three: Functioning in the Structures

# List of Tables

# List of Figures

# Authors

## Robert Strauss

Robert Strauss is owner of Global Perspectives Consulting in Highlands Ranch, Colorado. GPC clients excel in complex global marketplaces through the acquisition of cultural competence. Clients include the United States Department of Agriculture and City of Little Rock, Arkansas Police Department. Strauss is Lead Faculty of the courses *Program Development and Accountability* and *Research Methods* in the Anderson College of Business at Regis University in Denver, Colorado. Also, he is President of Worldview Resource Group, a not-for-profit organization that equips cross-cultural workers in a story-based worldview approach to mission. WRG works with agencies located in India, Southeast Asia, North Africa, Western Canada, Mexico, and all of Ibero-America. Strauss is a member of the International Academy for Intercultural Research. He is the author of *Introducing Story-Strategic Methods: Twelve Steps toward Effective Engagement*, published by Wipf & Stock in March 2017. He and his wife live near Denver, Colorado.

## Christopher Strauss

Christopher Strauss has two masters degrees from St. John's College, in the Western great books and the Eastern great books. He has taught and tutored at Pikes Peak Community College, the University of New Mexico, Santa Fe University of Art and Design, the Santa Fe Indian School, and Santa Fe Preparatory School. He owns and operates Sycamore Editing, and roasts coffee in Santa Fe, New Mexico for Ohori's Coffee Roasters. After reading full tilt for twenty years, he still comes across writers he cannot believe he did not find sooner. He lives in Santa Fe with his wife and two children.

# Acknowledgements

THROUGHOUT THE BOOK, I tell stories about my experiences travelling across the world. Along with my firsthand accounts of the behaviors I have observed, I apply insights from intercultural research. I do not offer new scholarship or break new academic ground. Most of what is shared in these pages rests on the inimitable scholarship of others—a debt I am glad to admit. I have made every effort to acknowledge the work of other researchers.

My wife Carole is an Accountant Manager for a software company based in the Western United States. Her every day interactions are with colleagues in Ireland, Germany, Australia, New Zealand, Japan, Singapore, and China. Interestingly, her college degree is in intercultural studies. She travels also, mostly enjoying regions of Italy and the rivers of Europe.

I am grateful to Dr. Elena Tartaglione, my business partner in Global Perspectives Consulting, whose curiosity is never satisfied. She has traveled, lived, and researched throughout the world. Along with her native English, she speaks German and French. I can always count on her penetrating questions and informed insights. As I write in the chapters to follow, I give credit to her contributions.

My son, Christopher, joins me as co-author. He worked tirelessly to bring wording to life and make meaning clear. He shares his insights based on his background in classic literature and philosophy.

# Introduction

THE MONSOON SEASON OF India had begun. The noisy, city air of Bhubaneshwar was hot—over 100°F—and impossibly humid. This air was not the dry, thin stuff of the Colorado high desert, my home. It was the wet, sticky air of Orissa, a state on India's east coast. I was in Bhubaneshwar on a short teaching trip with Dr. Bhargava, a university president from Bangalore, Karnataka. Having just finished teaching at a university extension, we were leaving town. We found a taxi to the airport and settled into the backseat. Dr. Bhargava's assistant, an Orissa local, took a customary seat in front, on the driver's left. The university president turned to me in a panic: "Dr. Strauss, where are the documents?"

"Dr. Bhargava, I don't know what you're talking about," I said. At the same time, to my surprise, overlapping my remark, his assistant said, "We have done everything possible to retrieve the documents, but the hotel staff must have failed to provide them." In fact, neither I nor the assistant knew what Dr. Bhargava meant. We soon learned he was asking about boarding passes for our flight back to the south of India. He expected the hotel to have printed them.

This simple exchange may seem unremarkable. Exchanges like it happen hundreds of times a day. The small confusions they create are usually smoothed over and forgotten. But this time the question would not leave me—why had the assistant and I responded so differently to Dr. Bhargava's question? The more I pondered it, the more I realized this simple exchange had all the complexities of culture.

Our diverse responses showed differences in "overarching patterns" of culture. I responded truthfully. I did not know what Dr. Bhargava was talking about. I gave little thought to my reputation, to appearing to those around me to possess important information, or to Dr. Bhargava's reputation, to how my answer might make Dr. Bhargava appear in front of me, his assistant, and the driver. I was raised up in a culture that is justice-oriented. We tend to speak the truth. We do so as clearly as we can.

But Dr. Bhargava's assistant gave little thought to the truth. His answer saw to it that all present maintained face. He protected reputations. He did not know what Dr. Bhargava meant. Still, he honored our assumed efforts and shamed the unrepresented hotel staff for its unbeknownst failure. He was raised up in an Orissa culture that is honor-oriented. They tend to show honor to whom it is due.

The differences between the high-desert climate of Colorado and the two monsoon seasons of India are easy to notice. Trickier, though, is understanding the differences between overarching patterns of culture. To an outsider, cultural differences may seem strange. We often lack the language to describe them.

In *Overarching Patterns*, I introduce four frameworks of culture found worldwide. The book provides language and concepts to help us talk about cultural differences and understand them. In Part One, I define culture and discuss the unseen layers that make culture so complex. Then, I explore two cultural perspectives—those of the insider and the outsider—and explain their significance. Next, as a segue to the patterns themselves, I explain what a pattern is, how it can be "overarching," and that these specific patterns are not new. So much for Part One.

Part Two of *Overarching Patterns* analyzes in depth each pattern of culture—justice, honor, harmony, and reciprocity. It gives a template for considering other patterns. Part Three applies insights from the four overarching patterns of culture to everyday life across cultures.

By no means are these four patterns of culture the only ones. Other patterns are noticeable, especially on a smaller scale, and deserve serious study.[1] But the four patterns I take up are widespread; they inform and form the lives of millions of people every day. Several of these patterns have been discussed in academic literature for decades, but I also show the pattern of reciprocity warrants more attention.

---

1. A more localized pattern of culture is provided by Shweder et al., in "The 'Big Three' of Morality." They refer to karma (coupled with personal responsibility) as "an overarching moral metaphor" (150–57). The concept, supported by precedent literature, comes from India, specifically the state of Orissa. In karma, an individual takes responsibility to live out a code of ethics sourced in divinity but also part of the natural order of life. Fulfilling one's dharma duties enhances this life and bodes well for the next life. See Footnote 80 for a contrary perspective about patterns from Richard Shweder.

I name each of the four patterns according to its defining feature, and present each using a model of culture indebted to the anthropologist G. Linwood Barney.[2] Both Worldview Resource Group (in the third sector) and Global Perspectives Consulting (in private and public sectors) have refined Barney's model into a more sophisticated presentation tool for understanding four interactive layers of culture and how the layers work across time. These four layers are evident in each pattern of culture.

This work tries to get beyond simple pairs of opposites. You often see handy graphs of opposite cultures, charts that pin down societies into pairs (individual vs. collective or hierarchical vs. egalitarian).[3] True, most societies can be classified or ranked on such scales. But these categories are too often presented as polar opposites, obscuring a society's inner tensions. Cultural factors underlie these value orientations, factors that are brought to the surface by considering the overarching patterns of culture.

*Overarching Patterns* explains a complex model of culture and explores some major cultural patterns. But it does not address every question related to culture and its study. An ocean cannot fit in a cup. The book touches in passing on the origin of certain ideas and terms but does not discuss in detail how anthropological theory has evolved. I do not address how cultures are passed on or change. Clearly, culture is passed from generation to generation. People are not automatons that passively internalize norms. People matter in the complicated process of passing culture down.[4] But my book could only tackle so much. For a good overview of cultural anthropology, interested readers should consult Alan Barnard's *History and Theory in Anthropology*. A good source on how cultures change, one that explains cultural themes and counterthemes, is Paul Hiebert's *Transforming Worldviews: An Anthropological Understanding of How People Change*.

Other parts of culture *Overarching Patterns* does not speak to are ethnography and acculturation. I do not discuss data collection techniques—inquiry, data management, or data analysis.[5] Here, too, I have not had the space to sufficiently explain cultural adjustment. But on that topic, I

---

2. Barney, "Supracultural and Cultural," 48–55. See *Appendix A* for a more complete description of Barney.

3. See, for instance, Hofstede's "6-D Model of National Culture."

4. See Thompson et al., *Cultural Theory*, 218.

5. I do touch on field methods in my earlier book, *Introducing Story-Strategic Methods* (2017); see Appendix A in that book, beginning at page 151.

recommend the work of John Berry, Professor Emeritus of Psychology at Queen's University.

One charge that can be laid before the book is that of reductionism, a fallacy in analysis when a complex phenomenon is described in overly simplistic terms. *Overarching Patterns* avoids reductionism, I believe, in two ways. First, its cultural descriptions are overviews, describing broad patterns of observed behavior. The book does not claim to predict what every person will say and do. It simply describes what has been observed in the aggregate. Second, the book's descriptions are anything but simple. These sophisticated models are based on established theoretical constructs to understand complex actions. Repeatedly, the book emphasizes that even these sophisticated models may not be subtle enough to capture the nuances of human thought and behavior.

Predicting a specific person's behavior in a given circumstance, then, may be impossible. Still, in the aggregate, we may identify overarching patterns of behavior. This, the book does. If researchers only expect the prototype or the ideal (emic) when observing a pattern of culture, normal variations will thwart the effort. Conversely, if all researchers see are normal variations (etic), they may never conclude an overarching pattern is there.

As a starting point in laying a foundation in Part One, we ask, "What is culture?"

# Part One: Laying a Foundation

Chapter 1

# Culture

## Opening Remarks

WHAT DOES *CULTURE* MEAN? In this book, it does not mean highly culti-vated. It does not mean high-brow sophistication, or some airy realm of ex-istence, the purview of wealthy elites who wear monocles, sip champagne, drive sports cars, own rare Picassos, and listen to Vivaldi. *Culture*, as it is used in this book, is something everyone has. It is so deep and so familiar that it seems to lie in our very blood and bones.

Figure 1: Definition of Culture.

In this chapter, we try to pull it out into the light and articulate what feels like instinct. After comparing dozens of definitions of culture as a trainer and consultant, I have settled on one that seems best: "culture is our learned, shared patterns of perception and behavior."[1] The definition's five main words pinpoint important components of culture.[2] Before unpacking these five, here are several stories to provide a real-world framework for thinking about what culture is and how it works.[3]

For ten years, I have been traveling to India. I almost always stay with my host, Dr. Bhargava. His home is on the northeast side of Bangalore, the capital of Karnataka, in the residential colony of Banaswadi. Dr. Bhargava is from the southern state of Tamil Nadu. He speaks Tamil as his native language. Like all educated people in India, he also speaks English. His father worked as a businessman in the city of Madras (now Chennai) but was a native Telugu speaker from the state of Andhra Pradesh. He was also a devout Hindu. Contrary to what a Westerner might expect, Dr. Bhargava does not speak Telugu, his father's language, does not speak Hindi, and is not a practicing Hindu. Dr. Bhargava's daughter, unlike her father, speaks four languages. Her native tongue is English, but she is also fluent in Hindi, Tamil, and Kannada, the local language of Karnataka, a Dravidian language with almost 50 million speakers. Her English is flawless, partly due, no doubt, to her postgraduate education in speech pathology. She speaks with a lyrical British accent.

Recently, sitting in Dr. Bhargava's living room one afternoon, I was talking with a lecturer from Texas. (His scholarly research had looked at the impact of rhetoric in human exchange.) As a grandfather of six, I was older than my living room companion, who had two young children at home in Austin. A disagreement had surfaced in our conversation. I suggested that "culture" was learned over time and patterned, generally amidst endearing relationships. My living room companion countered that "culture" was a manifestation constructed at any given moment based upon need. Just then, Dr. Bhargava's daughter entered from the kitchen and addressed me. It was about three o'clock.

"Uncle, may I offer you tea?"

---

1. See Strauss, "Culture." This definition is adapted from Martin and Nakayama's in *Experiencing Intercultural Communication*, 32.

2. For a more detailed analysis of the definitions of culture with academic resources, see *Appendix A*.

3. Ward Goodenough (1919–2013), an American anthropologist, shows how our term *culture* comes from the nineteenth-century German word *Kultur*, which referred to the customs, beliefs, and arts of the better educated classes of Europe. At the time, societies were ranked by comparing them to European elites. See *Culture, Language, and Society*, 47.

I smiled. What further evidence did I need? This told everything. Her culture was not a mere spontaneous generation but was deeply patterned: the fictive kinship title "uncle,"[4] normal India tea (hot and sugary with boiling milk), a beverage of choice offered at the customary time, the usual honor shown to the family friend, her use of English but with a British accent. I felt like an attorney who had just argued compellingly in a court of law, although I had argued nothing. The immediate circumstance said it all. Case closed. I turned to my companion and held up my hands, as if to say, "What did I tell you? Learned patterns!" As you might imagine, he took my gesture differently.

"Yes, I would love some tea," he said.

In a recent class at Regis University, where I teach, I was able to exchange stories about perception with a graduate student from Senegal, West Africa. He had come from Dakar to play basketball at Georgetown, another Jesuit institution in Washington D. C., which he did for four years, playing with later All-Star Allen Iverson. My student, a Muslim, explained to me why some soldiers in the Senegalese military wear amulets containing verses of the Qur'an. (The armed force of Senegal has about 20,000 soldiers. Many are Wolof, the country's largest ethnic group.[5] Most are Sufi Muslims.) Wolof soldiers wear amulets, my student explained, for protection in battle. They claim not to need the West's Kevlar armor.[6] Soldiers across North Africa often wear amulets with verses from the Qur'an written on parchment, rolled up, and placed inside. Scriptures that invoke the name of Allah and the Prophet Muhammad are considered especially powerful.[7] This practice is common throughout the Muslim world. A talisman (it could be clothing, a banner, art, a container, weaponry, or another object) is inscribed with sacred designs or words and thus gains power to protect.

Some Westerners may find such practices superstitious. My student, however, compared a Wolof wearing an amulet to a Christian wearing a cross. There is no difference here, he said, between a Muslim and Christian. True, on the surface the practices seem similar. But is there a difference

4. See Ibsen and Klobus, "Fictive Kin Term Use," 615–20.

5. *Race* refers to physical characteristics based upon genetic ancestry. These biological features are not alterable. *Ethnicity* refers to shared cultural traditions, including the language of a geographic region. *Nationality* refers to the political country of origin or in which one enjoys citizenship.

6. An amulet is an object worn to protect its owner from danger or harm. See González-Wippler, *Complete Book of Amulets and Talismans*.

7. For images of such talismans, see Al-Saleh, "Amulets and Talismans."

at the level of perception? Does a Christian wearing the cross perceive it merely as an identity marker? A good luck charm? An amulet powerful enough to deflect bullets?

All cultures have artifacts. Any artifact's role depends on people's perceptions. Is a necklace with a cross an identity marker and nothing more? Is the value of art merely aesthetic? Does an amulet provide protection? Do the large, deep-set eyes of some dolls cause harm?[8] Will an icon of the Feng Shui three-legged money toad, placed properly in one's home or business, bring prosperity and wealth? Can the grotesque appearance of a gargoyle perched on a roof corner in Bangalore, India ward off evil spirits?

People will answer these questions differently, depending on their culture—depending on the patterns of perception and behavior they have learned from their families and share with their society. [9] Their answers will seem right to them. All groups of people assume that what they learn and share, what they think and do, is right and real. Culture works for them. It explains the past, justifies the present, and offers trajectory for the future.[10]

Let's go on to unpack the definition of culture—our learned, shared patterns of perception and behavior—step by step. I proceed in reverse order, starting with behavior and perception, and then look at how our actions and thoughts become reinforced into patterns, how we learn them from our elders and share them with our community.

## Behavior

Behavior is the most obvious face culture shows us. It is what strikes us at first glance. In a new society, we soon find ourselves surrounded by strange things—the way people look and dress, the way they walk and talk, their food, their music. We realize we're not in Kansas anymore. (Being struck by strangeness is actually a good thing. Too often, travelers end up minimizing cultural differences—their visits may be brief or their hosts tolerant and

8. See Kearney, "World View Explanation of the Evil Eye," 175–92.

9. In this work, the term *society* refers to an aggregate community of people living together according to commonly held assumptions and values. Society and culture are not synonyms. Society refers to the group, whereas culture refers to the mindset common to the group.

10. At times, a culture *may* also make promises that are not fulfilled, predict consequences that prove false, and create blind spots that lead to calamity (see Thompson et al., *Cultural Theory*, 218–19). When a culture fails, especially repeatedly, people tend to raise questions and explore new, more sensible ways of life.

obliging. Guests that trivialize or even romanticize cultural differences may be stuck in what experts call an early, ethnocentric stage of intercultural sensitivity.[11] Admitting differences is a first step to moving beyond ethnocentrism into greater cultural sophistication.) Pretty much everything we do can be considered a behavior. Since I look at behavior more closely in the next chapter, here I want focus on one part of it—language.

Wherever we go, we find people speaking a local language (they may speak others, too). At home a child learns a first language—an arterial language, a mother tongue—on which her sociolinguistic identity is based.[12] Native speakers usually master their language in childhood. Once it is mastered, they more or less intuitively know what to say, and when, where, and how to say it. They think in their language, dream in it. They are fluent not just in mundane, daily communication but also in spontaneous higher-level discourse. Their skill includes far more than just using the right words in the right order. Besides apt vocabulary and correct grammar, native speakers seemingly instinctively use appropriate nonverbal cues and gestures. They use tone, volume, and other subtle conventions to convey their point. They usually self-identify by their language. They display a local dialect, an accent, most often outside of their awareness.[13]

Language is also a repository of culture. Through language, a society preserves its culture and passes it on to the next generation. The two are inextricably linked. It is no exaggeration to say if I do not know the language, I do not know the culture.

Language is a key display of observable behavior in culture, but only one. Chapters to follow expand on behavior, showing how behavior works not only in individuals but on the social level, too. For behavior also involves a social collective, the way a society is structured and how it functions for the wellbeing of its members. Behavior is usually driven by *perception*. The next section explains how.

11. For a fuller account of Milton Bennett's model of how intercultural sensitivity develops, see my blog post "Developmental Model of Intercultural Sensitivity."

12. Catholic monks coined the phrase *mother tongue* to identify the language they used "speaking from the pulpit," instead of Latin. See Illich, *Shadow Work*.

13. See Lee, "The Native Speaker," 152–63.

## Perception

Our behavioral habits are only one part of the puzzle. Culture also includes our patterns of thought. What we notice about the world, the way we interpret reality, the categories we use to think—all these are part of our culture. Culture is a set of perceptions in the mind.[14] Along with apprehension and comprehension, both suggesting a sense of awareness, there is a third common and pervasive characteristic of perception. It is that we are often not consciously aware of our perceptions. Some cultural perceptions are outside our awareness. True, culture includes the relationships we enjoy, the status and role we have in those relationships. It includes the structure and function of socio-cultural institutions. As Eugene Nida writes, "There is no culture apart from society."[15] As Clifford Geertz says, "Culture is public."[16] But in addition to being a social construct, culture is a mental construct as well. Anthropologist Paul Hiebert suggests, "Cultures are the *mental* worlds societies construct [in order] to live in a confusing world—to give it order and meaning."[17] He explains that perceptions (he calls them "deep assumptions") are sorted in the mind into themes and counterthemes. These deep assumptions define and explain reality.[18] Culture is in the mind. It is bound up in our perceptions. There is no culture apart from the unseen abstraction of perception.

These mental constructs form lenses through which we see and interpret all aspects of life. Our conceptual constructs determine what is in focus and tells us what it means. Philosophically, the constructs can be analyzed as a set of assumptions that shape and sort what we see. Sociologically, the constructs can be analyzed as a nest of symbols, rituals, and stories.

We see the symbols and know what they mean. We participate in rituals that reinforce the way things should be. Culture orients us. We live and relive the stories. From them we apprehend expressive meaning. We may feel sympathy at a child's cry. We often smile when another person laughs. Most of us feel discomfort when an injured person moans. These

14. In this chapter, *perception* refers both to "awareness of the surrounding environment acquired through the physical senses (apprehension) and conceptual images in the mind (comprehension) formed through observation." See *Webster's New Collegiate Dictionary*.

15. Nida, *Customs and Cultures*, 28.

16. Geertz, *Interpretation of Cultures*, 12.

17. Hiebert et al., *Understanding Folk Religion*, 234. My emphasis.

18. Hiebert, *Transforming Worldviews*, 50.

feelings come from a set of assumptions the mind remembers.[19] Culture is how we perceive.[20]

Table 1 provides several examples of the way different cultures ascribe different meanings to symbolic forms.

Table 1: Symbolic Meaning across Cultures

|  |  | USA | India | Argentina |
|---|---|---|---|---|
| Color | Red | Danger, emotion | Matrimony, feminine energy, purity, spirituality | With blue, the color of liberal parties, socialism, and gauchos |
|  | Black | Formality, power, death | Wards off evil | Formality, mourning |
|  | White | Purity, innocence | Death, mourning; but also, the color of high caste attire | A national color prominent in the flag |

19. Professor Emeritus at the University of Washington, John Toews refers to cultural perspectives as "intellectual maps" (Toews, *The Communist Manifesto*, 13). Through apprehension we know something took place, whether or not we understand it. Through comprehension we gain insight into the why behind the what. Once in rural Karnataka, a woman bent down and touched the bottom of my pant leg. I saw her do it: apprehension. I didn't understand why. My driver said it was a common display of deep respect in that locale: comprehension.

20. For more details related to signs, see Hiebert et al., *Understanding Folk Religion*, 231–56. For rituals, see 257–81. The meaning ascribed to symbols is phenomenological. It is not universal and certainly there would not be universal agreement as to what is and is not real. A passage in an obscure Old Testament book illustrates the disagreement: "Of what value is an idol, since a man has carved it? Or an image that teaches lies? For he who makes it trusts in his own creation; he makes idols that cannot speak. Woe to him who says to wood, 'Come to life!' Or to lifeless stone, 'Wake up!' Can it give guidance? It is covered with gold and silver; there is no breath in it." (Habakkuk 2:18–19, NIV). No doubt, the conquering Babylonians believed their symbols and images were potent. The Jewish prophet clearly did not. Robert Priest, et al., highlight the dilemma of conflicting cross-cultural meaning in "Missiological Syncretism," 9–87.

|  |  | USA | India | Argentina |
|---|---|---|---|---|
| Image | Swastika | Associated with Germany's Nazi Party and its WWII atrocities | An important Hindu symbol representing Brahman; a lucky charm painted on auto rickshaws, etc. | Similar association as USA but dissimilar to India |
| Photo | Che Guevara | Infamous Marxist revolutionary, seen by some as an enemy of the USA | Folk or cult status | National hero and icon |
| Monument | Statue of Liberty | A gift from France in 1886, celebrates freedom | Not the same meaning as USA | Not the same meaning as USA |
|  | Great Buddha Statue | Not the same religious history and meaning as India | Located in Bodhgaya, Bidar and consecrated in 1989 by the Dalai Lama, the statue marks a holy place in the Buddhist pilgrimage. | Not the same religious history and meaning as India |
|  | Obelisk | Washington Monument: erected in 1888, honors the first US president | Srirangapatna Fort Obelisk: erected in 1907, honors soldiers killed in the Fourth Anglo-Mysore War | Obelisco de Buenos Aires: designed by Alberto Prebisch, erected in 1936, commemorates the city's 400th anniversary |

Many cultural perceptions are taken for granted. An example is our perception of time. Just what is time? It is linear and constantly in motion, we say. Time flows from an instantaneous present toward the inaccessible future, we say. The past is a memory and is "the past" only if it is remembered. Time has a beginning, an end. Time is a cherished commodity to be used productively in its designated increments of minutes, hours, days, and more. Time is money, we say. But we may not be aware that other cultures perceive time differently. For them, time may be an endless cycle, without beginning or end. Time may not be a prized commodity so much as an opportunity to enjoy relationships with others.

Regarding culture as perception, Greg Bahnsen writes, "Presuppositions form a wide-ranging foundational *perspective* (or starting point) in terms of which everything else is interpreted and evaluated. As such, presuppositions have the greatest authority in one's thinking, being treated as one's least negotiable beliefs and being granted the highest immunity to revision."[21] If Bahnsen is right, then any starting point shapes its conclusions. The perceptions of culture determine what a person feels ought to be and thinks is real. Our presuppositions transcend our experiences. Our experiences cannot touch or change them. In fact, our experiences seem to be what they are because our presuppositions are what they are. "Culture is not a random assortment of traits," says Hiebert, "but an integrated coherent way of mentally organizing the world."[22]

Our perspective, then, shapes the world we know. Ernest Bormann, professor of speech-communication at the University of Minnesota, asserts that we do not interpret and evaluate based on indolent and isolated ideas, but rather with "rhetorical vision."[23] Our rhetorical vision (*rhetoric* not in the sense of bombastic blurbs, but as the art of discourse) forms the grid through which we see. Story is our way of knowing.[24] That is, cultural perceptions are not sequestered items in a mental filing cabinet. Instead, they permeate the stories we remember.

Although culture includes our patterns of perception, we may be largely unaware of them. Consider the rules of the language we speak. Most native English speakers know little about phonetics but nevertheless skillfully aspirate unvoiced bilabial and alveolar consonants like "p" and "t." We may never have heard of bilabial stops or nasals, but we proficiently say "puppy" and "mommy." When communicating, we focus our attention on the intended message but may know little about morphology. We add

---

21. Bahnsen, *Van Til's Apologetic*, 2. His emphasis.

22. Hiebert, *Transforming Worldviews*, 16.

23. Bormann, "Fantasy and Rhetorical Vision," 398.

24. See Bradt, *Story as a Way of Knowing*. A fascinating example of the use and power of story is found in Thomas Johnson's article about the "Night Letters" written by Taliban leaders. See his "Taliban Insurgency," 317–44.

the negative morpheme "dis-" to "trust" to express a lack of confidence. We combine the preposition "under" with the noun "weight" to create an adjective, "underweight." We manifest these language skills in communication but are not always able to explicitly describe the morphological structures of our own speech patterns.

Our perceptions "stick out" on rare occasions—when an outsider enters our culture, say, or when we travel into a new geographic area where language and culture differ from our own. Then we notice differences. Our own perceptions come to the surface. A stranger's perceptions challenge the perceptions we unknowingly embrace.

The "surfacing" of our own perceptions, that is, mindfulness or self-awareness, is a first step toward cultural competence. In Spanish, the "t" in *tiempo* (time) is not aspirated. If I want to speak Spanish with less of an accent, I need to know that as an English speaker, I always aspirate an initial alveolar "t." Only then can I work to curb my aspirations. Likewise, when I travel to a foreign country, I need to know that I am time-oriented rather than relationship-oriented. Only then can I try to avoid treating time like a commodity in a way that seems bizarre to the people I am with. Someone with advanced cultural competence is aware of their own perceptions and can change their speech and behavior to fit the expectations of those around them.

We have looked briefly at behavior and perception. A moment's thought shows us that the way we act and think often falls into familiar forms. We are creatures of habit. Though we do have spontaneity and freedom in choosing how to respond to situations, our habits are governed by *patterns*.

## Patterns

Chapter 4 describes patterns of culture in detail. But a few words are needed here. If only one person or a handful of people exhibit a behavior or a perception—a strange turn of speech, say, or an enigmatic gesture— we call it an idiosyncrasy. If more people embrace a behavior but it lasts only a short time, we call it a fad. If enough people show a behavior for a long enough time, if it "goes mainstream," that is, if it is *strongly-patterned* enough, we call it culture. (Just how many people must embrace a pattern of behavior or thought, and for how long, before it becomes *culture*, is an open question—one we pass over here.) My point is that *all* societies show patterns of thought and behavior. Even the most individualistic societies, ones that prize idiosyncrasy, radical behavior, innovation—the United States, say, or Canada—have distinct habits of thinking, speaking, and behaving that recur and repeat. These free thinkers and rugged individualists likely will not admit it, but they are more conditioned than they know. Their behavior follows patterns.

Over time, a culture's patterns of behavior and perception are worn into place. In any given situation, the behavior that people feel is appropriate gets repeated and reinforced. Almost always, people are unaware of the patterns of their culture, both how a given pattern has been formed and how it is reinforced and passed on. It just feels right. It just feels normal.

As a thought experiment, let's imagine a society that has no patterns of culture, *at all*. First, though, a description of a society with patterns: As I write now, I sit in a café in downtown Little Rock, Arkansas. In front of me, two large glass garage-type doors are open to East 3rd Street. Cars are driving past. The available side street parking is full—it's now almost noon—and people pay for parking in individual meters—a quarter gets you thirty minutes. On either side of the street, pedestrians are walking on sidewalks. At the cross street, River Market Avenue, is an all way stop. Cars are stopping. Drivers look both ways before proceeding. Inside the restaurant, patrons sit enjoying sandwiches and drinks. Wi-Fi is available. "Time in a Bottle" by Jim Croce is playing quietly. The turkey sandwich is available cold or hot. The meat is FDA approved. Everything is more or less normal. Predictable. Nothing out of the ordinary. Nothing irregular. The patterns are fixed, but mostly outside the awareness of the patrons sitting in Adina Café and Coffee Roastery.

Now imagine if this society's patterns were suddenly removed. What if people parked their cars in the middle of the street? What if cars were driven not on streets but on sidewalks? What if drivers gave up their habit of stopping at stop signs? What if pedestrians began walking in the streets, or shaving themselves in the streets, or sleeping there? What if Nita, the owner of Adina Café, decided patrons must pay for their lunch by singing "Time in a Bottle"? What if Nita decided to grill the turkey out in one of the lanes of East 3rd Street? What if a competing restaurateur decided to build a new restaurant in the middle of the intersection of East 3rd Street and River Market Avenue? *What if there were no Wi-Fi?* Disorder ensues. Mayhem. Chaos.

As my thought experiment shows, we mostly take patterns of culture for granted. They provide predictability, order. They give a society a certain structure and help us function within it. They have a certain convenience—we usually do not *have* to think about them or talk about them. They work for us, and allow us to work.

But what feels normal is not always *right*. Not all cultural patterns are morally or ethically correct. Some may be unrighteous or dishonorable or exploitative. I would like to illustrate the more pernicious side of patterns of culture by retelling a story from the civil rights movement in the United States. Like my thought experiment, the story takes place mostly in Little Rock.

Not long ago in Denver, I was able to sit down with Carlotta Walls Lanier for a conversation over coffee. Carlotta is a champion of the civil rights movement in the United States. She is one of the Little Rock Nine. Below is a brief excerpt of her life story, revealing fixed, deep-seated, and seemingly unalterable patterns of culture.

Carlotta was born in Little Rock on December 18, 1942, the oldest of three sisters. Despite the *Emancipation Proclamation*, an executive order signed by President Lincoln on January 1, 1863, that freed the slaves in Confederate states, despite the Thirteenth Amendment to the Constitution in 1865 that abolished slavery and involuntary servitude, Carlotta and her family, like all Black Americans, were deeply and daily confronted with issues of race.

Following the Civil War (1861–1864) and during the years of Reconstruction (1865–1877), Jim Crow laws replaced Black Codes, state laws that restricted free activities of blacks and isolated them.[25] *Plessy v. Ferguson* (1896) upheld state racial segregation. Homer Plessy was one-eighth black by descent, with one black great-grandparent and seven white great-grandparents. This negligible biracial mix was sufficient to segregate him to a black railway car in Louisiana. Laws supported and enforced separation.[26]

25. Jim Crow was a fictitious song and dance character in a performance by white actor Thomas Rice (1808–1860). The name became a pejorative expression meaning "Negro." Over time, the name was associated with laws enforcing racial segregation in the United States.

26. The Supreme Court ruling between Homer Plessy and John Howard Ferguson, a Louisiana judge, was 7–1. Justice John Marshall Harlan (1833–1911) was the lone vote against seven. In his dissent he wrote, "But in view of the constitution, in the eye of the law, there is in this country no superior, dominant, ruling class of citizens. There is no caste here. Our constitution is color-blind, and neither knows nor tolerates classes among citizens. In respect of civil rights, all citizens are equal before the law. The humblest is the peer of the most powerful. The law regards man as man, and takes no account of his surroundings or of his color when his civil rights as guaranteed by the

In Little Rock, Carlotta attended Dunbar Junior High School, an all-black school. She and her family occasionally traveled by bus, sitting, of course, in the back. She drank from a water fountain marked "colored." Waiting rooms were segregated. When shopping, a black person could not try on or return clothes and shoes. Almost all black mothers were seamstresses, as was Carlotta's. Black people sometimes had to enter and exit a store from the rear. On the sidewalks, as people walked, blacks gave way to whites.

But then, on May 17, 1954, the landmark Supreme Court case *Brown v. Board of Education of Topeka, Kansas* declared, in a unanimous 9–0 vote, that state laws establishing separate public schools for black and white students were unconstitutional. *De jure* racial segregation was said to be a violation of the Fourteenth Amendment (equal protection under the law). Segregation had ended. It was a monumental decision. It took place one year before my birth.

What did this ruling mean? In the immediate, it meant Oliver Brown, a Santa Fe Railroad welder and assistant pastor of a local church in Springfield, Missouri, along with 13 plaintiffs, was free to send his daughter to the white school only six blocks away. More generally, the ruling meant that if black students wanted to attend a white school, they were legally permitted to do so. Institutionally, the law had changed. But, functionally, white people's patterns of perception and behavior had not.

Subsequently, in the fall of 1957, in Little Rock, Arkansas, nine black students with the support of their families decided to attend Little Rock Central High School. They would later become known as the Little Rock Nine. At fourteen years old, Carlotta was the youngest of the nine.

Even though the Supreme Court had changed segregation laws, local white residents and white political figures vehemently and violently opposed integration.[27] In early September 1957, the nine black students were blocked at the steps to the high school by the Arkansas National Guard, who had been called out by Arkansas Governor Orval Faubus.[28]

---

supreme law of the land are involved. It is therefore to be regretted that this high tribunal, the final expositor of the fundamental law of the land, has reached the conclusion that it is competent for a state to regulate the enjoyment by citizens of their civil rights solely upon the basis of race." See https://louisville.edu/law/library/special-collections/the-john-marshall-harlan-collection/harlans-great-dissent.

27. Today, we correctly make a distinction between "desegregation" and "integration." Almost everyone is for desegregation but few support forced integration. This differentiation is important in any conversation about diversity, inclusion, equity, and mutuality.

28. A marble bust of Faubus sits on a stand in the north wing of the Arkansas state

An angry group of white residents jeered and insulted the students and had to be forcibly restrained by soldiers. The students were denied entrance to Central High.

It is helpful to remember that in Little Rock, Reverend Wesley Pruden, pastor of Broadmore Baptist Church, was enjoined by local white leaders to articulate "white fears" related to "black aspirations."[29] White fears were rooted in stories told by white parents, pastors, and politicians. From Pruden's congregation, the Mothers League of Central High School emerged to champion the defense of white girls from black boys, if desegregation were to take place. Thereby, the politics of segregation were inseparably tied to the providence of God.

So egregious were the behaviors in and around Central High School (see footnote 36 for examples—the reader should be aware that the content of the footnote may be disturbing)[30] that on September 24, 1957, President Dwight D. Eisenhower ordered the 101st Airborne Division of the U.S. Army to accompany and protect the Little Rock Nine. Later, to counter the president's order, Governor Faubus closed all Little Rock public schools for the 1958 academic year. The period came to be known as the Lost Year. The schools reopened in 1959, and Carlotta returned to Central. In 1960, she was the first female black student to graduate from Central High School.

---

capital building. Statues of General Robert E. Lee and his horse Travelers Rest have been in jeopardy in 2017, but presumably few know about the existence of this bust.

29. See Daniel, "Bayonets and Bibles: The 1957 Little Rock Crisis," a paper presented at the 1998 inauguration of the Women's Emergency Committee. A copy of Pruden's speech is in the archives at the Butler Center in downtown Little Rock. Dr. Johanna Miller Lewis, professor of history at the University of Arkansas at Little Rock, alerted me to the vast array of archival material housed in the Butler Center, most of which focuses on the Little Rock Nine and all associated events related to September 1957 at Central High School.

30. Governor Faubus ordered the National Guard to block entrance to Central High School. No black children were to be granted passage. In a media interview, Faubus said no black child would enter the school. In subsequent days, as the Little Rock Nine attempted to do so, crowds of white protestors jeered, called the children names, and at times attempted to storm them, only to be held back by the very soldiers who were blocking the entrance. Protestors called the children "niggers" and yelled at them to stay out of "our school." Reporters for *The Arkansas Gazette* and *The Arkansas Democrat* covered these events. See Dhonau, "Negro Girl Turned Back," 1–2; Douthit, "CHS Emptied" 1; Lewis, "Governor Gets Plea," 1–2; Trout, "Crowd Jeers," 1–2; "High School Off Limits," 1; "Growing Violence," 1.

Figure 2: Little Rock Central High School.

After high school, Carlotta attended Michigan State University. She finished her baccalaureate degree in Colorado. She started a real estate company in Denver and has worked successfully in that capacity for over forty years. Frequently today, she speaks about her experiences, especially in Colorado schools, where she helps young people understand the history of Black Americans in the United States.

Six decades later in Denver, Carlotta told me that even though time had passed, she still remembers everything that took place on the steps of the high school. She hears the angry voices, sees the soldiers, and recalls her confusion. She was confused, she clarifies, because she assumed that the white people in the crowd who jeered, mocked, and resisted only misunderstood the change in federal law. At the time, in her innocence, she did not know that people were not misunderstanding at all. They were acting out ingrained perceptions—in this case, prejudices—about people of color and acting out shared values about what ought and ought not to be. White locals felt that there ought to be segregation. Without question, they assumed it was what God wanted. They believed white girls must be protected from black boys. The patterns were deeply worn and seemingly unalterable.

Knowing that I had been hired by the City of Little Rock to provide culture training to the police department, Carlotta gave me the brass commemorative coin pictured in Figure 3.

Figure 3: Congressional Gold Medal of Freedom.

She shared that if I kept it in my pocket while facilitating the training, it might bring me good luck. In honor of Carlotta, I facilitated eight months of training in 2017 to command staff, field officers, and police academy recruits. During every training, I kept the coin in my pocket.

Inside the Presidential Library of William J. Clinton in Little Rock is a tribute to the Little Rock Nine. Their powerful story is told in brief through a display of artifacts and speeches by President Clinton and Ernest Green, one of the Little Rock Nine. The display aims to expose and change patterns of perceptions.

Often, a generation or two must pass before people see and behave in different cultural ways. At times, it takes longer. Sometimes it seems cultural patterns, however insidious, are not alterable. People's self-perception is so clear to them and seems so right, whether it is or not. Where do these patterns come from?

## Learned

Patterns of behavior and perception—regardless of their moral standing—are learned. Children born in the South in the early twentieth century did not have a preprogramed schematic in their minds; at birth they had no disposition to racism and segregation. It was a pattern of perception they learned from their society—from their parents, their families, their friends, their elders.

Likewise, children the world over are born without such patterns of perception and behavior in place. Just as children are not born speaking a particular language, they are not born with a particular culture. Children do not automatically know how to behave suitably. Adults and others teach them what they ought to say and do. Through enculturation, children pick up the patterns present in their society—assumptions about how the world works, a local language, a way of behaving that seems fitting. They acquire wisdom, a capacity of homo sapiens—and they perhaps acquire more pernicious behaviors and prejudices. For better or worse, they internalize a preexisting system of symbols, rituals, and meaning.[31] This symbolic system is learned situationally—every day, through formal instruction or informal socialization, at school and at home, with individuals and with groups, our culture is solidified, reinforced, and made more nuanced.

Figure 4: Children Learn Culture through Hearing and Observing.

Remarkably, what we learn early likely lasts a lifetime, and what we learn may take a lifetime to master. It is as children that we are most impressionable, most sponge-like, ready to soak up whatever our culture can offer. Social psychologist Geert Hofstede writes, "Every person carries

31. Kottak, *Mirror for Humanity*, 22–24.

within him or herself patterns of thinking, feeling, and potential acting which were learned throughout [his/her] lifetime. Much of [these patterns are] acquired in early childhood, because at that time a person is most susceptible to learning and assimilating."[32]

Learning over time means acquiring new knowledge or reinforcing and modifying existing knowledge, values, and skills. It involves communication and observation. It requires practice and benefits from reflection. In Table 2, Global Perspectives Consulting describes activities in the learning process.[33]

Table 2: Activities in the Learning Process

| Activity | The Learner Asks: | Role of Society |
| --- | --- | --- |
| Tell | "Tell me." | Someone or a group has the status and role of telling and showing. Not everyone does. Status is ascribed or achieved—a teacher, mentor, coach, trainer, supervisor, or expert. Telling takes place in both informal and formal settings. |
| Show | "Show me." | |
| Do | "Let me try!" | Learners practice in social contexts. The phenomenon of experience is immediately engaged as a device of learning. |
| Reflect | "How did I do?" | Based upon assumed standards, a learner hears, "Well done!" or "Let's try that again." Summative evaluation of outcomes is a key component in any program of learning. |

© Used by permission of Global Perspectives Consulting
and may not be replicated.

32. Hofstede, *Cultural Consequences*, 4. Hofstede's use of the term "assimilating" may be derived from Piaget but differs from John Berry. See Berry, "Psychology of Acculturation," 232–53.

33. Adapted from a presentation in Green et al., "The Practice of Management," reprinted in Margolis and Bell, *Understanding Training*, 59–64. The four features of the management skills method are originally from Wexley and Latham, *Developing and Training*, 86–90. Wexley and Latham label the features as *goal setting, behavior modeling, active practice*, and *evaluative feedback*. In my work for Global Perspectives Consulting and Worldview Resource Group, I have renamed the learning activities: *tell, show, do*, and *reflect* in an adaptation for training across cultures. I also add the perspective of the learner reflected in the four questions. It would be interesting to know if trainers have seen these features in Addelston, "Child Patient Training," 27–29, who suggests "tell, show, and do" as a means of managing dental anxiety.

Two particularly important activities in the learning process are practice and evaluative feedback ("Let me try!" and "How did I do?"). Figure 5 highlights the benefits of when learners are proactive—of practice. Edgar Dale was on the faculty at Ohio State University for over forty years. In 1946, he introduced "The Cone of Experience" to gauge teaching that uses audiovisual methods. His model was not derived from formal research, and so Dale urged others to take his model with a grain of salt. (They did not listen.) Today his model is known by a commonly-used image called "The Cone of Learning." The cone of experience (or the cone of learning) suggests that learning increases as one descends through the cone's layers. That is, proactive learners learn more.[34]

Figure 5: Cone of Learning *Adapted from Edgar Dale.*

Children learn culture following the same repetition. They begin by hearing and observing. They may quickly move to practicing. Only later might they be able to explain abstractly what they did and why they did it. (They are not always able to. Even as adults, we cannot explain everything we do to the satisfaction of an outside observer.) A similar progression appears in Swiss psychologist Jean Piaget's theory of cognitive development, according to which children assimilate and accommodate new information and experiences. Piaget understood mental development as a movement from the concrete to the abstract. The cone of experience works in the same way.

34. For additional insights, see Dale, *Building a Learning Environment.*

An example from India of children being enculturated sheds light on the cone of experience. In India, as in many other places, one honors guests by serving them first at meals. The practice stems from Hindu assumptions about god as guest and guest as god. (The role model, in this case, is Krishna in the *Bhagavad Gita*.) The word for "guest" in Sanskrit is *atithi*, which means "without time." It is customary in India to visit friends without notice. Regardless of their other tasks, the host and hostess will suspend what they are doing to graciously entertain. One's home and wealth are, in fact, good fortunes attained to provide hospitality to guests. The Ministry of Tourism in India has even adopted as its tag line *Atithi Devo Bhavah*—"guest as god." In Dr. Bhargava's home in Bangalore, even though he is not a practicing Hindu, I am still served first at meals. (The practice has a certain oddity for me, used as I am to families eating together at the same time. But his whole family expects it.) I am given the seat of honor at the table. Only Dr. Bhargava sits with me, no one else. His wife Hema serves me. His children and grandchildren, waiting in the living room for their turn to eat, watch expectantly. At times, the grandchildren linger in the doorway, eager to hear and observe. Without explanation from the adults, they learn hospitality by example, relationally, concretely. They hear the conversations, observe the activities of the host and hostess. They watch what foods are served to the guest and how. They hear which phrases fit which gestures. They are immersed in the conversations, though not actively. Perhaps after I leave, they play guest, reenacting what they have watched.

But learning involves more than just concrete relational activities in lived experiences. Learning also includes cognition and affect. In 1956 and 1964, Benjamin Bloom and David Krathwohl, educational psychologists at, respectively, the University of Chicago and Michigan State University, introduced taxonomies of educational objectives. Their taxonomies, often called domains of learning,[35] include cognition, affect, and psychomotor skills. These taxonomies help us see that learning requires far more than mere mimicry: Behavior is discussed and explained. There is a "why" behind the "what." Parents and educators make explicit what is implicit. Cognition is developed. Schematics etched by experience are colored by explanation.

The taxonomy of cognitive learning starts with rudimentary information that is retained in memory and moves toward higher levels of learning through stages of deeper comprehension, application, analysis,

---

35. Quinonez, "3 Domains of Learning."

synthesis, and, ultimately, the implementation of knowledge from one application into others.[36]

When I was a boy, my dad's dad taught me how to play golf. He was a member of the Augusta Country Club in Georgia. I used hand-me-down golf clubs and equipment. We spent hours on the driving range, practicing. I learned verbal and behavioral etiquette that was to be sustained throughout eighteen holes of golf. This etiquette was transferred into the club house, too.

Figure 6: Sam Edward Strauss, Senior Vice-President of the Georgia Power Company.

36. See https://en.wikipedia.org/wiki/Bloom%27s_taxonomy. This knowledge-based domain has six levels of progressive difficulty:

1. Remembering: Locate, label, and describe (what)
2. Comprehending: Distinguish, match, and explain (how)
3. Applying: Organize and choose
4. Analyzing: Subdivide and prioritize
5. Synthesizing: Design and develop
6. Evaluating or creating: Evaluate effectiveness and recommend adaptations

My grandfather taught me how to greet people, how to show respect to the Country Club's employees, and how to conduct myself at lunch in the men's grill. There, I met my great uncle, editor of the Augusta Herald, a prominent newspaper in the city. Also, we sat in the grill listening to Judge Edward James Slayton expound the law. Judge Slayton had served in the Army as a Brigadier General during World War II and the Korean War. He was a member of the Baptist church.

As an adult, I transferred the rules of etiquette from the golf course into my business practices. The implementation represents the highest order of learning in the cognitive taxonomy. This is what happens with culture. Culture is learned.[37]

Before we leave the topic of "learned," consider how much of a culture, though learned, remains tacit to its own members. In our culture, we notice speech and behavior. Yet, most of the time, the deeper values and assumptions that shape what we say and do are outside our awareness. For example, those of us in an individualistic culture may behave with strong individualistic tendencies, but likely we are not able to self-identify as individualists vs. collectivists. We may not know that individualism is a prominent pattern in egalitarian societies. And, often those societies are wealthy. Yet, the anthropologist from the outside does observe the tendencies and understands how the tendencies fit together into an overarching pattern of culture. As American anthropologist Edward T. Hall writes, "Culture hides more than it reveals, and strangely enough what it hides, it hides most effectively from its participants."[38] Paradoxically, culture is passed on through language but also through silence. What is *not* said gets passed on, too.

## Shared

Our culture knits us together into a community: "Shared cultural beliefs, values, memories, expectations, and ways of thinking and acting override differences between people."[39] Each society shares a common story. People know the story; it shapes their identity. Within the common story, people are united through shared experiences. From their common story springs a people's unique common sense. As characters in their common story with

37. For a comprehensive overview of learning, see Jerome Bruner's *The Culture of Education* and John Dewey's *Experience and Education*.

38. Hall, *The Silent Language*, 29. For more about self-awareness, see Appendix C.

39. Kottak, *Mirror for Humanity*, 24.

common sense, people live in community. From the perspective of sociology, that community is structured and is made up of parts, each of which has a function. A community's common story and common sense play out daily on life's stage. What is done each day on this stage seems familiar. There is a common vernacular. There are everyday behaviors. Things are predictable. Everything is normal. People feel comfortable in their communities.

Figure 7 depicts a model of culture highlighting the layers of commonality.

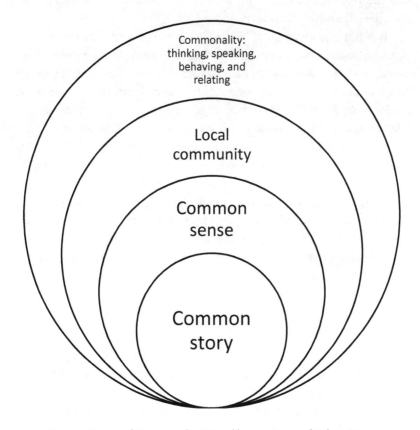

Figure 7: Layers of Commonality© *Used by permission of Robert Strauss. Informed by the research and insights of Michael Matthews. This image may not be replicated without permission.*

Culture is shared, it is common. But what makes something common? At least four things: The elements of commonality are (1) an ability to communicate (2) in relationships with others (3) at a particular time and (4) in a local place.

Hall writes, "Culture is communication and communication is culture."[40] First and foremost is the ability to communicate in the local vernacular, verbally and nonverbally. Communication through speech is uniquely human. And, it is through communication that culture is transmitted. Language provides labels for symbols, objects, and rituals.[41] Through language, people develop relationships with one another, ranging from the mere acquaintance to the intimate. Building intimate relationships, deep friendships, takes time.

It is this phenomenon of "shared" culture that underlies the need for cultural adjustment when a person moves from one region to another. What was common and familiar at home is not in the new locale. When people change locations, they encounter a different story—a story common to the new location, but unlike their own. In the new location, common sense is different. Elsewhere, common sense feels uncommon. It is not universal. It arises from local common stories. Common sense is, one could say, local sense. This is why local people often say an outsider is strange.[42] And, the outsider says the same thing about locals. Also different is the new community, its structures and functions. And what happens on the daily stage, so to speak, what is said and done, differs from culture to culture. The outsider experiences deprivation of norm. The observer does not see what he expects. One is unable to predict what will happen. Familiar patterns are missing. There are new patterns of culture to learn and share.

## Closing Comments

I have reasoned in chapter 1 that culture is our learned, shared patterns of perception and behavior. Though they feel so natural, no one is born with cultural norms in place. Culture is learned. Everyone develops a cultural framework over time. They get it from a group of people who share the

---

40. Hall, *The Silent Language*, 169.

41. For a complex analysis of the relationship between language and symbols, see Deacon, "The Symbol Concept." Also, see Deacon. *The Symbolic Species.*

42. Eugene Nida writes that the outside observer (whether a descriptive linguist, cultural anthropologist, or simply a visitor) usually has a "tourist's viewpoint" which consists in judging everything strange and different on the basis of things found at home. See *Morphology*, 1.

same perceptions and behaviors. Even in the most individualistic societies, such as the USA and Canada, speech and behavior are shared and patterned. Certain ways of thinking and behaving become normal.

But there is more to culture than simply what is said and done. Culture has depth. Culture has layers, most of which are not immediately visible. What is said and done derives from those unseen layers. The most powerful aspects of culture are not visible. Chapter 2 exposes and explores culture's layers.

Chapter 2

# Culture's Four Layers

## Opening Remarks

IN A NEW CULTURE, it does not take long for us to see behavior that is different, strange, perplexing, even downright shocking. But it takes longer to figure out a culture's core—to get beneath the behavior we see and get a feel for a foreign culture's institutions and deeper values. These social structures and values can be radically different from our own—and hard to understand. Western institutions, for example, emphasize equality between people. But elsewhere, institutions often distribute power unevenly. Why? Other cultures may be structured by an informal hierarchy of power based on kinship ties. Other cultures may believe that gender makes a difference in roles and responsibilities. There could be many more reasons why institutions function differently. There is always more to culture than meets the eye.

Scholars have long been aware that culture is like an iceberg. In his work on American cultural patterns, psychologist Edward Stewart proposed a basic distinction—objective culture vs. subjective culture. He defined objective culture as the "institutions and artifacts of a culture, such as its economic system, social customs, political structures and processes, arts, crafts, and literature." Subjective culture is the "psychological features of culture, including assumptions, values, and patterns of thinking."[1] Stewart correctly treated objective culture as an externalization of subjective culture. That is, what is observed outwardly—speech, behavior, social systems—springs from harder to see patterns of thought and value. See Figure 8.

---

1. Stewart and Bennett, *American Cultural Patterns*, 2.

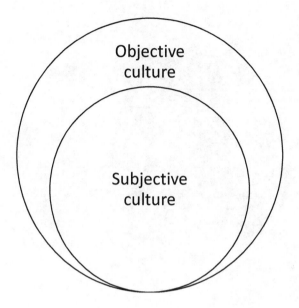

Figure 8: Stewart's Two-Tier Model of Culture.

Stewart's two-tier model helps us appreciate how much of a culture we cannot see at first glance. But this book prefers a four-tier model. As noted in the *Introduction*, this book uses the work of G. Linwood Barney to suggest a model of culture with four layers—outward observable behavior, socio-cultural institutions, values, and worldview assumptions.[2] Barney's outer two layers correspond to Stewart's objective culture, while the inner two layers correspond to subjective culture. Barney's more specific and detailed model gives us more of a handle on culture's complexity.

The earth and its layers is a helpful metaphor for understanding culture's layers.[3] The earth's crust, outwardly visible, is relatively thin—only five kilometers deep at its thinnest places on the ocean floor. Below the surface, the crust is upheld by a mostly solid mantle. Beneath the mantle are two cores, one outer and another inner. See Figure 9.

2. Barney, "Supracultural and Cultural," 48–55.

3. It was at the Pike's Peak Public Library in Colorado Springs, Colorado during 2010 where my business partner, Dr. Elena Tartaglione, suggested the layers of the earth as a visible model for the layers of culture. With a PhD from the Arizona State University Hugh Downs School of Human Communication, Dr. Tartaglione sees three components of worldview: position, agency, and morals.

Figure 9: The Layers of the Earth (Gary Hincks, Science Photo Library)
*Proposed by Dr. Tartaglione and Copyrighted Image Used
by Permission of Global Perspectives Consulting.*

Just as the earth's crust is thin, so is a culture's outward observable *behavior*. We hear and see only a fraction of the whole culture. What is said and done, the visible aspects of culture, are promoted and prohibited by socio-cultural *institutions*, that is, a culture's mantle. These institutions give a society its unique structure and help it function. Beneath these institutions are even deeper, shared cultural *values* that influence what people should say and do. At first, to an outsider these deep values are hidden. In fact, even cultural insiders have trouble talking about the values they act on. Finally, at culture's deepest core are *worldview* assumptions. These speak to what is and is not real, and, for an outsider, can be the hardest part of a culture to uncover. Let's look at each layer of culture in depth.

## Observable Behavior

A culture's outward observable behavior is what we see first. Behavior includes people's bodily actions, reactions, mannerisms,[4] and speech. It in-

4. Mannerisms are mostly involuntary. Still, they are habitual traits of behavior. They include physical posture, hand gestures, and facial expressions. A culture's insiders tacitly understand the meaning of various mannerisms.

cludes the ways we greet each other, how we prepare and take meals, how we celebrate, dance, and play. Behavior includes the way we woo, court, and marry; how we solve problems and avoid danger; how we interact with family, friends, and strangers. It includes the ways we dress and how we honor our dead. Observable behavior varies across cultures, often subtly—but with dramatic consequences. Here are a few examples from my experiences traveling and training in intercultural environments. The examples are close to home. Though we may not realize it, the U. S. has its own culture, too, just as much as more exotic places like Mongolia, Rhodesia, or Borneo.

1. In the United States, police officers are invested by the state with authority to enforce the law. A field officer arrives on scene in uniform, wearing a badge, carrying a firearm. These symbols of state power represent legality. Depending on the situation, an officer has the prerogative to escalate the display of power. Every police department trains officers to follow a use-of-force continuum. The continuum starts with an officer's "presence" in a setting requiring service and protection. Next is an officer's use of "voice." From there, an officer may regrettably have to respond with physical force. All field officers are also trained in de-escalation tactics. Still, the use-of-force continuum guides their behavior. Such behavior invested with state authority is germane to law enforcement. It is part of police culture. In contrast, you and I do not have the same kind of use of force continuum in our personal friendships. Our actions are not emblems of state power. Our arm, however long, is not the arm of the law.

2. American television often uses differences in behavior for comic effect. Take a sitcom from the sixties, *The Beverly Hillbillies*, about an impoverished mountain family that strikes oil on their land and moves to upscale Southern California. After the Clampett's discover $25 million worth of oil on their Ozark property, Jed Clampett sells his land to Mr. Brewster of the OK Oil Company, and the family moves into a mansion in Beverly Hills. Mr. Drysdale, owner of Commerce Bank, convinces Jed Clampett to deposit the fortune into his bank. In Episode 5, Mr. Drysdale recommends that Jed invest his fortune by purchasing stock. Jed does—goats, pigs, cattle, chickens. Jed attempts to order the animals over the telephone, directly from the operator. Somehow, the livestock arrive by truck and are corralled in the tennis court. The Clampett's commence to tending to them. Throughout the episode,

there are countless miscues and missteps as two cultures collide—the hillbilly lifestyle clashes with Southern California sophistication.

3. Risk is a daily factor for everyone along the Southwest border of the United States and Mexico. Along with the regular border commerce are drug and human trafficking, with profits in the tens of billions. Residents and workers north of the border mitigate risk differently from residents south of the border. Before Global Perspectives Consulting could travel into the region as contractors, the US Department of State required our team to undergo security training. The training—in classic "north-of-the-border" style—gave practical instructions: how to drive, where to park, and on which floor of a hotel to book a room.

Residents with roots in Mexico may also try to avoid danger by following similar safety protocols. But first and foremost, they rely on relationships. For instance, one federal officer in a major border city relies on friendships across the border to remain alert to both general danger and specific incidents. The officer went to high school with the current mayor of a city south of the border.

Figure 10: Resident of the Southwest Border.

They remain in routine contact. Through relationships, the officer mitigates risk. Residents north of the border are less likely to use relationships in this way, relying instead on their own wherewithal, feel for their surroundings, and common sense. The two ways of avoiding danger were so different, the Department of State hired Global Perspectives Consulting to train its employees in a more balanced approach to risk mitigation.

4. Recently, laying over at the Denver International Airport during a consulting trip, I met an elderly Black American man. Dressed in a sports jacket, I had just eaten at a restaurant chain from Southern California, which offered an arrangement of classic cheeses and rustic breads served on a wooden board and paired with a Spanish red wine. After

sitting down beside me, the gentleman, wearing overalls, rustled into his carryon suitcase and retrieved a plastic bag with two homemade bologna sandwiches. He noticed me watching him and said hello.

We talked for a while, mostly about his life. He had been raised up in the Mississippi Delta. He worked as farmer; his father, his grandfather, worked as farmers. They farmed mostly potatoes, he said, as there wasn't much money in cotton and cotton was so difficult to harvest. He said he was eighty. For much of his life, he had been a heavy drinker, always vowing to himself and his family every Sunday evening that he would never drink again. At fifty, he had a religious experience—and hadn't drunk since. He shared with me that he could not read or write, but that he could count.

I was struck by the outward differences in our lifestyles—our clothing, our food, our work. Still, I was not entirely unfamiliar with his story. My mother's father was a cotton farmer in rural South Carolina. Cotton was hauled to the gin in a wagon pulled by two mules. He leased land and rented a rural farm house. He drew water from the well. He used an outhouse, as the main house did not have running water. My grandfather could not read or write.

Figure 11: My Grandfather's Wagon and Mules in the Late 1930s.

As these examples show, behaviors vary subtly yet importantly *within* cultures. How much more *across* cultures. What people say and do are visible. Most of culture is not. Below a culture's surface, beneath people's behavior, are institutions that give a society shape and help it work.

## Socio-cultural Institutions

The development of our perception is related to our social environment, as the Soviet psychologist Lev Semyonovich Vygotsky (1896–1934) understood. He argued that a child's mental development is tied to human interactions. People's behavior is encouraged or discouraged by the institutions present in their social environment.[5]

Going further, what people say and do is not created instantaneously in the moment, contrary to the assertions of my colleague in India from Texas. Our behavior is learned, shared, and patterned. It is shaped by our perceptions. So, despite my surname, I did not grow up speaking German. My family and entire community are English speakers. I grew up speaking English, only because that was the language of my socio-cultural context. My family name is German, but the language of our home was English. And, this phenomenon of socio-culture dictates everything. We ate grits seasoned with butter and salt. As a child, I played fast pitch baseball on several teams, ultimately playing as the starting third baseman on my high school team. We did not play cricket. I knew nothing of the India-Pakistan rivalry in that sport. My exposure was to Three Dog Night and the Charlie Daniels Band, not Los Gatos of Argentina.

Socio-cultural institutions are numerous. First and foremost is the family—as defined by a specific culture or subculture. Other institutions are the extended family, the neighborhood, the local community, civic groups, formal and informal networks of relationships, religion, government, a judicial system, law enforcement, art, play, and more. Kinship is also a key socio-cultural institution. Despite its obscurity in the West, kinship plays a fundamental part in socio-cultural roles and responsibilities throughout the world.

Each of the above institutions is a cultural pattern, practice, or relationship that is organized and reinforced by the community. Said

---

5. Eugene Nida concurs as he writes about morphology. Environment shapes meaning. The meaning of every word and phrase is learned from its sociolinguistic setting. See *Morphology*, 152.

differently, it is a formalized way of thinking, speaking, behaving, and relating according to community-derived codes and categories. Table 3 visually unpacks these descriptions.

Table 3: Institutions of Culture

| A local community institu-tionalizes thinking, speaking, behaving, and relating by . . . | | Types of Institutions | | |
|---|---|---|---|---|
| | | Patterns | Practices | Relationships |
| | | *Thinking—speaking—behaving—relating* | | |
| *Formation* | *Reinforcement* | Genre | Judicial System | Kinship |
| First, core as-sumptions and shared values | Reward | Protocols | Religion | Society |
| | | Standards | Language | Family |
| Then, meaning, codes and categories | Retribution | Law | Means of Production | Marriage |
| | | Status | Financial Exchange | Government |

A local community first mutually assumes what is real and what ought to be. Then, collectively, people define what they mean, quantity or qualify, and organize perceived reality into categories, most of which are complex and detailed. If a person generally says and does what is expected, that person is prized and rewarded. If not, that person may be penalized by some means of retribution. For most people in any society, the socio-cultural institutions are just there. The structures are already in place and function somewhat effectively.[6]

Take a typical financial exchange in the United States. When shopping, Americans may look for sales but usually will not haggle over the price or try to barter with other items of value. If you try to pay your water bill at the local utility company with beaver pelts, more than likely the exchange would not take place. We have set ways of performing economic transactions. More generally, local communities establish, over time, their own patterns, practices, and relationships. Within such structures, people live out their lives.

6. See Appendix E for a detailed parallel between language and culture. Just as language has rules and patterns, so culture displays the same organization, thus making behavior predictable and providing a sense of normalcy.

Clearly, given the power of institutions, a few new words or behaviors are not enough to change a culture. Lasting cultural change requires institutional change, which itself requires a change in shared values and core assumptions.[7] See Figure 9 for the layers of culture with worldview at its core.[8]

## Values

Values define what must or should be done. In our layers-of-the-earth metaphor, values lie near the core of culture and determine its manifestations.[9] What people feel ought to be said or done shapes what they will say and do at the level of outward observable behavior. Consider, for example, these somewhat contrary pairs of values and the behaviors they could give rise to: (a). The environment must be protected. The economy must grow. (b). Elders ought to be respected. We must invest in our youth. (c). Time should be used wisely. We must not be slaves to the clock. (d). Relationships are more important than tasks. Tasks are more important than relationships. (e). Individual needs take precedence over group needs. The group takes precedence over individuals. (f). Men should take the lead. Men and women are equal. (g). Nation states should have strong borders. We are all global citizens.

In each of these pairs, we find an explicit or implicit "should," an imperative that demands a certain sort of action or behavior. It is this "oughtness" that suggests a value is at work. Oughtness bespeaks necessity, obligation, and duty. Such and such is the right or honorable thing to do. From an early

7. British anthropologist Bronislaw Malinowski (1884–1942) realized through empirical observation that cultural institutions function to meet the basic psychological needs of a society's people (McGee and Warms, *Anthropological Theory*, 154). He identified those needs: nutrition, reproduction, bodily comforts, safety, relaxation, movement, and growth. During the same era, A. R. Radcliffe Brown (1881–1955) understood that cultural institutions function to maintain social equilibrium and cohesion. Structural functionalists are concerned with laws and norms that maintain social organization.

8. This chapter presents the formation of culture such that core worldview assumptions are the basis for shared values. Codified values become institutionalized. Then, institutions promote and prohibit outward observable behavior. A flow can be traced from the inside out or from the outside in toward the middle of the model of culture. However, this is not to suggest that the starting point is always worldview. I would argue that causality may flow in any direction. Therefore, worldview is not always the independent variable with values, institutions, and behavior always the dependent variables.

9. Hofstede, *Cultures and Organizations*, 8.

age, children take on the values of their family and community. After that, values rarely change. Most children and adults are not consciously aware of the specific values they embrace. They just live them out.

Values drive what people think about—their ideas, the way people think, the topics they talk about, how they behave, and with whom and how they relate. All people think, speak, behave, and relate. But all people are not the same. They differ culturally. They live in different places and at different times. The time and stage upon which people live out their lives has both differences and similarities for people.

Although people live in the same world, they interact with their circumstances differently due to their value orientations. As an American, I tend to speak in terms of first-person pronouns, "I", "me", and "my." This way of speaking seems normal and natural to me. My society tends to prize self-reliance, the individual. But my university colleague Li Jun, a professor from China, tends to speak in terms of plural pronouns. This seems natural to her. Her society tends to prize collective endeavor, the group. At Regis University in Denver, Colorado, my students call me "Robert." In Bangalore, India, I am always addressed as "Dr. Strauss." These titles of address reveal differences in value: people in India recognize social hierarchy more so than people in the United States.

Though hard to see initially, these differences in values are ultimately observable. They can even be measured quantitatively and qualitatively. Once measured, a value may be described dimensionally.[10] Often, dimensions of culture are presented in contrasting pairs, but the juxtaposition does not imply one side is better. In other words, it is not helpful to think of the dimensions of culture in terms of right or wrong. Table 4 compiles several value dimensions with accompanying descriptions.[11]

10. The following are interchangeable terms: value, value dimension, dimension of culture, and value orientation.

11. The dimensions of culture have been analyzed and organized by qualitative research studies, including Kluckhohn and Strodtbeck, *Variations*; Hofstede (1980, 1991, 2001), Trompenaars and Hampden-Turner, *Riding the Waves*; Schwartz, "Universal Aspects"; Robert House et al., *Culture, Leadership, and Organization*; Minkov (2007), and Hall (1959, 1966, and 1976).

### Table 4: Dimensions of Culture

| Dimension | Contrasting Pairs | | Description |
|---|---|---|---|
| Basic orientation of self and "other" | Individualism | Collectivism | In societies where rule of law is dominant, people tend to become more wealthy and individualistic. They enjoy being self-sufficient. |
| Status in society | Egalitarian | Hierarchical | Individualistic societies tend to be egalitarian. Everyone is viewed as being the same in essence. |
| Status acquisition | Achieved | Ascribed | Status is acquired through achievement in justice cultures or ascription in honor cultures. |
| Power distance: the degree of inequality | Low | High | If a society values equality, power distance is low. |
| Vulnerability | Exposed | Concealed | In honor societies, vulnerability tends to be concealed in order to save face. |
| Information processing | Dichotomistic | Holistic | A data set may be processed singularly or in its relationship to the whole. |
| Mental processing and communicating style | Low context | High context | In low context communication, the meaning resides in the words. In high context communication, meaning is derived from the larger context of historical circumstances and relationships. |
| Time | Linear, monochronic, and a commodity | Nonlinear, polychronic, and an opportunity | Time may be viewed linearly with a past, present, and future. In contrast, it may be viewed circularly. |
| Status quo | Change | Tradition | In entrepreneurial contexts, rapid change may be prized. In honor societies, tradition is maintained. |

| Dimension | Contrasting Pairs | | Description |
|---|---|---|---|
| Planning, rules, and clarity | Uncertainty avoidance | Comfort with ambiguity | People in the Global West tend to hope for the best but plan for the worst. |
| Gender roles | Overlapped | Clearly distinct | In some societies, the roles of males and females overlap. Anyone can do anything. |
| Focus | Tasks | People | People in the Global South tend to value relationships and may put people ahead of tasks. |
| Preferred way of learning | Abstract conceptualization | Concrete relational/sequential | Some societies prefer to learn through concepts rather than concrete experiences. |

So vast and impactful are the value dimensions tabled above that each represents a potential book. Take mental processing and communication style. Typically, in the West, especially in urban centers and business activities, people tend to be "low context" communicators. "Context" refers to the communication situation—where one is, who one is speaking to, who one is. To what degree does the overall environment, past, present, and future, make a difference in processing information and the way it is communicated? In a low context setting, the environment is less consequential. Past relationships may be less important than the topic at hand. The impact of what is said on identity is less important than the task to be performed. Table 5 shows the differences between low and high contexts.

Table 5: Contrasting Low and High Context Communication

| | The Context | |
|---|---|---|
| | Low | High |
| Time | How long participants have known each other matters less than factual information, the results of empirical research, or the task at hand. | Historical context is so important. What happened in the past? Who did what? With whom? What time of year is it? What year is it? In what ways did your father know my father? |

| The Context | | |
| --- | --- | --- |
| | Low | High |
| Setting | Setting matters little. Anyone can connect with someone else almost anywhere. A business meeting at a local coffee café is normal. | Setting is key. Does the place, its decorations, and surrounding environment befit the status of the people participating? Does the place bestow appropriate honor? |
| Relation-ships | Personal relationships are impor-tant but not vital to effectiveness. | Relationships may be the most important part of high context communication. Credible mes-sengers share credible messages. |
| Identity | In egalitarian societies where people are more or less equal, voice and vote are often granted to almost anyone. Everyone may feel they have a right to "be at the table" of decision-making. | The ascribed status of one or more of the participants may be the most important factor in processing of information (what is or is not accepted as fact), the manner of communicating (who speaks, to whom, when, and how), and how decisions are made. |

A community's shared values shape how its members will act. These val-ues are not just whimsical fancies that come out of the blue. In our model of culture, values are underpinned by deep assumptions about reality—what we call core *worldview* assumptions. Worldview, then, is the critical component of culture. These assumptions are often hidden from those who hold them; they seem so natural and normal that their embracers have trouble noticing and articulating such basic beliefs. Some researchers think worldview is too complicated to consider. We argue it is too important to ignore.

## Worldview

Worldview is a story-grid through which a person sees and interprets all aspects of life. A person may or may not see reality as it really exists, but every person sees through a cluster of socially-constructed stories. These stories determine what is "real"—and what that reality means. Worldview is like a lens we look through, a lens fashioned by our society, its curvature determined by the stories a society holds dear. Every person has a lens, but the prescription in the lens differs from group to group.[12]

Over time, people pass their experiences along through storytelling. The stories clump together into story sets. Some powerful stories emerge as controlling stories or master narratives.[13] At any moment in time, a person looks through the story-grid and interprets everything—self, other, one's relationships with other, causality, time, and space. As Craig Rusbult says, "Worldview is a view of the world, used for living in the world."[14]

While similar, worldview is not the same as culture. Culture is the broader term. Worldview is one part of culture, at its core.[15] We can define worldview more precisely. Michael Kearney analyzes worldview into seven universal elements: classification, self, other, relationship, causality, time, and space.[16]

There are patterns to worldviews.[17] The Porteños of Buenos Aires speak alike, with a distinct Castellano accent, and display a conjoint bravado. The Black American police officers I am privileged to train in cultural competency think in similar patterns, that is, almost always from the perspective of the civil rights movement. Their story grid is the history of slavery in America and their own place in the unfolding story. Table 6 identifies how worldviews are patterned and offers brief descriptions.[18]

12. This illustration of different prescriptions comes from Jerry Solomon, "Worldviews," par. 4.

13. Halverson et al., *Master Narratives of Islamist Extremism*.

14. Rusbult, "What Is a Worldview?" par. 1. Rusbult's definition is likely informed by Walsh and Middleton, *Transforming Vision*, 32.

15. Naugle's *Worldview* gives an in-depth analysis of the definition of worldview beginning in the 1800s.

16. Kearney, *World View*.

17. Some writers mistakenly refer to the overarching patterns of culture as paradigms or worldviews. An example is Thomas and George's article about guilt, shame, and power, "Impact of Worldviews," 24–33. True, worldviews have patterns, as do most things, but this book's overarching patterns are not themselves worldviews. Each overarching pattern can have different, particular worldviews at its core.

18. Most sociologists and anthropologists agree about a worldview's components. Robert Redfield's *The Primitive World* and Michael Kearney's *World View* use strikingly similar language in their analyses.

Table 6: Worldview Patterns

| Pattern | Description |
|---|---|
| Common | The elements that make up a worldview are shared by the group. They are common. Markers of self-identity are shared. |
| Consistent | The core assumptions are basically the same person-to-person. Citizens in North Mexico along the USA border know that illness is caused by the evil eye. Almost everyone in India recognizes the differences in caste and these differences dictate occupations. |
| Coherent | Overall, the core assumptions fit logically together. The logic used is locally defined. It is phenomenological. In McAllen, Texas, I know to stroke the newborn's arm and say, *Pa no dale* (*Para no darle el mal de ojo!* Roughly in English, "So as not to give you the evil of the eye."). This feels right to the mother holding her newborn. It makes sense. |
| Comprehensive | The set of assumptions are broad in scope. A worldview charts enough territory to explain the whole of life. |
| Correspondence | The elements are similar to lived experiences. Endocrinologists with PhDs who work for the US Department of Agriculture in McAllen, Texas swear that the evil eye is real and cannot be persuaded otherwise. |
| Coordinated | The assumptions are synced together through themes emphasized in master narratives. |

The chapters on the four overarching pattern of culture explain more about worldview and how it works.

# Closing Comments

Culture—our learned, shared patterns of perception and behavior—has layers, some of which are deep, hidden from sight, outside of our awareness. The layers of culture have their own complexity. Shared values and core worldview assumptions are at the center of culture. These are rarely made explicit. They are the most difficult to identify. They change slowly, if at all.

Often, people coming into a new locale from the outside are able to see manifestations of culture that insiders do not. Consequently, researchers make a distinction between the emic and etic perspectives of culture. Chapter 3 tells more.

Chapter 3

# Two Inroads into a Culture

I cannot boast that [this book] contains much which a reader could not have found out for himself if, at every hard place in the old books, he had turned to commentators, histories, encyclopaedias, and other such helps. I thought . . . the book worth writing because that method of discovery seemed to me and seems to some others rather unsatisfactory. For one thing, we turn to the helps only when the hard passages are manifestly hard. But there are treacherous passages which will not send us to the notes. They look easy and aren't. Again, frequent researches *ad hoc* sadly impair perceptive reading, so that sensitive people may even come to regard scholarship as a baleful thing which is always taking you *out of* the literature itself. My hope was that if a tolerable (though very incomplete) outfit were acquired beforehand and taken along with one, it might lead *in*. To be always looking at the map when there is a fine prospect before you shatters the 'wise passiveness' in which landscape ought to be enjoyed. But to consult a map before we set out has no such ill effect. Indeed it will lead us to many prospects; including some we might never have found by following our noses.

—C. S. Lewis, "Preface," *The Discarded Image: An Introduction to Medieval and Renaissance Literature*, ix

"If you want to learn about water, don't ask a fish."

## Opening Remarks

I KNOW WHAT YOU are probably thinking. "If culture is *that* big, *that* complicated, with all those layers—with parts of it hidden even from the people who know it best—how in the world am *I* supposed to learn anything about the culture I'm traveling to? In just the short time I have before I leave? And in the short time I'll be there? I hardly have time to make my travel arrangements. You really expect me to read a five-volume history of the colonization of Indonesia? Or spend six months practicing the tones of Cantonese? Or puzzle out how the melodic lines of Indian *ragas* correspond to seasons, times of day, colors, and emotions? Forget it. I'm flying blind."

You are right. In only a few weeks, you are not going to become an expert on the culture you are visiting. You only have so much time before your trip. And on your trip, too, down time will be sparse. But not preparing at all is probably the worst thing you can do, and you would be surprised at how far a little preparation goes. So where should you focus your efforts in the time you *do* have to prepare? Well, there are two ways of learning about a given culture, two types of field research you can do. Social scientists call these two avenues of approach by an odd pair of terms. These four-letter words your parents probably never let slip: *emic* and *etic*. (No, they are not acronyms. But if you suspect they looked lopped off from larger words, you are on to something.) Each avenue of approach leads downtown, so to speak, straight to a culture's heart. But each takes you past different scenery. Each requires a different style of driving. Each has potential traffic snarls and clear stretches that get you right where you want to go. I will explain the advantages and drawbacks of each. And while combining both approaches gives a well-rounded sense of a particular culture, we will see that one inroad may be the better starting point.

## Emic—the View on the Ground

The terms *emic* and *etic* come from linguistics, the scientific study of language.[1] Over half a century since their coinage—over time all words drift in meaning—social scientists now use the terms a bit differently. But I want to honor their origin by unpacking the difference between an emic and an etic point of view using an example from spoken language.

Just south of Denver, my home in Colorado sits at an elevation of almost 7,000 feet. Out back is an unobstructed view of the Rocky Mountains' Front Range dominated by Pike's Peak. Now, when I say the word "mountain," I

---

1. Kenneth Pike (1912–2000) coined the terms *emic* and *etic* in 1954 in his ambitious book *Language in Relation to a Unified Theory of the Structure of Human Behavior.* Pike earned his PhD in linguistics from the University of Michigan, studying under Edward Sapir (1884–1939). For 37 years, Pike was president of the Summer Institute of Linguistics (known internationally as Wycliffe Bible Translators) based in Norman, Oklahoma.

think I say all the consonants and vowels in the written word. (If asked, "do you pronounce a 't' when you say 'mountain'?" I will say yes.) We all know how to spell "mountain." Its spelling is fixed. We spell it with a "t." And we think that this "t" stands for the same sound we use in words like "top," "pot," and "butter." Such a sound is what linguists call a *phoneme*, an abstract unit of sound perceived by the speaker to be a single distinct sound.

But let's bring in an outside observer, an expert in *phonetics*, who can tell me what sounds I really make when I say "mountain." Because of my southern American English accent, the linguist tells me, what I actually say, phonetically—and I know this looks pretty weird—is [mąwʔn̩]. Let me explain. First, I make an initial nasalized consonant—"m." Next is a vowel glide—that is the "a" with the little sickle under it and the levitating "w"— which gets nasalized, too, being so close to the nasalized "m." (You can hear almost the same vowel glide without the nasalization if you say "cow.") In the middle of the word "mountain," despite my confession above, I do not bring my tongue against my teeth to make an "n" or a "t" sound. Instead, my tongue is low in the mouth, nowhere near the upper teeth, and I briefly restrict the air coming out of my throat—a glottal stop, represented by what looks like an upside down 5. (In terms of distance in the mouth, a glottal stop is actually about as far as you can get from a "t.") Finally, after the glottal stop is simply a syllabic "n." Even though the written word has a cozy pair of vowels—"ain"—I do not actually pronounce them. What I say does not rhyme with "rain" or "train." Instead, it rhymes with "fountain," which I also pronounce with a glottal stop and final syllabic "n."

A trained linguistic easily hears my sounds and records them using the International Phonetic Alphabet (see Figure 12), as I have done above. The linguist points out that the "t" sound in "top," "pot," "butter," and "mountain"—which I think of as being the same—is actually four differ-ent sounds. (In "top," it is aspirated; in "pot," it is unreleased; in "butter," it's actually a medial flapped "r"; and in "mountain," a glottal stop.) The *phoneme* "t"—an abstract unit of sound which I perceive to be a single distinct sound—actually varies slightly depending on the sounds around it. These contextual variations are unconsciously considered nonsignifi-cant and nondiscriminatory.[2] As a native English speaker, I do not notice the variations, unless I am consciously wearing my linguistics hat and paying very careful attention to the actual sounds I make. Indeed, apart from studying linguistics in college, I would have no idea whatsoever

2. Harris, "History and Significance," 332.

which sounds I was actually making. I would simply think I was saying "mountain" as it was spelled.

If the linguist—or some other foreigner or outsider—asks me to explain the writing system I use to transcribe my language, I may not be able to give a very good account. Perhaps the best I could do is something like this: The English alphabet has twenty-six characters, five vowels and twenty-one consonants. Each letter in the alphabet may be written in uppercase or lowercase depending on the dictates of grammar. Each has a name, derived mostly from French or Latin. In American English, "e" is the most frequently used vowel and "t" the most frequently used consonant. The letters of the alphabet represent particular phonemes or sounds. This is how it looks to a native English speaker untrained in linguistics. This is the view from the ground. But there is another view—that of the outside expert.

## Etic—the Bird's Eye View

If asked to describe English sounds, an untrained native speaker would give an emic account. In answering, he would follow his gut or use a bit of local knowledge about the English alphabet and grammar. His local knowledge—a pattern of perception—hides from him the fact that he pronounces "t" differently in different contexts. But our example above has already given us a glimpse of a different view, an *etic* view. The trained linguist uses a schematic totally unknown to most native English speakers to accurately describe the sounds an English speaker makes. As good as our gut feelings often are, the trained linguist has a much better tool—an alphabet that can describe *exactly* what sounds someone's mouth is making, whether that person is speaking English, Navajo, or Chinese. What interests the linguist, here, is the multiple pronunciations of phonemes depending on their environment (that is, their position in a word and overall speech context). Linguistics record the sounds they hear using the phonetic alphabet, shown in Figure 12.

## THE INTERNATIONAL PHONETIC ALPHABET (revised to 2015)

CONSONANTS (PULMONIC)                                                        © 2015 IPA

| | Bilabial | Labiodental | Dental | Alveolar | Postalveolar | Retroflex | Palatal | Velar | Uvular | Pharyngeal | Glottal |
|---|---|---|---|---|---|---|---|---|---|---|---|
| Plosive | p b | | | t d | | ʈ ɖ | c ɟ | k g | q ɢ | | ʔ |
| Nasal | m | ɱ | | n | | ɳ | ɲ | ŋ | N | | |
| Trill | B | | | r | | | | | R | | |
| Tap or Flap | | ⱱ | | ɾ | | ɽ | | | | | |
| Fricative | ɸ β | f v | θ ð | s z | ʃ ʒ | ʂ ʐ | ç ʝ | x ɣ | χ ʁ | ħ ʕ | h ɦ |
| Lateral fricative | | | | ɬ ɮ | | | | | | | |
| Approximant | | ʋ | | ɹ | | ɻ | j | ɰ | | | |
| Lateral approximant | | | | l | | ɭ | ʎ | L | | | |

Symbols to the right in a cell are voiced, to the left are voiceless. Shaded areas denote articulations judged impossible.

CONSONANTS (NON-PULMONIC)

| Clicks | Voiced implosives | Ejectives |
|---|---|---|
| ʘ Bilabial | ɓ Bilabial | ' Examples: |
| ǀ Dental | ɗ Dental/alveolar | p' Bilabial |
| ǃ (Post)alveolar | ʄ Palatal | t' Dental/alveolar |
| ǂ Palatoalveolar | ɠ Velar | k' Velar |
| ǁ Alveolar lateral | ʛ Uvular | s' Alveolar fricative |

OTHER SYMBOLS

ʍ Voiceless labial-velar fricative     ɕ ʑ Alveolo-palatal fricatives
w Voiced labial-velar approximant     ɺ Voiced alveolar lateral flap
ɥ Voiced labial-palatal approximant   ɧ Simultaneous ʃ and x
ʜ Voiceless epiglottal fricative
ʢ Voiced epiglottal fricative          Affricates and double articulations
ʡ Epiglottal plosive                   can be represented by two symbols joined by a tie bar if necessary.   t͡s k͡p

DIACRITICS Some diacritics may be placed above a symbol with a descender, e.g. ŋ̊

| | | | | | | |
|---|---|---|---|---|---|---|
| ̥ Voiceless | n̥ d̥ | ̤ Breathy voiced | b̤ a̤ | ̪ Dental | t̪ d̪ |
| ̬ Voiced | s̬ t̬ | ̰ Creaky voiced | b̰ a̰ | ̺ Apical | t̺ d̺ |
| ʰ Aspirated | tʰ dʰ | ̼ Linguolabial | t̼ d̼ | ̻ Laminal | t̻ d̻ |
| ̹ More rounded | ɔ̹ | ʷ Labialized | tʷ dʷ | ̃ Nasalized | ẽ |
| ̜ Less rounded | ɔ̜ | ʲ Palatalized | tʲ dʲ | ⁿ Nasal release | dⁿ |
| ̟ Advanced | u̟ | ˠ Velarized | tˠ dˠ | ˡ Lateral release | dˡ |
| ̠ Retracted | e̠ | ˤ Pharyngealized | tˤ dˤ | ̚ No audible release | d̚ |
| ̈ Centralized | ë | ̴ Velarized or pharyngealized | ɫ | | |
| ̽ Mid-centralized | ě | ̝ Raised | e̝ ( ɹ̝ = voiced alveolar fricative) | | |
| ̩ Syllabic | n̩ | ̞ Lowered | e̞ ( β̞ = voiced bilabial approximant) | | |
| ̯ Non-syllabic | e̯ | ̘ Advanced Tongue Root | e̘ | | |
| ˞ Rhoticity | ɚ a˞ | ̙ Retracted Tongue Root | e̙ | | |

VOWELS

Where symbols appear in pairs, the one to the right represents a rounded vowel.

SUPRASEGMENTALS

ˈ Primary stress          ˌfoʊnəˈtɪʃən
ˌ Secondary stress
ː Long          eː
ˑ Half-long     eˑ
̆ Extra-short    ĕ
| Minor (foot) group
‖ Major (intonation) group
. Syllable break     ɹi.ækt
‿ Linking (absence of a break)

TONES AND WORD ACCENTS

| LEVEL | | CONTOUR | |
|---|---|---|---|
| e̋ or ˥ Extra high | | ě or ᷄ Rising | |
| é ˦ High | | ê Falling | |
| ē ˧ Mid | | e᷄ High rising | |
| è ˨ Low | | e᷅ Low rising | |
| ȅ ˩ Extra low | | e᷈ Rising-falling | |
| ↓ Downstep | | ↗ Global rise | |
| ↑ Upstep | | ↘ Global fall | |

Figure 12: International Phonetic Alphabet.

A trained linguist can use the International Phonetic Alphabet to transcribe sounds in any language in the world. It's quite a powerful tool. But the linguist still has his work cut out for him, especially if he is not a native English speaker. While able to transcribe sounds very accurately, the linguist still has to figure out which sounds in a language are phonemes—that is, whether or not an English speaker thinks of those four "t" sounds as being different or the same. (In a similar vein, whether the hissing sound at the end of "cats" is the same, in the speaker's mind, as the buzzing sound at the end of "dogs.") This is important if the linguist is creating an alphabet for a language not yet written down. He needs to know whether to use one letter, "t," for four different sounds or use four completely different letters. And beyond orthography, the linguist will have a host of other questions about the more complicated aspects of language, questions only an insider with an emic view can answer.

## From Language to Culture

To get a handle on another culture, you do not have to become a master linguist. You do not have to know the International Phonetic Alphabet and practice scribbling down everything your friends say in its strange characters. All I mean to imply is that scholars of culture and anthropologists have developed tools *like* the International Phonetic Alphabet, tools that use categories gleaned from large-scale patterns shown by cultures all over the world. Just as the linguist's tool allows him to notice sounds a native speaker does not, these cultural tools reveal patterns of culture an insider does not see. Every emic view has its blind spots. Stepping back to get a bird's eye view of a culture, an etic view, can reveal truths about a culture that you might never reach, even after a thousand interviews.

I often work as a consultant for organizations in Western Canada, mostly with executives. I travel into the region from the Lower Forty-Eight. As an outsider coming into a new place, I tend to notice cultural differences, like communication style. When I communicate, I tend to be direct. In a conversation, I often summarize or condense points. I rarely tell stories. My counterparts in Canada, however, the insiders to the locale, tend to be less direct. They amplify details. They speak concretely. They enjoy descriptive storytelling. They like luxuriating in the past. These Canadian executives notice when someone communicates in a style different from theirs. Most of them see me, the outsider, as a stranger,[3] and find my communication style odd. But few of them could describe their communication style in an abstract way. They would have trouble adjusting their communication style to a new context. As a trained outsider, however, I am familiar with categories of communication style across cultures. I have terms to describe communication styles. I am less likely to experience "conversation shock." I can adapt my default communication style to fit new situations. So in Canada, instead of shutting down, or being baffled by people's indirectness, or impatiently waiting for them to get to the point, I tell more stories and allow more room for details. Having an etic view lets me act with awareness.

The terms *emic* and *etic* were lopped off from the linguistic terms *phonemics* and *phonetics*,[4] descriptors of the dichotomy in all languages between the perceived sounds in the mind of native speakers and the actual sounds that they articulate when they speak.[5] Pike and others subsequently broadened the application of *emic* and *etic* to all aspects of human behavior in culture.[6] Pike credits his teacher Sapir with the initial insights about insider vs. outsider perspectives.[7] He quotes from Sapir's *Selected Writings*:

> It is impossible to say what an individual is doing unless we have
> tacitly accepted the essentially arbitrary modes of interpretation

3. Georg Simmel's 1908 essay "The Stranger" explores the unique status of the stranger in society. Strangers, he suggests, are simultaneously near and far from the group and are often in a position to offer an impartial and objective view of what is happening within a society.

4. Pike, *Phonemics*, 57.

5. Procedures of phonemic analysis are based upon premises about the way sounds function in their environments. See Pike, *Phonemics*, 58–60. The premises:

1. Sounds tend to be modified by their environment (sounds tend to slur into one another, like the nasalization of vowels contiguous to nasalized consonants)

2. Sound systems have a tendency toward phonetic symmetry (if "t" and "d" are phonemically different, then "p" and "b" likely will be also)

3. Sounds tend to fluctuate (a "t" may sound different depending on its position in a word)

4. Characteristic non-suspicious sequences of sounds exert structural pressure on the phonemic interpretation of suspicious segments or suspicious sequences of segments

These remarkable phenomena are replicated in culture. See Appendix E. Observable behaviors are modified and differentiated. Meaning is largely derived from context.

6. For the emic and etic perspectives as a way to describe human behavior or culture, see Pike, *Language*, 8. Appendix E compares the attributes of language with culture.

7. Pike, *Language*, 10.

that social tradition is constantly suggesting to us from the very moment of our birth. Let anyone who doubts this try the experiment of making a painstaking report of the actions of a group of natives engaged in some form of activity, say religious, to which he has not the cultural key. If he is a skillful writer, he may succeed in giving a picturesque account of what he sees and hears, or thinks he sees and hears, but the chances of his being able to give a relation of what happens in terms that would be intelligible and acceptable to the natives themselves are practically nil. He will be guilty of all manner of distortion. His emphasis will be constantly askew. He will find interesting what the natives take for granted as a casual kind of behavior worthy of no particular comment, and he will utterly fail to observe the crucial turning points in the course of action that give formal significance to the whole in the minds of those who do possess the key to its understanding.[8]

You will notice a difference of emphasis here. Sapir thinks the natives have "the cultural key" an outside observer lacks. The observer, says Sapir, will mistake the ceremony's significance until he gets the native interpretation. This may seem to counter my claim that the outside observer has a cultural key that insiders lack. Yet I would argue Sapir's remark shows how important it is that the outside observer have proper *training*. (Not just any outsider's view qualifies as an etic view. The tools and categories of anthropology are essential.) And Sapir also suggests that an etic view alone, without any emic input, will likely get it wrong.

Social scientists have, in the decades since Pike, debated the exact meaning of the emic-etic distinction. They have also differed on which view, the insider's or the outsider's, is the better view—more accurate, more useful, truer—or if the best perspective is one that combines the bird's-eye view with the view on the ground, using both to obtain a binocular vision of a culture.[9] Some, like Marvin Harris, find the local perspective to be, well, local. Cultural insiders usually have only a limited and parochial view of their society, not

8. Sapir, *Selected Writings*, 546–7.

9. The rift between emic and etic approaches in the social sciences, and their respective drawbacks, was nicely described back in the sixties by Berreman, in a cuttingly-titled article "Anemic and Emetic Analyses in Social Anthropology," 346–354. Berreman suggests etic approaches too often sacrifice life to rigor and end up overly dry, anemic— lacking the blood and verve of real life—while emic approaches flout rigor in favor of intuition and gut feeling, often nauseatingly so. In fact, Berreman wonders if these categories from linguistics should be seen as a cure all for the problems ethnographers face when describing cultures.

often being in a position to compare it extensively with others. Harris says the local is "ineluctably bound" to the emic universe of his own culture.[10] (At the same time, Harris wants to avoid the notion that one view is superior and the other inferior.[11]) Pike, in turn, argued that the student of culture must start with etic categories but push toward emic descriptions: "etic data provide access into the system—the starting point of analysis . . . [but] the initial etic description gradually is refined, and is ultimately—in principle, but probably never in practice—replaced by one which is totally emic."[12]

Pike's desire for a total emic description of a culture, a comprehensive account from an insider's point of view, is a nice ideal. It requires years of study: professional training in anthropology, mastering a local language or two, interviewing dozens if not hundreds of locals. But it may not be the best goal if your incursion into another culture is going to be brief. Instead, what will help the short-term traveler is a tool for getting a foot in the door. A few terms and contrasts for getting a handle on a new culture's blooming, buzzing confusion. In short, etic categories—overarching patterns that form the invisible backbone of a culture. The rest of this book offers just such a tool, a sort of international cultural alphabet. It gives the student of culture a framework for describing strange behaviors, foreign values, and mysterious assumptions about reality.

As a summary, Table 7 compares the two perspectives and clarifies how they differ in language and culture.

Table 7: A Comparison of Emic and Etic

| Emic: an "insider" perspective | Etic: an "outsider" perspective |
|---|---|
| In linguistics, there are the sounds I think I say (a "t" in *top*, *pot*, and *butter*) based on phonemics or correct alphabetical spelling. | In linguistics, there are the sounds I actually make (an aspirated "t" in *top*; an unreleased "t" in *pot*, and a medial flapped "r" in *butter*) as analyzed by articulatory phonetics. |
| An emic unit ("t") is constant in the speaker's mind in spite of its etic variability. In all three words, I assume I make the "t" sound. | An etic unit varies to the outside observer in spite of its emic constancy. |

10. Harris, *Anthropological Theory*, 582.

11. Harris, "History and Significance," 331.

12. Quoted in Harris, "History and Significance," 333.

| Emic: an "insider" perspective | Etic: an "outsider" perspective |
| --- | --- |
| Related to research methods, the primary data collection techniques are participant observation and in-depth interviewing in the local vernacular. The quest is to know the mindset of the insider. | Related to research methods, the primary data collection technique is direct and indirect observation (often ethnographers will transition from emic to etic). |
| In linguistics, etic is used to discover emic. | In culture, emic is used to discover etic. |
| The research approach tends to be qualitative. | The research approach tends to be quantitative. |
| Categories of meaning are described based upon phenomenological definitions derived from the host society that are culturally and historically bound. "I am making the 't' sound every time." | Categories of meaning are described based upon scientific definitions from universal patterns of culture that are empirically documented across space/time history. What is outside of my awareness, is that I am actually making three distinct phonetic sounds. |
| Helpful descriptions are culture-specific, related to particular domains in the locale. | Helpful descriptions are culture-general, related to broader comparisons across cultures. |
| Constructs are grounded in self-understanding (consciously or unconsciously). | Constructs are predetermined from insights that apply equally well to all cultures. |
| Emic systems are not necessarily transparent to the insider without exposure to others or training. | Etic systems in a local cultural context are transparent to a trained outside observer. |
| An example of emic variation is changing sports from football to baseball. | An example of etic variation is playing an extra inning in a tied baseball game. |
| Personal ideas and values (core worldview assumptions) are assumed to be the ultimate cause of observable behavior. | Impersonal factors, especially material conditions, are assumed to be the causes of observable behavior. |

## Closing Comments

When it comes to learning about a new culture—a society's learned, shared patterns of perception and behavior—there are two main inroads, the emic and the etic. Emic research seeks to gain an insider's point of view, how it looks in the thick of things or on the ground, most often by intensive interviewing of local people and paying attention to the categories and explanations they use to describe their behaviors, institutions, and beliefs. Etic research uses a trained outsider's point of view, a loftier, bird's-eye-view perspective, informed by categories developed by the prior comparison of many cultures, to find patterns of behavior locals may not be able to articulate or even notice. While a full appreciation of a culture involves both approaches, etic categories are the better place to start. An etic view arms the traveler with a framework. It makes some sense of the jumble of emic experiences that the traveler often encounters at random.

To summarize, culture is learned. We are not born with it. We are born into a social context. Culture has layers. It is deep. Beneath the surface of what is said and done are powerful drivers of culture. And any culture looks different depending on whether one is a local or an outsider. Just as language is patterned, so is culture. The patterns are not abstractions constructed by the analyst or outsider observer. They are real. The locals tacitly know the units that make up the patterned system and the structural classes overall. Actions and reactions of locals are predictable.[13]

So, what is a *pattern* of culture?

13. Pike, *Language*, 8.

# Chapter 4

# Patterns of Culture

## Definition of Pattern

A *PATTERN* IS SOMETHING deliberately repeated and thereby predictable. A pattern can be a natural configuration, a mechanical design, a musical arrangement, an artistic work, or a personal preference (like the arrangement of my shoes in Figure 13). A pattern is generally intelligible.

Figure 13: Shoes *Image used by permission of Robert Strauss.*

By intelligible, I mean an observer with adequate knowledge gets the intended form and may even comprehend its function and meaning. A skilled observer may be able to tell what comes next.

Recently, a barista at Starbucks asked me how long I had been ordering a grande caramel macchiato. Rather bemused, I responded (truthfully, of course), "For the past fifteen years!" Apparently, she detected a pattern in my drink preference. At my local store, I do not need to order, but only arrive and pay. I walk in the door, and even before I approach the counter, a barista straightway makes my drink. My preference is patterned.[1]

## Four Components of Observed Behavior

When it comes to patterns of culture, not only are observable forms themselves predictably repeated. Also repeated are the way such forms function in a social setting, the meaning people give them, and the ways people use them. The anthropologist Ralph Linton (1893–1953)[2] introduced this

1. Are there patterns to human behavior that can be observed, known, and defined? Yes: "it is possible to make statements of regularities that help in explaining and even predicting the human construction of meaning" (Thompson et al., *Cultural Theory*, xiii). In fact, sciences like psychology would not exist without such patterns. Social psychology studies people's reactions to the real or imagined presence of others. It looks at topics like attraction, influence, human exchange, and group dynamics. Notable social psychologists include Kurt Lewin, Gordon Allport, Stanley Milgram, Albert Bandura, Don Campbell, Erik Erikson, and others. Behavioral psychology studies the relationship between one's thoughts and behavior. How much does observable behavior influence thinking and vice versa? Seminal scholars include Edward Thorndike, Ivan Pavlov, B. F. Skinner, and Lev Vygotsky. If every human interaction were entirely random, there could be no social or behavioral psychology, for there would be no patterns of observable behavior. Indeed, there would be no such thing as meaning and learning. There would be no meaningful human communication. But there is communication. We often know what each other means. We learn from one another and our experiences. All because there are patterns of observable behavior. Beneath these observable behaviors lie layers of culture. There are patterns of culture, too, likewise observable, knowable, and definable. The patterns are not necessarily rigid. Variations within patterns occur due to contiguous circumstances.

With an opposing perspective, cultural psychologist Richard Shweder writes, "Much less is 'glued together,' much less is integrated, than most of us have imagined" (Shweder, *Thinking through Cultures*, 269). He cites broad and varied research, especially highlighting method bias. Marvin Harris (1927–2001), professor of anthropology at the University of Florida, argued likewise as a cultural materialist. Harris writes, "To explain sociocultural differences and similarities exclusively in terms of more or less reasonable thought and action is to omit any statement of conditions" (Harris, *Anthropological Theory*, 39). Harris understood that the material world and its present conditions at any moment of time drive human behavior. As such, for him, patterns are not as significant as being presented in *Overarching Patterns*.

2. When Franz Boas retired in 1937 as the head of the Department of Anthropology at Columbia University, many expected his mentee Ruth Benedict to replace him. But she did not. Instead, the university choose Ralph Linton. Linton's culture classification of form, meaning, use, and function has been timeless, although his differentiation of *use* from *function* is difficult for some readers to comprehend. A broader culture classification posited by Linton has been less popular or useful. He saw culture "units" like wood and string assembled as a "trait" or what may be called a bow. Traits are combined

classification of form, function, meaning, and use. His framework offers a deeper view into the patterns of culture.

In his 1934 book *The Study of Man*, Linton shows how these categories—form, function, meaning, and use—fit together. A few examples will help. Table 8 explains Linton's terms, via the way people in Western cultures use flowers in social relationships.

Table 8: Flowers as an Example of Linton's Categories

| Form | Function | Meaning | Use |
|------|----------|---------|-----|
| Flowers | A relational expression of goodwill, nuanced for each occasion. Note how function derives more from meaning than from form. Understanding meaning is a key element in effective cross-cultural communication. | What do they mean? 1. *Sympathy* if related to sickness or death 2. *Congratulations* if related to a birthday or wedding 3. *Thanks* if brought by a dinner guest to share with the host 4. *Love* if given in courtship  Note how the form remains somewhat constant (one could say "universal") but the meaning changes significantly based on the purpose associated with a setting (particular). | Delivered in a timely manner, appropriately arranged for the circumstances with the "right" kind and color of flowers (in the West, white for sympathy and red for love), and perhaps accompanied by a written note or brief verbal statement. |

In the example from Table 8, the form—flowers—remains constant. But what giving flowers *means*—love, gratitude, congratulations, or sympathy—changes based on the situation, depending on the particular nuance of goodwill the giver wants to convey. The form is universal or essential. The function is particularistic. So is the meaning and the use. These four components are everywhere in culture.

---

functionally as a "trait cluster," for example, the bow, arrows, and a quiver (each of which are traits). Trait clusters (the weaponry set, animal tracking, and archery techniques) are integrated to form an "activity" or the cultural behavior of hunting.

Another behavior that illustrates Linton's classification is the hand-shake. Although quite complex mechanically, a handshake is easily recognized by its look. Its form typically remains the same. We usually use the right hand. There is some gripping action. The fulcrum is the elbow, not the shoulder. The motion is up and down rather than side to side. The duration is often only a few seconds. Handshakes have patterns. Pretty simple, right? Actually, while a handshake seems simple and straightforward, its meaning, function, and use are quite complex. Consider Table 9, which analyzes common handshake behavior.

Table 9: Handshake to Illustrate the Complexity of "Use"

| Form | Function | Meaning | Use |
|---|---|---|---|
| Handshake | When and where? (numbers match the "Meaning" column) 1. A social exchange 2. Informal greeting 3. Congratulations 4. Economic exchange 5. Business agreement | What does a handshake mean? 1. Indicates friendship 2. Gestures courtesy or goodwill 3. Bestows honor 4. Signals a transaction is final 5. Assures obligations will be met | How long? How firm a grip? How rigorous a shake? Eyes looking where? Other hand? Body position—seated or standing? Verbal accompaniment? Other accompaniments—hug, kiss, or other? Optional for other party? When—meeting, departing, middle of conversation? Dry vs. sweaty palm? Grip four fingers? Thumb? Speed of body movement? Motion of wrist, elbow, and shoulder? Substitutes if hands are full? What if wearing gloves? Dirty hands? With whom? Who initiates? Illnesses? |

How does Linton's framework—form, function, meaning, use—impact communication across cultures? All communication is made possible because a society understands the meaning associated with cultural forms. Forms have some degree of consistency. They remain essentially the same anywhere in the world. But meaning differs setting-to-setting and culture-to-culture. Meaning is particularistic. Meaning is diverse. The same form in another culture has some difference in meaning. The same meaning in another culture is often represented by a different form. An informal greeting in Argentina, for example, may not be a handshake, but an air kiss on the cheek. True, handshakes are not unheard of when Argentine friends greet. But more likely they will touch cheeks and kiss the air. Closer friends may even receive air kisses on both sides. In fact, very close friends may literally kiss each other on the cheeks, call each other *Che*, and speak in a seventh conjugation of verbs using the pronoun *vos*. In communicating across cultures, if one uses an inappropriate form, the meaning will be unclear, at best, and wrong or insulting, at worst.

Even within a culture, the same handshake can be used for different functions, each with its own meaning. I saw a friend yesterday at the same Starbucks described above. We greeted each other with a handshake, a demonstration of friendship. Two weeks ago, after a two-day training in McAllen, Texas, for the US Department of Agriculture, a participant came up to me and shook my hand. Complimenting me, he said, "Great job facilitating the training. I learned a lot!" The handshakes in Texas and at the Colorado Starbucks had the same form. But the function and meaning were different. At Starbucks, the function was a friendly greeting. In Texas, it was congratulatory. Further, at a garage sale my wife organized last Saturday, I gave a radio/CD player to an immigrant family. The father shook my hand and said, "Thank you!" Again, the form of the handshake remained unchanged, but the function this time was gratitude, not greeting or congratulations.

The handshake is but one of thousands of possible behaviors in human exchange. All over a culture, these interrelated patterns of form, function, meaning, and use are repeated. Within any one culture, locals tacitly or explicitly know the forms and their associated meanings.

Figure 14: The Layers of the Earth *Used by permission*
*from Global Perspectives Consulting.*

All we say and do is patterned. Yet our outward observable behavior is only a fraction of our whole culture. Much more of culture is unseen, below the surface. Chapter 2 compares the deep layers of culture to the layers of the earth. See Figure 14. The earth's crust is only five kilometers thick in some places. Seismologists say that its thinness is like the skin of an apple. So, too, with culture. Observable behaviors represent only a thin veneer of all a culture's patterns. Below a culture's surface, at the mantle layer, are socio-cultural institutions. Examples include kinship, the family, religion, judicial systems, law enforcement, and community groups. These structured institutions function in ways that promote and prohibit observed behavior.

Still deeper in culture, at the outer core layer, are identity markers and value orientations. Values represent what a group of people feel ought or ought not to happen. Then, at the center of culture, at the inner core layer, are core worldview assumptions about what is and is not real. Michael Kearney asserts that worldview is made up of six categories. They include assumptions about self, other, relationships, causality, time, and space.

Core worldview assumptions vary from culture to culture. But every culture has them, solidly in place. They do not change easily or quickly. These assumptions drive values. Codified values become institutionalized. From these unseen, hidden layers of culture come outward behaviors.

In Bhubaneshwar, Orissa, why did I, without thinking, tell the truth? Why did the assistant shame the hotel staff and maintain our honor? Neither of our responses to Dr. Bhargava's question was random. Both responses were patterned. Both came from deeper layers of culture, layers which themselves are patterned. Both responses were culturally conditioned. Mine was natural to me but no doubt appeared strange in Orissa. The assistant's response was natural to him and appeared normal in Orissa.

## Patterns without Essentialism

Cultural patterns exist. But some people are afraid to admit it. They worry that doing so means falling into errors like overgeneralizing, or stereotyping people, or discriminating based on race. That need not be the case, though. We can recognize cultural patterns without embracing a cluster of errors I call, for convenience, *essentialism*.[3]

Broadly, essentialism assumes that any entity (a physical object, a geographical place, an observable behavior, or a group of people) has a set of requisite attributes essential to its form and function. A chair, for example, has a determined function that dictates its form. Consequently, one expects to find a chair in a particular place for a specific time. Generally, in the United States, most Americans speak English. The behavior of murder is wrong in an absolute sense because it violates a shared, universal code of moral conduct. The "whatness" of a chair is typically not disputed. Nor is the claim that in the United Sates English is usually spoken, or that murder is wrong. Essentialist concepts work for these sorts of things. But when it comes to characterizing groups of people, essentialist concepts cause evident problems. A person with a certain form does not have a fixed function. Specifically, essentialist assumptions are criticized if applied to people's gender, sexuality, and ethnicity,[4] if one (a) infers permanent traits, (b) discounts possible variations, and/or (c) speculates a single source of influence.

---

3. A version of this section about essentialism also appears in the *International Encyclopedia of Intercultural Communication* under my entry "Essentialism and Universalism."

4. Tadmor et al., "Not Just for Stereotyping Anymore," 99–105.

Used as an illegitimate form of evaluation, essentialism may declare that all people from India, say, have a predisposition toward social stratification, or that residents of Barcelona, Spain are futbol aficionados who frequent matches at Camp Nou. In point of fact, neither of these may be true. If taken to its ultimate end, in these applications essentialism is always a false assumption.

However, every global traveler does see and experience bona fide differences in people and cultures. Going further, there are not only differences but also patterns of differences in behavior, socio-cultural institutions, values, and core worldview presuppositions. It is generally true that the overall society in India is to some degree socially stratified. Likely, it is also true that many people in Barcelona are Barça fans. In such cases, there are unmistakable patterns.

If indeed patterns of differences do exist (and they do), what then is the problem with essentialism? I would argue that essentialism is fallacious philosophically if presented as absolutism and is fallacious socially if leveraged as a means of power. To explain further, if the term *essentialism* means that everyone in a group of people must necessarily display the same essential traits at all times and in all circumstances, then of course the term has little value in the real world, except as a label for thinking that may cause harm. In similar fashion, if the term *essentialism* is used to deny access to individuals from a unique group of people strictly because they are from such a group, then such denial of access is an abuse of power.

Given these problems with essentialism, we should be wary of it. However, differences and patterns of differences do exist, and we should not conflate recognizing patterns with straitjacket essentialism. Interculturalists, then, should not deny or minimize differences, nor defend one difference over another. Differences are a normal part of human exchange across cultures. One may integrate some difference from other people into one's own life and relationships. This type of cultural adaptation occurs not only at the individual level but also among groups and beyond.[5] Empirical evidence shows that patterned differences do exist. One may desire that a rabbit climb a tree, but it cannot. A squirrel can. It is easier for humans to see in the day than at night. Argentine friends speak Castellano. Much of Western culture is steeped in a justice pattern of culture. Most Muslim cultures are just as rooted in a cultural pattern of honor. Still other people groups are influenced by a pattern of reciprocity or harmony. These types of differences are true

5. See the research and academic writings of John Berry.

everywhere. To deny them means assured ineptness in human relationships. To respect them is not giving space to an illegitimate essentialism, but is simply displaying Cultural Intelligence (CQ).[6]

Further analysis is needed. Is everything different or is nothing different? Take again the example of a chair. We may assume that a chair is what it is. Plainly, a chair's form is primarily designed for an intended function, sitting. Here, the essence of the chair is fixed and hard to fault. It is not wrong nor dishonorable for a chair to be a chair. If this is so, then four underlying presuppositions make up this type of essentialism (this construct is copyrighted by Robert Strauss):

1. *Configurability*: Although it bears different brands, materials, colors, and auxiliary features, generally we easily recognize a chair. A chair has a look. It always has a certain and recognizable configuration. At a local coffee café, patrons sit in the chairs. Not one patron has confused the configuration of chair for a table.

2. *Immutability*: For the most part, a chair remains a chair throughout the course of its existence. Because of the reciprocal relationship between its required form and intended function, its determined purpose remains fixed. Therefore, its configuration remains basically unchanged.

3. *Determinability*: In a practical and rational world, manufactured physical objects are designed for a purpose. Their existence meets a need. Granted, a wooden chair may be used for other purposes—firewood or an impromptu ladder. However, such irregularities belie the determined purpose of a chair. Using factory-made wooden chairs for firewood would be expensive. Using a chair for a ladder might be dangerous.

4. *Locality*: Often it is expected that a chair (or any variation in form and function albeit called by another name, such as the front seat of a car or a park bench) will be situated in a location determined by need. This chapter is not arguing that locality is a requirement. No, a chair is a chair regardless of time and space. However, we presume chairs to be situated in given locales. There is a space in which they need to be.

These underlying premises seem plain and simple when describing chairs and things like them. Essentialism in regards to physical objects is obvious. But would they be plain and simple if applied to a group of people?

6. See Appendix B for a detailed introduction and explanation of CQ.

Let us attempt to apply these underlying presuppositions to people. It's clear it does not work:

- Configurability: Would we say that a person is preconfigured not just physiologically but also connotatively and functionally? Are such boundaries appropriate? By connotatively, I am asking if there is a fixed "meaning" inextricably associated with a person. By functionally, I am asking if there are fixed tasks inseparably connected with a person. Or, on the other hand, are people category-free?

- Immutability: Would it be accurate to say that who a person is and what a person does are unalterable?

- Determinability: Is it true that a person exists for fixed purposes and not others? Apart from cultural boundaries, are there essential boundaries?

- Locality: Where is a person expected to be? What is the space in which one expects a person to be?

If the four presuppositions that apply to essentialism about objects, places, or behaviors are applied to a group of people, it's quickly clear that in the Global West each presupposition is inappropriate. What may be categorically essential for a physical object is not essential when applied to a group of people. Yet we still face a dilemma. Is the term *essentialism* useful? To answer this question, it may help us if we see differences more clearly.

The term *diversity* means different things to different people. At its core, the term simply refers to differences. How does one see diversity? How can one see differences but avoid essentialism? The US Department of the Interior has said the term *diversity* is used broadly to refer to many demographic variables, including race, religion, color, gender, national origin, disability, sexual orientation, age, education, geographic origin, and skill characteristics (http://www.doi.gov/pmb/eeo/what-is-diversity.cfm).

In any conversation about diversity, it is easy for the focus to turn—fittingly so—toward political positions and legal standings. These are important. Political dialogue and debate help clarify what ought and ought not to be, especially if broadly sufficient voices are heard. Law declares what is and is not. Politics and law stress differences. Yet, interestingly, the field of social science does something different with differences. Rather than accentuate differences, the social sciences attempt to celebrate and bridge them.

As a social scientist, I see diversity not so much in terms of making space between two entities that are different. It is much more than simply legalized or begrudged accommodation. I see patterns of diversity as an opportunity to bring together what is different to create a whole that is greater than the sum of component parts. Therefore, diversity is a basis for synergy. It is more about integration. This way of seeing diversity requires proximity to others, effective communication between sender and receiver, mutual respect, creativity, ethnorelativism, adaptation, and leverage of polarities toward a common good.

Occasionally, people downplay differences. Perhaps they want to avoid inappropriate essentialism. Their assumptions about this de-emphasis are often unstated. What a person may mean is that essentially there are no differences between people, human beings are similar the world over. This is certainly true to some extent. Paul Ekman's research, for example, on the worldwide commonality of facial expressions, found universal patterns for five basic emotions: enjoyment, sadness, anger, disgust, and fear.[7]

But there are differences relatively. In India, people in a queue do stand very close together. I cannot understand Mandarin, even though I speak some Castellano from Argentina. Some cultures relate hierarchically, while others are more egalitarian. Just because one sees patterns of differences in people does not mean one stereotypes groups in an unsophisticated manner. Observing and describing differences is not a bias. On the contrary, these are actually intercultural skills. Without them, we are ineffective in the intercultural environment, and perhaps even brutish.

We do not see all men and women as being exactly the same, and therefore we do not relate to them in the same manner. There are differences. We do see patterns of culture, and therefore we adapt speech and behavior to effectively relate.

Next, what criteria make a pattern of culture *overarching*?

7. Ekman, *Emotions Revealed*.

Chapter 5

# The Four Overarching Patterns

## Opening Remarks

THE IDEA OF LARGE-SCALE patterns of culture is not new. For at least a century, scholars have talked about these patterns, albeit in different ways. In the thirties, anthropologist Ruth Benedict used the expression "great arc(s) of potential human behaviour."[1] In the forties, Morris E. Opler spoke of cultural "themes" that control behavior and whose interplay and balance give a culture its unique structure.[2] In their study of Navajo society, Clyde Kluckhohn and Dorothea Leighton described "highest common factors . . . implicit in [people's] doings and sayings," as well as "recurrent themes" and "unstated premises" that offer social coherence.[3] In a more recent work, Michael Thompson, Richard Ellis, and Aaron Wildavsky discuss "fundamental ways of life."[4] Culture experts agree: overarching patterns exist. Comparing such patterns brings out each culture's unique assumptions and behavioral trends.

Culture experts also agree that cultures change. Their patterns are not static or monolithic or everlasting. More often, a culture is a web of patterns in tension. Old ways are challenged by new ways. The patterns of an outside group challenge the traditional patterns of the clan. The previous chapter defines a *pattern* as something deliberately repeated and thereby predictable. But predictable patterns are not necessarily immutable.[5]

1. Benedict, *Patterns of Culture*, 219.

2. Opler, "Themes as Dynamic Forces in Culture," 198.

3. Kluckhohn and Leighton, *The Navajo*, 296. Kluckhohn built on the work of pioneering American anthropologist Alfred Kroeber, a student of Native American cultures and father of the writer Ursula Kroeber Le Guin.

4. Thompson et al., *Cultural Theory*, 223.

5. As previously noted, the dynamics of cultural change are complex. This book

In any culture, one can find the four patterns this book describes. Each pattern is present to some degree. But one pattern will be more important. One will be overarching. The adjective *overarching* signifies influence or dominance, and both senses apply here. My orientation toward justice influences everything I think, say, and do. Someone oriented toward honor is similarly influenced.

## Preview of the Four Patterns

Two overarching patterns of culture—justice and honor—were mentioned earlier in my anecdote of the taxicab in India (where my spontaneous reaction was to tell the truth instead of save face). The other two patterns of culture are harmony and reciprocity.

*Justice* has been the dominant cultural framework of people in the West for two centuries, ever since the rise of constitutional democracies. Consciously or not, most people in the West have a strong awareness of right and wrong. Their sense of morality is generally rooted in an obligation to the rule of law. In democratic societies, the rule of law ultimately relies on constitutional documents ratified by a widely-accepted process of development and implementation.[6]

For millennia, *honor* has been the dominant cultural framework of most people in the East and Middle East. Here, people know that speech and behavior display respect or disrespect. While pervasive in all relationships, honor and shame are most important in the family, extended family, and local community. In the East, honor is not necessarily an internal feeling, as it is in a justice culture. Honor is more often an external attribution bestowed by others rather than claimed by oneself.

*Harmony* is prevalent globally in indigenous cultures. Many indigenous peoples do not distinguish between the supernatural and natural worlds. All aspects of life are connected. Interactions with spirit beings are the key to maintaining harmony in order to be secure.

*Reciprocity* is a common cultural framework in the Global South. Here, one learns to develop connections with the right people in given circumstances for needed resources. These connections may or may not be characterized as "friendships" and provide not so much close friendships

---

doesn't address them in depth.

6. A significant exception in the Global West is indigenous people groups, who are orientated toward honor and also have a strong sense of harmony.

as reciprocal exchange. In some places, reciprocity is the means whereby one survives.

Again, any culture will display tendencies from each pattern, but generally one pattern will be dominant.[7] When this book refers to a "justice culture," it uses a convenient shorthand. It does not mean that in a justice culture no one gives a hoot about honor or about investing in reciprocal relationships. "A justice culture" is short for "a culture in which all four patterns are present and important but whose overall bent is toward matters of justice."

7. Do the four overarching patterns arise in any order—historically, developmentally, morally, or some other? There does seem to be a historical progression. Some of the earliest human cultures valued harmony. (Consider the stories in the Old Testament.) Honor societies, as well as feudal clientelism, predate justice cultures, which are more prevalent in modern nation states. The concept of a nation state may be traced to the sixteenth and seventeenth centuries. Nation states began to rise out of empires in continental Europe throughout the eighteenth and nineteenth centuries. See the research of Andreas Wimmer, professor of sociology at Columbia University.

Is the chronological progression developmental? That is, do civilization and modernization represent human progress? In *Manifest Destiny: American Expansion and the Empire of Right*, Anders Stephanson, professor of history at Columbia University, captures many of the assumptions of colonization. Across the new continent of America and throughout the world, Europeans and ultimately Americans "knew" that God had called them to territorial expansion. Their way of life was exemplary, exceptional. Expansion was "manifest destiny." The people of God had been chosen. The hand of God was upon them. It was their mission. It was common sense to them. Yet, how do these assumptions square with cultural relativism? Cultural relativism means the anthropologist suspends moral judgment. The perceptions and behaviors of people are viewed through the perspective of the people themselves. The emphasis is not right or wrong, but how people's perceptions explain their world and work for them. Interestingly, the Declaration of Human Rights from the Commission of Human Rights of the United Nations challenges the assumption of cultural relativism in favor of moral standards. While an individual or group may judge a perception or behavior to be right or honorable, it must be understood that such judgments are not self-evident universals. See Renteln, "Relativism and Human Rights," 56–72.

Finally, does one pattern represent a stronger morality? Yes, though not exclusively. Each pattern of culture has its upsides and downsides. The downside to an "all" justice view of life is that justice may become inhumane. The upside to a justice culture is a just, fair, and equitable lifestyle for all people. It provides equal opportunity for all. However, justice should not exclude the enjoyment of family (honor), the value of strategic networks (reciprocity), and the role of spirituality (harmony), all upsides to other patterns of culture.

## History of the Four Patterns

The four patterns presented here have a long history. Allow me two examples. Over two thousand years ago, the *Analects* of Confucius compared statecraft based on justice (clear laws and harsh punishments) with statecraft based on honor (personal virtue and ritual practices): "Guide them with policies and align them with punishments and the people will evade them and have no shame. [But] guide them with virtue and align them with *li* (protocol and etiquette) and the people will have a sense of shame and fulfill their roles."[8] Similarly, in Homer's epics—the *Iliad* and the *Odyssey*—heroes act out of a concern for *kleos*: good reputation, glory, fame, or honor. "A warrior culture is constructed on two notes," says one Homeric scholar, "prowess and honor. . . . Every value, every judgment, every action, all skills and talents have the function of either defining honor or realizing it. . . . even life must surrender to honor."[9] Many other examples from ancient cultures are possible.

Nor have these four patterns ceased to be discussed—especially, the patterns of justice, honor, and harmony. In the early twentieth century, the sociologist Max Weber analyzed the role of guilt in Protestantism and its impact on western capitalism.[10] In 1946, Ruth Benedict described the role of honor and shame in Japanese culture in her well-known work *The Chrysanthemum and the Sword*.[11] Later in 1954, in a work seminal for the discipline of missiology, linguist Eugene Nida mentioned three orientations of culture: guilt, shame, and fear.[12] Following Durkheim, British anthropologist Mary Douglas described a variation of honor and shame in *Purity and Danger*.[13] Perhaps informed by Nida, Roland Muller (a pseudonym) compared and contrasted guilt, shame, and fear cultures.[14]

In my work for Global Perspectives Consulting (GPC), we describe each pattern by its core feature rather than its outcomes. So, we refer to a pattern of *justice* instead of guilt/righteousness; a pattern of *honor* instead of shame/honor; and a pattern of *harmony* instead of fear/power. GPC also

8. Confucius, *Analects* 2.3.

9. Finley, *The World of Odysseus*, 120.

10. Weber, *The Protestant Ethic and the Spirit of Capitalism*.

11. Benedict, *The Chrysanthemum and the Sword*, 222–7.

12. Nida, *Customs and Cultures*, 150.

13. Douglas also addresses purity and pollution as a pattern of culture, which it is, but this book does not address this polarity as an overarching pattern.

14. Muller, *Honor and Shame*.

argues that the fourth pattern—*reciprocity*—has been unduly neglected and is worth setting alongside the other three.

But if each culture contains all four patterns, how do we tell which one is dominant? By what criteria can a pattern of culture be said to be overarching?

## Four Criteria of an Overarching Pattern

The research of a forefather in sociology can answer this question. Emile Durkheim (1858–1917) was a French sociologist, a contemporary of Karl Marx (1818–1883) and Max Weber (1864–1920). Durkheim identified four characteristics of society to measure the influence of a cultural pattern. He tried to assess the continuity of the "conscience collective"—a set of ideas that work as a unifying force in any society—to understand how traditional societies become modern.

Durkheim called the four factors *volume, intensity, rigidity,* and *content*. Each factor impacts how easily, quickly, and completely someone would embrace a cultural norm—or choose to act against it. Table 10 analyzes Durkheim's matrix, suggests more contemporary terms, and applies his insights to overarching patterns of culture. [15] Durkheim's four factors assume that the conscience collective is the totality of assumptions and values common to a group. It preexists and survives any one individual. It shapes what we say and do.

Table 10: Analysis of Durkheim's Four Factors

| Durkheim's Factors | Description | Contemporary Terms | Application to Patterns of Culture |
|---|---|---|---|
| Volume | How many individuals within a society embrace beliefs and values common to all other members? High volume means any individual is likely a microcosm of societal beliefs and values. | prevalent  dominant | Justice, honor, harmony, or reciprocity is an overarching pattern of culture if a prevalent number of society members embrace its beliefs and values. |

15. The table's descriptions draw on Anthony Giddens. See his "Introduction," *Emile Durkheim: Selected Writings*, 5–7. See also Durkheim, *Division of Labor*, 105–6.

| Durkheim's Factors | Description | Contemporary Terms | Application to Patterns of Culture |
|---|---|---|---|
| Intensity | How strongly do common beliefs and values sway an individual's mind and heart? High intensity means the conscience collective has powerful influence. | passionate<br><br>devout | How passionate are people about right and wrong or honor and shame? Guilt and innocence are not only legal labels. They are also feelings. |
| Rigidity | How clear are the definitions that prescribe beliefs and social practices? High rigidity means people do not have to interpret rules of conduct for particular situations. | precise<br><br>defined | How strongly are people socialized into believing in the rule of law, the importance of a family name and heritage, or the value of networks? |
| Content | What form does the conscience collective take? In traditional societies, it is religious; religion pervades society.[16] In modern societies, the "cult of the individual" gradually replaces religion, stressing individual dignity and personal development. | prescriptive<br><br>dogmatic | What is the history of the constitutional system in a justice-oriented society? How much is honor tied to religion? Is the network of relationships vital to survival? |

Perhaps the best place to see a society's conscience collective at work is in celebrations and ceremonies:

> There can be no society which does not feel the need of upholding and reaffirming at regular intervals the collective sentiments and the collective ideas which makes its unity and its personality. Now this moral remaking cannot be achieved except by the means of reunions, assemblies and meetings where the individuals, being

16. Among others, two contemporary authors concur with Durkheim's assertion about the vital role of religion in society. See Watt, "Religion as a Domain of Intercultural Discourse," 482–95. Watt is a professor of linguistics at Geneva College. See also Rieff, *My Life Among the* Deathworks. Rieff (1922–2006) was an American sociologist who taught at the University of Pennsylvania for over 30 years.

closely united to one another, reaffirm in common their common sentiments.[17]

Durkheim thus ties together the concepts of belief and ritual, both "social facts" he sees as institutions. Ritual celebrations and ceremonies validate the cosmological order or worldview present in the minds of participants. Ritual reinforces belief.

## The Core of the Collective

But what generates the consensus? By the volume of what is the conscience made collective? Is there any one group of people in a geographic region that influences the whole? While it can be tricky to pinpoint the core of a conscience collective, especially for today's modern, heterogeneous societies, Raphael Patai's work on Arab cultures and Max Weber's study of German national character both suggest that we look for an influential social strata. Patai discusses the national character of Arab cultures in terms of the cultural focus, or dominant concerns, of a modal personality. (Patai here follows American anthropologist Melville Herskovits (1895–1963).[18] Patai comments:

> One must keep in mind that to speak of the focal or dominant concerns of a culture is merely a convenient shorthand for saying that most individuals who make up a society are more concerned with those particular aspects of their culture than with others. Or, to put it in even more precise terms, the dominant (or focal) concerns in a culture are those cultural features which constitute the prime preoccupation of the modal personality in that culture. Another important feature in the interrelationships between cultural focus and modal personality is that the latter not only puts high value on the focal aspects of his culture, but considers them ethnocentrically as superior to corresponding features in other cultures.[19]

Like Patai's emphasis on a modal personality,[20] Weber suggests we look for a social group that supplies a prominent behavioral model for the rest

17. Durkheim, *Elementary Forms*, 474–5.

18. Herskovits, *Man and His Works*, 542–4.

19. Patai, *The Arab Mind*, 437.

20. *Modal personality* was an expression used by anthropologist Cora Du Bois (1903–1991) in her 1944 monograph *The People of Alor: A Social-Psychological Study of an East Indian Island*. The expression suggests that society has a personality structure. For more

of society. In his essays, Weber observes the impact of Junkers sensibility on German national character.[21] The Junkers (from the German *Juncherre*, "young lord" (*jung* + *Herr*) were members of landed aristocracy in Prussia during the nineteenth century. They were educated, had social status, influenced politics, and controlled the military.

Which social strata might generate the conscience collective in various societies? Table 11 offers suggestions, using examples from each overarching pattern of culture. [22]

---

on this approach to studying culture, prominent in the first half of the twentieth century, see Chao et al., "Culture and Personality."

21. Weber, *Essays in Sociology*, 386–95.

22. In *Developing Intercultural Awareness*, Kohls and Knight identify these cultural values of US Americans (14):

1. *Individualism*: A concern for justice emphasizes individual legal rights. The USA is considered the most individualistic nation in the world.

2. *Equality/egalitarianism*: A natural outcome of individualism

3. *Personal control of environment and fate*: A natural outcome of individualism

4. *Action orientation*: If I control my fate, then I must act.

5. *Problem-solving orientation*: A natural outcome of action orientation

6. *Practicality*: A natural outcome of problem-solving orientation

7. *Future orientation*: There is a correlation between individualism and wealth. A wealthy society enjoys the luxury of looking ahead toward the future rather than being absorbed in daily sustenance. An individual can shape his own future. "Do not wait for it to happen—make it happen."

8. *Free enterprise and competition*: Because the individual is sustained (not in need of others), one is able to compete with others.

9. *Materialism*: A natural outcome of enterprise

10. *Change is inevitable and desirable*: A natural outcome of future orientation

The cascade effect of the values is easily observed. Legality begets individualism. From there, individualism impacts all aspects of life and relationships. Would one agree that Weber ties the justice pattern of culture ("the Spirit of Capitalism") to Protestantism in his 1930 work *The Protestant Ethic and the Spirit of Capitalism*? Weber seems to connect pietism and rational labor. Paradoxically, the resulting individualism, especially in its more extreme forms, defies the New Testament emphasis on "one another" (see John 13:34–35, Romans 12:10, Galatians 5:13–15, Ephesians 4:32, and 1 John 4:11–12).

Regarding American practicality, consider Richard Hofstadter's *Anti-Intellectualism in American Life*. Hofstadter, a historian at Columbia University, analyzed the impact of 1950s anti-intellectualism on society. In Part 4, "The Practical Culture," 236, Hofstadter writes, "The anti-intellectualism of businessmen, interpreted narrowly as hostility toward intellectuals, is mainly a political phenomenon. But interpreted more broadly as a suspicion of intellect itself, it is part of the extensive American devotion to practicality

Table 11: What Group Impacts the Conscience Collective?

| Overarching Pattern: | Justice | Honor | Reciprocity | Harmony |
|---|---|---|---|---|
| Society | U. S. American | Arab | South American Cone Countries | Japanese |
| Strategic Influence | Judeo-Christian | Bedouin of the Arabian Peninsula | Latin culture | Confucian-ism |

## Closing Comments

Table 12 gives a framework for the four patterns, using a four-tier model of culture with worldview at the core (see Figure 9). The table's far-left column lists the layers of culture represented in Figure 9,[23] and also adds the categories "obligation," "identity" (status or role), "spotlight," and "place." The chapters to come will fill out this framework for each main pattern.

---

and direct experience which ramifies through almost every area of American life."

23. Some presentations refer to patterns of justice and honor and the like as paradigms or even worldviews. My view is that such labels are mislabels. The terms *paradigm* and *worldview* do not fit as a broad label for these patterns. I call the sets "overarching patterns of culture." Within each, worldview is a part but not the whole.

Table 12: Four Overarching Patterns of Culture

| | Justice | Honor | Harmony | Reciprocity |
|---|---|---|---|---|
| Worldview | | | | |
| Value | | | | |
| Obligation | | | | |
| Identity | | | | |
| Spotlight | | | | |
| Key Institutions | | | | |
| Outward Observable Behaviors | | | | |
| Place | | | | |

Chapter 6 explores justice cultures founded on the rule of law. Chapter 7 surveys honor cultures, often using Arab societies, though the honor pattern applies to other societies, too. Chapter 8 uses examples from indigenous societies throughout the world to introduce harmony cultures. And Chapter 9 tackles the topic of reciprocity, manifested in the clientelistic affiliations so prevalent in Latin America and Africa. As we begin to build out the frameworks, let's look more closely at the overarching pattern of justice.

# Part Two: **Building the Frameworks**

Chapter 6

# Justice

## Opening Remarks

FOR SEVERAL CENTURIES, THE global West has been dominated by an over-arching pattern of culture that this book refers to as *justice*. The term *justice* implies administrative activities that are objective, neutral, equal, and fair. Justice is personified in the statue of Lady Justice, a blindfolded woman holding scales and a sword. Her scales bespeak fairness, and her sword signifies authority. Justice presupposes legality. And legality or lawfulness is derived from the authority of the law. What is just is what is right.

The concept of justice dates from antiquity. The idea of criminal law can be traced to Hammurabi (1792–1750 BCE), the sixth king of Babylon. His Code of Hammurabi, a set of laws, established a system of crime and punishment.[1] Later, Aristotle writes, "And the rule of the law, it is argued, is preferable to that of any individual. On the same principle, even if it be better for certain individuals to govern, they should be made only guardians and ministers of the law."[2]

The World Bank has established "worldwide governance indicators" that include six dimensions of governance.[3] It measures some 200 countries, giving results as percentiles. Scores show how confidently a populace feels its government follows the rule of law. Justice cultures like the United States, Canada, Western Europe, and Australia always score in the 90–100 percentile. Nations where the overarching pattern of culture is reciprocity always score in the lowest percentiles.

---

1. Siegel, *Criminology*, 14.
2. *Politics*, Book 3, Part 16.
3. World Bank, "Worldwide Governance Indicators."

As noted earlier, the dominance of a justice pattern does not negate the presence of honor, reciprocity, or harmony. These other patterns exist within the justice pattern of culture, and may be important. Figure 15 depicts this coexistence through a Venn diagram.

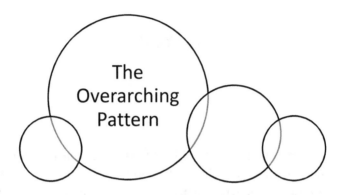

Figure 15: All Present and One Dominant.

In a justice culture—indeed, in any culture—other patterns still have influence. In the global West, it is easy to see the effects of reciprocity and harmony.[4] We see reciprocity at work, for instance, when a friend recommends us for a job (as we say, "it's not what you know, but who you know"). Similarly, in the global South, harmony and reciprocity compete for dominance. There, even within a social hierarchy, people strive for calm relationships. In their book *Cultural Theory*, Michael Thompson, Richard Ellis, and Aaron Wildavsky identify research showing that "competing ways of life exist within a single nation."[5] Still, despite the presence of other patterns, justice remains dominant in the West.

## The Foundations of Justice

What are the roots of justice? The principle of justice is (a) grounded in shared socio-historical assumptions of righteousness (in Greek, the terms *justice* and *righteousness* are from the same root, *dike*), (b) manifested by moral conduct, and (c) administered impartially.[6] Right and wrong, then,

4. See Appendix F for more about combinations of patterns.

5. Thompson et al., *Cultural Theory*, 215.

6. The single most important progenitor of the justice pattern of culture is the legal

are not arbitrary or situational. Instead, they maintain essential validity and reliability because their underlying assumptions have a historical basis. Right and wrong are valid because they are derived through unprejudiced processes. They are reliable because anyone can administer the processes to derive the same results. Here are some of the traditional bases of justice:

- Natural law[7]

- Sacred texts (for example, the Mosaic Covenant in the Torah or Pentateuch)[8]

- Essential attributes of divinity (for example, the essential attribute of *holiness*, in contrast to a relative attribute such as *omnipresence*)

- Resulting written documents, such as a country's constitution, clauses from the Magna Carta, or the United Nations Charter for Human Rights[9]

The bases for justice are assumed to be valid and reliable given the following five factors:

1. The fixed standards of right and wrong are written and retained within lawful and official documents. This factor may contrast with

---

system of ancient Rome. Simply stated, Roman law has three divisions: (a) laws applicable to citizens, (b) laws governing foreigners who related to Rome, and (c) laws common to all humanity derived from what was perceived to be common sense. Elements of Roman law are seen in constitutional republics today: separation of powers, term limits, vetoes, and the Electoral College. In contrast to the legal codes of today's nation-states, the Roman constitution was not written but resided in understood precepts. Today, globally, two primary legal systems are in use, both with elements of Roman law. In the United States, Canada, England, Australia, and several other nations, common law prevails, in which jurisprudence depends on precedent law adjudicated by courts. In Continental Europe, all Latin America, China, and portions of Southeast Asia, civil law rules, in which statutes guide rulings by judges.

7. Natural law is a system of justice common to all humans and derived from nature. It asserts that there are universal morals, which are the foundation for human rights.

8. Reformed theologian Loraine Boettner argues in *Roman Catholicism* that Protestantism is more closely linked to the sacred text: "One of the strong contrasts between Protestantism and Roman Catholicism is found in the moral codes which distinguish the two systems. In Protestantism, this code is taken directly from the Bible. But in Roman Catholicism the moral code is based primarily on Canon Law and only secondarily on the Bible, and in the main is imposed on the person from without," 385. While some Catholics have found Boettner's critique unfair, the larger insight is that in global contexts the justice pattern is not predominant in societies where Catholicism is prevalent.

9. See United Nations, "Universal Declaration."

arbitrary fiats pronounced impromptu by (a) autocratic leaders in a dictatorship, (b) family heads in an honor culture, or (c) patrons in clientelism. In a justice culture, justice is defined by the state.[10] It is not determined by kinship or friendships. The key question is "Is the individual in a right relationship with the state?"

2. The standards are embedded in timeless and broadly accepted conventions of human behavior that transcend any one family dynasty or a prominent business leader.

3. The framers of the written standards are credible. Most often this factor requires framers to be appointed proxies of the populace. An illustration of this in India is Dr. B. R. Ambedkar, who chaired the drafting committee of the India constitution and is considered its chief architect.

4. The standards are enforced through civil and military relations.[11] The state requires a military, strong enough to execute the civil government's commands, but subordinate enough to do only what citizens authorize it to do.[12] This common characteristic of contemporary societies requires people to "keep covenant with one another."[13]

5. The application of the standards is objective, legislated by elected representatives, and adjudicated by magistrates. Race, religion, class, and status (whether achieved or ascribed) are not factors of arbitration. Right and wrong are established and time-honored. All people are equally accountable to the rule of law.[14]

10. Siegel, *Criminology*, 5.

11. Strauss, "Civil-Military Relations." See also Bruneau and Matei, "Democratization and Civil-Military Relations," 909–29.

12. Feaver, "The Civil-Military Problematique," 149–77.

13. Volf, *Exclusion and Embrace*, 152, 157. Volf, from Yale University Divinity School, reminds readers of Thomas Hobbes' *Leviathan*, 1651, in which Hobbes describes a civil government whereby people transfer authority to the state—yes, a potential "sea monster," but if the relationship is balanced properly, that entity provides peace and defense. Volf's assumptions about the concept of covenant are rooted in his theological understanding of the God of Scripture living in covenant relationship with humankind and the broader creation.

14. These five factors presuppose a nation-state defined by geographic borders and populated by allegiant citizens (compare the Fourteenth Amendment of the U.S. Constitution from 1866). As Erler claims, "Constitutional government only succeeds in the nation-state, where just powers of government are derived from the consent of the governed." It is through the nation-state that rights, responsibilities, and liberties exist.

Table 13 unpacks key components of the overarching pattern of justice. Its cultural participants value righteousness. They are obligated to follow written standards. Through codified law, they enjoy individual rights protected institutionally by a judicial system. Notwithstanding social status, all individuals are protected equally. This spotlight on individualism spawns an egalitarian society. In the West, individualism and wealth are correlated, although it is debated which is the cause and which is the effect.[15]

Table 13: Four Overarching Patterns of Culture—Justice

|  | Justice | Honor | Harmony | Reciprocity |
|---|---|---|---|---|
| Worldview | Legality |  |  |  |
| Value | Righteousness |  |  |  |
| Obligation | To written standards |  |  |  |
| Identity | Guilty or not guilty |  |  |  |
| Spotlight | Individual rights |  |  |  |
| Key Institutions | Codified law, justice system, law enforcement |  |  |  |
| Outward Observable Behaviors | Truth, individualism, self-efficacy, achieved status, equality |  |  |  |
| Place | The West |  |  |  |

# Worldview

In a justice culture, the underlying core assumption is *legality*. The bottom-line arbitrator of people's social interactions is the law. The basic lens through which people see and interpret all aspects of life—even if people

---

This is the essence of a liberal democracy, in contrast to an administrative state as seen in the current European Union. For more, see Erler, "Who We Are as a People," 1–5.

15. Hofstede, *Cultural Consequences*, 253.

have not memorized any laws or read specific statutes—is a legal lens. Right and wrong are ultimately tied to the law.[16] Criminal activity is defined by written statute and determination of guilt is adjudicated by the state in a court of law. Crime is specific, not arbitrary. Larry J. Siegel, criminal justice professor at the University of Massachusetts, explains: "In order for a crime to occur, the state must show that the accused committed the guilty act, or *actus reus*, and had the *mens rea*, or criminal intent, to commit the act."[17] Technically, the criminal act is not a legal crime until a judge and jury rule in the prosecution's favor. In other words, the accused is innocent until proven guilty, a principle that goes back to Roman law.

In this pattern of culture, the victim of a crime may rightly pursue justice—by means of the judicial system. A victim is less likely to invoke the spirit world to curse the perpetrator, as one would in a harmony culture. A victim probably would not seek revenge through a strong man, as in a reciprocity culture. Instead, victims call local law enforcement or an attorney. Though tempted to seek revenge, a victim usually opts to trust the established system of justice.

Of course, not everyone in the West trusts the justice system. The core worldview assumption of *legality* per the law does not automatically equate to *legitimacy* in day to day relationships, especially for some minority communities. For many, a rift exists between legality and legitimacy, and attempts have been made to heal this wound. A 2016 study by the Obama administration, the *White House Task Force on 21st Century Policing*, found that lasting collaborative relationships between law enforcement agencies and the diverse communities they serve require building trust and nurturing legitimacy. If lasting collaborative relationships are developed through nurturing legitimacy, then legitimacy is attained by means of procedural justice. Criminology research shows that procedural justice involves four central values:

1. Treating people in the local community with dignity and respect

2. Giving "voice" to people during encounters with law enforcement

3. Remaining neutral and being transparent in decision-making

4. Conveying a trustworthiness in motives[18]

16. Siegel, *Criminology*, 14–16.

17. Siegel, *Criminology*, 18.

18. Fischer, *Legitimacy and Procedural Justice*, 3–4.

Embracing and living out these four values builds community trust in law enforcement. Ultimately the proof of lasting collaborative relationships between law enforcement agencies and the communities they serve is manifested through the following three community behaviors:

- People within the community feel an obligation to follow the law and situational dictates of legal authorities

- People cooperate with law enforcement

- People engage legal authorities in their local community[19]

Legality assures equal treatment under the law and protection from arbitrary bias—from the whim of the monarch or warlord. The enforced rule of law assures individuals, families, and communities. One can live in peace and venture outside in safety. Agreements and contracts decrease risk. In his analysis of US civilization, political theorist Russell Kirk (1918–1994) follows Simone Weil in asserting that "order is the first need of all human beings."[20] Here in the West, order derives from law.[21]

19. Fischer, *Legitimacy and Procedural Justice*, 3–4.

20. Kirk, *The Roots of American Order*, 1. See also Weil, *The Needs for Roots*, 11.

21. The concepts underlying the distinction between legality and legitimacy are not new. Law enforcement traces them to Sir Robert Peel (1788–1850), twice Prime Minister of the United Kingdom and the father of British policing. In 1829, he established the Metropolitan Police Force of London and guided it through nine principles. Note well principles two and three.

1. To prevent crime and disorder, as an alternative to their repression by military force and severity of legal punishment.

2. To recognise always that the power of the police to fulfil their functions and duties is dependent on public approval of their existence, actions and behaviour, and on their ability to secure and maintain public respect.

3. To recognise always that to secure and maintain the respect and approval of the public means also the securing of the willing co-operation of the public in the task of securing observance of laws.

4. To recognise always that the extent to which the co-operation of the public can be secured diminishes proportionately the necessity of the use of physical force and compulsion for achieving police objectives.

5. To seek and preserve public favour, not by pandering to public opinion, but by constantly demonstrating absolutely impartial service to law, in complete independence of policy, and without regard to the justice or injustice of the substance of individual laws, by ready offering of individual service and friendship to all members of the public without regard to their wealth or social standing, by ready exercise of courtesy and friendly good humour, and by ready offering of individual sacrifice in

## Values

In a justice culture, the fundamental value is *righteousness*. People expect others to act according to what is right and wrong. People expect equity and fairness in their society. They have a straightforward inner sense of right and wrong based upon authoritative written standards. They feel obligated to written standards. While this sense is present and powerful, locals may not be able to explicitly articulate the shared values by which they live and relate to others. People are taught these values as children, often tacitly; into adulthood, social institutions reinforce what is taught in the home.

## Institutions

In a justice culture, the function of codified law is paramount. Codification is a process of selecting and organizing laws into a subject-based codex. Here is a detailed example. The US federal government has an agency called the National Archives and Records Administration (NARA). NARA is responsible to compile the Federal Register (FR), an official journal of the federal government that contains department and agency rules. The resulting codex is called the Code of Federal Regulations (CFR). The CFR is divided into 50 titles, with rules and regulations that govern all aspects of the federal government's structure and function.

To illustrate further, CFR Title 9 contains rules and regulations pertaining to animals and animal products. CFR Title 9 Chapter 1 (in 199

---

protecting and preserving life.

6. To use physical force only when the exercise of persuasion, advice and warning is found to be insufficient to obtain public co-operation to an extent necessary to secure observance of law or to restore order, and to use only the minimum degree of physical force which is necessary on any particular occasion for achieving a police objective.

7. To maintain at all times a relationship with the public that gives reality to the historic tradition that the police are the public and that the public are the police, the police being only members of the public who are paid to give full-time attention to duties which are incumbent on every citizen in the interests of community welfare and existence.

8. To recognise always the need for strict adherence to police-executive functions, and to refrain from even seeming to usurp the powers of the judiciary, of avenging individuals or the State, and of authoritatively judging guilt and punishing the guilty.

9. To recognise always that the test of police efficiency is the absence of crime and disorder, and not the visible evidence of police action in dealing with them.

parts) covers definitions, standards, rules, and regulations for the Animal Plant Health Inspection Service (APHIS), one of many agencies within the US Department of Agriculture (USDA). APHIS has approximately 8,000 employees, including veterinary medical officers (VMO), botanists, and entomologists who work at all the ports of entry into the United States (seaports, airports, rail, and many lawful land ports of entry at the north and southwest borders). These highly trained professionals regulate animal, insect, and plant entrance into the country. The CFR guides their daily work of regulating imports and exports.

On a smaller scale and on a personal level, a resident of Denver, Colorado may own a plot of land zoned for a single-family dwelling—a house. The owner possesses a title of ownership, a legal document issued by the county. During the transaction for the home, the owner buys title insurance assuring the title is valid. By title, the land and house are private property. The owner rightly assumes that others will not trespass (enter the property without permission) on his private property. Another person will not enter the front yard to stake a claim, like a homesteader. Such a person would be trespassing. Law enforcement would remove that person, likely charge him with unlawful trespassing, and by ruling from the judicial system, the person would be fined and jailed.

It is understood that the residential road and public sidewalk in front of the house are open to the general public. The yard and driveway are not. There is no need to stand guard at a front window of the house to make sure neighbors and strangers do not enter the front yard. They will not. The homeowner, then, rests easy with the assurance that they will not. The institution of law and order makes this restful assurance possible.

Depending on the location of the private property and the improvements added to it, it has a financial value. A local municipality or homeowner's association may regulate what can and should be done at the private property to maintain the relative value of adjacent properties and the community as a whole. So even though the property is private, its location and appearance are not. It thus becomes subject to broader guidelines that protect the value of everyone's investment in the community and beyond.

The owner of the land and house will pay property taxes on the assessed value of the same. This revenue is used in turn to install and maintain the road in front of the house, to provide utility systems (electricity, water, natural gas, and sewage management) to the house, to offer a local public-school system for children, and to pay for the protection provided by law enforcement.

The structure and function of the institutional systems guide and regulate life. The systems are usually taken for granted. They operate in the background for most people. One expects that the roads will be repaired. Every house has running water. Law enforcement is only a phone call away.

An individual working internationally in a context where justice is not the overarching pattern of culture will naturally and tacitly assume that the host locale has a similar system of law and order that protects private property and promotes peace and security. One cannot but help project one's own culture and expectations onto another locale. However, the expectations may likely be wrong.

Legality, then, to summarize, is the core worldview assumption that forms the bedrock of many Western societies. People in such a society commonly and broadly embrace what ought and ought not to be said and done. These shared values, often unstated, buttress a complex framework of agreements upon which society is built. Without the agreements and adherence to them, society would collapse.

In political science, this framework of agreements rests upon the so-called "social contract."[22] The social contract addresses the relationship between the state, an entity with delegated authority, and individuals living within the jurisdiction of the state. It is assumed that all individuals in a society have rights. As I respect the rights of others, I may in turn be required to relinquish certain personal freedoms. By so doing, I and others both enjoy protected civil rights. People delegate authority to the state to administer those rights and relinquishments.[23] These shared values are far

22. The term "social contract" is taken from Jean-Jacques Rousseau's 1762 book *Du Contrat Social ou Principes du Droit Politique*.

23. Jean-Jacques Rousseau (1712–1778) was born into a middle-class family in Geneva. He was a fugitive, writer, philosopher, and composer. His ideas about the social contract have impacted all western civilization. If humans were not able to live in isolation (even though they were "born free"), Rousseau argued that to maintain social order (in his initial view, to protect private property) there should be an agreement between people and the state wherein people would oblige only legitimate power. That political power would guarantee the rights of people. Ten tenets of social contract theory:

1. People benefit from living together rather than in isolation
2. Living in a social community requires rules
3. Agreements are negotiated between people
4. Rules requires administration

more than simply cerebral pronouncements or inert morals. Born out of these values are behaviors distinct to the overarching pattern of justice.

## Behavior

People's core assumptions about justice and righteousness make them consider things to be straightforward. Reality is what it seems. People expect others to act in trustworthily ways. Describing the past, truth is what actually happened, the facts—the exposure of what was said and done. Epistemologically, truth agrees with basic laws of logic.[24] This is what was said. This is what is written. This is what was done. Statements about reality are valid and reliable. They are believable. They are based upon all likely relevant information. In such a culture, truth is truth, independent of the person who expresses it or one's title. Truth does not hinge on the speaker's lineage, or the location of the utterance, or the time of day.

Consistent truth, with its corresponding documentation, lays a foundation for personal rights, property ownership, wealth accumulation, and individualism. Truth is bigger than any one person. It transcends individuals. For example, as I write, it is daytime right now in Colorado. This is true whether I

---

5. A society is administered by a representative government (not family patriarchs, feudal lords, or powerful entrepreneurs)

6. Society guarantees beneficial freedoms, such as life, liberty, and property (noting that without established law and impartial adjudication, private property is in jeopardy) but also restricts harmful behavior (because people left to themselves tend to fight)

7. Government guarantees these beneficial freedoms and administers restrictions equally

8. If government is limited to these roles, it is valid

9. Therefore, people have social responsibilities (pay taxes and defend the state) and must give up freedoms (commit crimes)

10. The structure and function of society conforms to the general will of the people

24. There are three foundational laws of logic:

1. The law of identity: If a statement is true, it is true. For example, I say, "I live in Colorado." If this is true, then the statement is true. A is A.

2. The law of noncontradiction: A statement cannot be true and false at the same time, in the same place, and within the same relationship. If I live in Colorado, I do not simultaneous live somewhere else. A is not non-A.

3. The law of the excluded middle: A statement is either true or false. Either I do or do not live in Colorado. Something is either A or non-A.

am here or not. It is true whether I realize it or not. With truth and rule of law as bedrocks in a justice culture, the spotlight is on the individual.

How does justice beget individualism? Since the rule of law is authoritatively codified and officially recorded, the liberal democratic nation state provides a structure (the stage of life) in which individuals freely and equitably function. The individual person is granted personal rights and responsibilities. One learns to be self-reliant within the parameters of the social contract. The individual enjoys freedom of choice and expression.

Often, such individualism is contrasted with collectivism. Individualism shows three traits of behavior: (a) satisfaction with self (high self-esteem), (b) a quest for personal freedom, and (c) a direct communication style with appropriate emotional expression. Individualistic countries include the United States (particularly states such as Montana, Oregon, Nebraska, and Wyoming), Germany, Canada, Australia, and the Netherlands. By contrast, consider three traits of collectivist behavior: (a) social self-concept (a group orientation), (b) a need for affiliation, and (c) an indirect communication style with sensitivity to loss of face (embarrassment and rejection). Examples of group-oriented countries are Taiwan, South Korea, Indonesia, Pakistan, Guatemala, and many more.[25]

In a justice setting, personal rights, responsibilities, and accountability go together. The individual in a justice culture does not wait for things to happen. He or she tends to make them happen. Taking personal responsibility is common and respected. Over time, one may be able to accrue respect and increase status.

In a justice culture, status is often achieved, not necessarily ascribed as in an honor culture.[26] In the West, one can earn status through hard work, by developing talents and skills, by having unique experiences, by getting an education. But elsewhere, status may be ascribed by birth and based on immutable factors such as race and family name. Status may not be a thing one can earn. No matter how hard one works or studies, one's social position may be fixed instead of flexible. Table 14 provides additional contrasts.

---

25. Social researchers also consider horizontal and vertical dimensions of individualism and collectivism. The terms *horizontal* and *vertical* relate to the degree of hierarchy manifested in a society. For example, a horizontal individualistic culture values individualism, but sees individuals as equals, such as in Sweden or Austria. China is an example of horizontal collectivism. India demonstrates vertical collectivism.

26. For an early discussion of achieved and ascribed status, see Linton, *The Study of Man*, 115.

Table 14: Contrasts Between Achieved and Ascribed status

| Achieved Status | Ascribed Status |
| --- | --- |
| Justice pattern of culture | Honor pattern of culture |
| Earned by self | Attributed or assigned by others |
| By personal choice (voluntary) | By birth (involuntary) |
| Alterable | Immutable |
| Based on developed skills, abilities, efforts, experiences, acquired education | Based on race, ethnicity, gender, family name, heritage, land, extended family wealth, religion |
| Results in mutuality, equity, and opportunity for all | Results in privileged classes and unequal access to power |
| Depends on pragmatism | Depends on fate |
| Results in production | Results in consumption |

In a justice pattern of culture, the individual has the opportunity and freedom to achieve. Access to achievement depends on numerous factors, but begins with personal choice. Achievements result in self-efficacy, a confidence in one's ability to be effective, accomplish tasks, and succeed. Self-efficacy is derived from experiences.[27] Self-efficacy is different from bravado, which may be only a pretentious bluster and swagger without substance.

## Closing Comments

Throughout the Global West, justice is the overarching pattern of culture. The most vivid display is seen in the United States. Legality is the lens through which people see the world and interpret life. The bedrock of society is predicated on predictable rule of law. Based upon a body of codified legislations, institutions provide structure and function in the society. Safety and security mean personal freedom and equal opportunity for all individuals, regardless of diverse backgrounds. Life in the Global West attracts people from all over the world. Nevertheless, it is not the only overarching pattern, and per total population volume, it is actually the smallest.

27. Bandura, "Self-efficacy," 191–215.

Let's explore the overarching pattern of honor, a pattern of influence in the East and Middle East.

Chapter 7

# Honor

The noblest of you in the sight of Allah is the best of you in conduct

—Surah 49:13

## Opening Remarks

FOR MILLENNIA, LIFE IN the East, the Middle East, and elsewhere has unfolded according to an overarching pattern of honor.[1] If a justice culture is ordered by legality and the rule of law, an honor culture is inspired and restrained by community and family heritage. The family name comes first. At the forefront are personal, family, and communal pride. Instead of righteousness, resources, or outside relationships—important in other patterns

---

1. Also in North Africa and Central Asia. On a smaller scale, neighborhoods in minority communities, so common in urban contexts, display characteristics of an honor pattern of culture. In addition, there has been much research into the honor code in the South of the United States. Thomas Sowell, senior fellow at the Hoover Institution of Stanford University, analyzes Southern culture in his 2006 book *Black Rednecks and White Liberals*, which explores the honor code among Southern men. Sowell builds on Grady McWhiney's work in *Cracker Culture: Celtic Ways in the Old South*. These poor white uneducated rural farmers, referred to as "rednecks" around the 1900s, were mostly Democrats. Later, the term *redneck* came to imply bigotry and an unsophisticated ultra-conservatism. The same class of people in some areas of Georgia were called "crackers" (from the Middle English *crak*, "loud conversation." In the eighteenth century, runagates from northern Britain were referred to as crackers, a pejorative term that followed them to the New World, where they settled in the South.) Related to honor, Sowell writes, "It was not a pride in any particular achievement or set of behavioral standards or moral principles adhered to. It was instead a touchiness about anything that might be even remotely construed as a personal slight, much less an insult, combined with a willingness to erupt into violence over it" (*Black Rednecks*, 7).

James Bowman, a resident scholar at the Ethics and Public Policy Center, traces the story of honor from earliest civilizations in *Honor: A History*. His site—jamesbowman. net—has a comprehensive list of his articles on the topic. Of his dozens of posts, see "Whatever Happened to Honor?"

of culture—people value roles and reputations. In honor cultures, family members and communities feel an enduring obligation to an honor code derived from communal expectations.[2]

Honor cultures tend to be group oriented or collectivist, rather than individualistic. Their view of the world starts with community, not legality. Every honor culture is built on the backbone of a hierarchy of power, in which everyone has a place, a proper role and a specific duty. As an overview, Table 15 fills out the details this chapter will discuss.[3] Note the contrasts between honor and justice patterns of culture, especially at the institutional layer, where kinship supersedes codified law.[4] In such societies, honor and shame are positions, not necessarily behaviors.[5]

2. Jayson Georges refers to an overarching pattern as "the operating system of everyday life." See his "Resources" for an extensive bibliography on honor and shame. Also, Stewart and Bennett write, "Despite variations and contradictions, there exists an overall integration to the pattern of culture," *American Cultural Patterns*, 62.

3. Sources on honor cultures abound. See Neyrey, "Bibliography on 'Honor and Shame.'" (Jerome Neyrey, a retired professor of New Testament studies at the University of Notre Dame, is a contributor to the Context Group, a team of international scholars who combine insights from the social sciences with exegetical hermeneutics to interpret sacred texts.) The twentieth century saw ample empirical research into honor-based cultures. See Bodding's 1924 north India study, *A Chapter on Santal Folklore*; Pease's 1926 *Classical Philology* article, "Things Without Honor"; Musil's *The Manners and Customs of the Rwala Bedouins*; Margaret Mead's *Cooperation and Competition Among Primitive Peoples*; the works of French philologist Georges Dumézil; Erik Erikson's *Childhood and Society* (Erikson sees shame and guilt as stages of psychosocial development; but his definitions are Western and may not reflect shame in the East); Dodd's *Greeks and the Irrational* (especially his chapter "From Shame-Culture to Guilt-Culture"); Peristiany's anthology *Honour and Shame: The Values of Mediterranean Society* (especially Abou-Zeid's chapter "Honour and Shame Among the Bedouin of Egypt" and Pitt-Rivers's chapter "Honor and Social Status")—a seminal work often referenced today, but its authors sometimes confuse Western vs. Eastern definitions of honor. Pitt-Rivers, for one, incorrectly says that honor is the value a person feels in their own eyes.

4. In his 300-page 1913 treatise *Wild Tribes of the Afghan Frontier*, Dr. T. L. Pennell (1867–1912) describes the differences between justice and honor in Afghanistan in the early 1900s. Start at page 17.

5. Muller, *Honor and Shame*, 48.

Table 15: Four Overarching Patterns of Culture—Honor

|  | Justice | Honor | Harmony | Reciprocity |
|---|---|---|---|---|
| Worldview | Legality | Community | | |
| Value | Righteousness | Reputation | | |
| Obligation | To written standards | To an honor code | | |
| Identity | Guilty or not guilty | Shameful or honorable | | |
| Spotlight | Individual rights | Family name | | |
| Key Institutions | Codified law, justice system, law enforcement | Kinship, family, extended family, integrated community | | |
| Outward Observable Behaviors | Truth, individualism, self-efficacy, achieved status, equality | Conformity, collectivism losing or saving face in others' eyes, ascribed status, hierarchy | | |
| Place | The West | The East and Middle East | | |

To belong and relate communally is treasured. Inclusion is prized. Therefore, in a society where the overarching pattern of culture is honor, people's behavior conforms to collective norms instead of displaying their individuality.[6]

---

6. In *Face, Harmony, and Social Structure*, P. Christopher Earley attempts to explain behavior across cultures through the single lens of "face." Although he argues that his definitions of "face" are derived (his term is *harmony*) from differing social contexts, he still views cultures through the perspective of the individual ego, or self. His approach is purposefully simple, to be easily grasped and replicated in the business sector. *Overarching Patterns* looks at common behavior differently. In an honor culture, people may not have a strong sense of self in contrast to others. Earley, a professor of organizational behavior, participated in the early research related to Cultural Intelligence (CQ) with Soon Ang. He is not a cultural anthropologist.

## Contrasting Justice and Honor

Today, misunderstanding is rife between justice and honor cultures. Why? People with different core views of the world live alongside one another and tend to see others as they see themselves. People hastily assume that *guilt* in a justice culture translates to *shame* in an honor culture. It does not. They assume that *righteousness* or innocence in a justice culture is similar to *honor* in an honor culture. It is not. A comparison usually highlights resemblance, correspondence, and similarity, while a contrast highlights variance and dissimilarity. The identity markers of justice and honor cultures (guilt and shame) are best contrasted, not compared. See Table 16. At first glance, from the table below or in the thick of a society itself, guilt and shame may seem similar. Our itch to find likenesses is normal in any cross-cultural exchange, in which we experience deprivation of norm. When we are unable to predict the behavior of others, we want to find "cognitive similarities."[7] We want similarities to exist. But they may not.

Table 16: Contrasts Between Justice and Honor Cultures

|          | A Justice Culture | | An Honor Culture | |
|----------|-------------------|-------------|------------------|-------------|
|          | Righteousness | Guilt | Honor | Shame |
| Defined  | Innocent | Blameworthy | Attributed respect | Ascribed disgrace[8] |
| Basis    | The rule of law, clearly written codes | | A family code of honor, orally transmitted expectations | |
| Source   | The state | | Likely, a patriarch (family or elite class) | |
| Conferred | Achievement | | Ascription | |

7. Cognitive similarity is our tendency to tacitly assume another person's culture has the same values and assumptions as our own. It's our impulse to project our own values and assumptions on others who may be quite different. See the research of Dr. Angela Edwards for more about the concept of cognitive similarity.

8. Cultural anthropologist Raphael Patai (1910–1996) notes that "shame is more pronounced than guilt" when comparing personalities and societies in the East vs. West. See *The* Arab Mind, 113, republished in 2007 with a forward by Army Colonel Norvell DeAtkine, former director of Middle East Studies at a school in the running for the world's longest acronym, the John F. Kennedy Special Warfare Center and School (USAJFKSWCS) at Fort Bragg, North Carolina.

|  | A Justice Culture | An Honor Culture |
|---|---|---|
| Extent | Fixed but alterable through judicial process | Fickle per disposition of patriarch but perpetual |
| Situated | Internally: "I feel I am a bad person." | Externally: "They say I am a bad person." |

© Table used by permission of Robert Strauss

In a justice culture, a person usually knows whether he is innocent or blameworthy based upon fixed, clear written standards of right and wrong. He knows, on the inside, if he has done the wrong thing, even if no one else knows.[9] If the law has been broken, the person is culpable and merits punishment. But in an honor culture, things are not so clear. A person may not know if he has been given honor or esteem. To claim honor the community has not bestowed is folly. If one says or does something disgraceful, the family and community suffer shame along with the perpetrator. David Pryce-Jones describes how tricky it is to navigate reputation in an Arab context: "Between the poles of honor and shame stretches an uncharted field where everyone walks perilously all the time, trying as best he can to interpret the actions and words of others, on the watch for any incipient power-challenging response that might throw up winners and losers, honor and shame."[10] In honor cultures, this sort of watchfulness is especially bound up with hierarchy—one watches the reactions of those with power. The praise of the powerful bestows honor; their disapproval, shame.

In a justice culture, participants internalize the rule of law; they sense right and wrong in the gut. A Western individual's sense of shame is usually inward—one says to oneself, "I am a bad person." But in honor cultures, shame is usually external—more along the lines of infamy, a bad reputation, or public humiliation.[11]

9. See Ayers, *Vengeance and Justice*, 13–28. Social psychologist Edward Stewart analyzes American thinking patterns vs. people in the Global East. Stewart's research shows that Americans focus on process and production. They look for underlying causes and enjoy predicting outcomes. They assume there is more to anything and everything than meets the eye. It is natural for an American to internalize. It may not be natural in other cultures. And, it is not natural for immigrants to the United States. See Stewart and Bennett, *American Cultural Patterns*.

10. Pryce-Jones, *The Closed Circle*, 40–41.

11. Research professor at the University of Houston, Brené Brown addresses guilt and shame in the United States by noting that "guilt" in the West means that I did something

Moving beyond Table 16, biblical scholars see contrasts between justice and honor in the Bible.[12] They have found that the Old Testament is more oriented toward honor. Inappropriate speech and behavior break covenant relationships with others and Jehovah. Shalom is the mending of broken relationships and the restoring of peace and harmony. In contrast, portions of the New Testament are more oriented toward justice. Inappropriate speech and behavior violate the God's righteous standards. Substitutionary punishment and imputed righteousness are the only means to satisfy the righteous standards of God.[13] These contrasts have carried over into American culture. Edward Ayers, historian at the University of Virginia, writes, "Protestantism in the South stressed the harsher, fatalistic, patriarchal, Old Testament side of the Bible and Christianity, even as Northern Protestantism increasingly took on a rational, optimistic, 'feminized,' New Testament emphasis."[14]

Just as a religion can impact a culture, does culture impact religion? In Islam, for example, the Qur'an and Hadith emphasize the imperative of honor, but also highlight justice (Surah 5:8 and 49:9). Allah is called Al-'Adl (the Just One). The legal framework for a Muslim community is Sharia Law, which regulates all aspects of private and public life and is interpreted variously by five main legal schools. Some claim that Islam, as a religion, is itself an honor culture. Roland Muller (pseudonym), a Canadian historian and also an evangelical minister in the Arab world, writes, "Every part of the Muslim culture I lived in was based on honor and shame."[15] But assuming Islam itself resulted in this emphasis on honor may be mistaken. To what degree is the observed honor and shame more accurately part of the underlying regional culture vs. the pervasive monotheistic religion?

---

wrong, but "shame" in the West is an inner feeling that I am a bad person. See comments at 14:01 minutes in her TED talk "Listening to Shame." Her definitions of "shame" in the West should not be construed as "shame" in the honor pattern of culture.

12. See, for example, the work of John Goldingay, who studies how Old Testament themes are impacted by the honor culture of the Middle East.

13. In *Theology in the Context of World Christianity*, Timothy Tennent, president of Ashbury Theological Seminary, skillfully harmonizes the apparent contradiction between an Old and New Testament view of salvation history (see 77–103).

14. Ayers, *Vengeance and Justice*, 28. Ayers goes on to say, "Southern men who had undergone a conversion experience discarded the equation of manliness with boastfulness and pride, replaced honor's vulnerable strengths with an inner strength that could resist the scorn of the worldly" (28).

15. Muller, *Honor and Shame*, 47.

Whether derived from regional culture or religion, a set of core world-view assumptions drives the honor pattern of culture.[16] The paragraphs to follow explain and illustrate the layers of culture sketched previously in Table 15.

## Worldview

In a justice pattern of culture, the core worldview assumption is legality (see chapter 6). Legality is environed by logic and is expressed with clarity.[17] In an honor pattern of culture, however, the core worldview assumption is community. The lens through which a person looks out at the world is a lens of community, not legality. Most often, *group* starts with the extended family. This is the institution in focus. The aesthetics and experiences in this community form the grid through which one sees and interprets life.

The power a community has in shaping a society's worldview can be seen in Afghanistan. In the *Expeditionary Airman Field Guide*, the Air Force Culture and Language Center (AFCLC) writes, "Across all tribal and ethnic boundaries, the family remains the single most important institution in Afghanistan. A man's first loyalty is to his extended family, then to his tribe, then to his ethnic group."[18] Loyalty to clan, tribe, and family takes priority over national loyalty. In almost all circumstances, family and extended family live near each other.[19]

16. For chapter summaries of Sayyid Qutb's book *Milestones*, see Appendix D. The Appendix uncovers the assumptions underlying Islamism.

17. As F. S. C. Northrop (1893–1992), professor of philosophy and law at Yale, writes: "The Western type of knowledge tends to be formally and doctrinally expressed in logically developed, scientific and philosophical treatises. The syntactically constructed sentences of these treatises, by the very manner in which they relate to key factors in their subject matter, enable the reader, with but incidental references to items of his imagination or bits of his experience, to comprehend what is designated." (*The Meeting of East and West*, 315–316)

18. AFCLC Expeditionary Skills Team at Maxwell-Gunter Air Force Base, Montgomery, Alabama.

19. Afghanistan is a nation whose political borders sometimes split the lands of kinship-based tribes. Afghanistan's largest ethnic group is the Pashtun, who comprise 42 percent of the national population. (But more Pashtuns live in Pakistan than in Afghanistan!) The Pashtun speak Pashtu and are generally Sunni Muslims of the Hanafi School. Next, the Tajiks make up 27 percent of the Afghanistan population and are Persian-speaking (Dari/Farsi) Muslims. To a lesser extent, Afghanistan consists of Hazaras (of Mongolian descent, Shia Muslim, and agrarian) and Uzbeks (a Turkic language family). These tribal groups and others live in separated geographic regions that spill over from

Table 17 highlights the worldview components in an honor culture, using Kearney's worldview classifications. Kearney asserts that all world-views include a concept of self, how self relates to others (living and non-living), who has power and thus the facility of causation, and time/space conventions.

Table 17: Classifications of Worldview Assumptions in Honor Cultures

| Classification | Assumptions |
| --- | --- |
| Self | In an honor culture, there is an exaggerated self-consciousness, but individuality is not in view. In every circumstance, "self" is taken up with what others are thinking and saying. Self-identity comes from the other. Role and responsibilities are tied to community. |
| Other | The group is in continual focus: the extended family, lineage, village, the village *jirga*, the local community, the tribe, the mullahs, the *shura*, or simply an informal gathering of family and friends. The order just mentioned is prioritized. Group may also be the criminal gang that frequently emerges in disorganized urban neighborhoods when conventional institutions break down. Status is ascribed by gender, age, lineage reflected by family name, land, size of family, and religion. Decision-making is often by consensus, or so it may appear. Consent behind the scenes is often granted because a given individual has no power. But, publicly, everyone saves face through a facade of consensus style. In reality, hierarchy controls decision-making. |
| Relationships | Kinship is the connection. Societies tend to be patriarchal. Therefore, self and other are blood related. They speak the same language, have the same historical story, reside in the same land. In the USA, Black Americans feel an affinity with each other because of a shared historical experience of slavery. Even though they may have originated from different places in West or Central Africa, with their ancestors speaking different languages, Black Americans today share a common identity through common experiences. Allegiance is given to family above all other social groupings. Extended family obligations may supersede responsibilities to spouse or individual needs. |

---

Afghanistan into Iran, Pakistan, and Uzbekistan.

| Classification | Assumptions |
| --- | --- |
| Causality | The main factor in decision-making and the driving force behind actions is the family. Ascribed status markers determine hierarchy in societies that are high power distance. Tribal expectations and religious values dictate daily life. In many circumstances, the unseen spirit world plays a role in causation. Final decisions are the responsibility of the family patriarch, tribal elder, local politician, powerful businessman, or local mullah. |
| Time | The past is in focus—the remembered past, stories. Time-honored traditions are important. For everything there is a time and season (see Ecclesiastes 3:1). Honor-based cultures are backing into the future. |
| Space | Space is significant. Who has always lived in this region? To whom does the land belong? What spirits inhabit this space? What momentous events have taken place in this region? |

## Values

In an honor culture, what drives how one ought to act is reputation. To take another example from Arab culture, Raphael Patai notes that internal feelings are less important for Arab values:

> Since in the Arab view a man's self-respect depends primarily on the respect others have for him, the entire Arab ethical system is basically other-determined or outward-oriented. What is important for this type of ethical outlook is not feelings, intentions, and other internal values of morality, but the outwardly manifested behavior patterns which alone serve as the basis for the judgment others pass on the character of an individual.[20]

The judgment of others, especially patriarchal head and kin, is not fixed. As such, values are not fixed. Honor cultures have a certain degree of relativism, an ethical fluidity. Rule of law is not in focus. A specific righteous behavior is less in question. The role and word of family headship are

---

20. Patai, *The Arab Mind*, 329.

keys.[21] An honorable person respects kinship obligation. This may include remembering ancestors.

People feel an obligation to an honor code, which may have been passed down for millennia. This code may or may not be explicit. But it is embedded in the history and story of a group of people. Honor or attributed respect is tied to specific and expected behaviors. For example, in Bedouin culture, one would expect the following:[22]

1. Blood lineage: Having pure Arab blood, from both father and mother, is honorable.

2. Language: Arabic is bestowed the highest honor.

3. Kin group: A man is expected to exhibit adherence to his kin. Family solidarity is a "shroud of armor." *Asabiyya*, "kinship spirit," is sometimes the same term for honor. A loyal and united family displays honor. Loyalty is unconditional. By maximal extension all Arabs are united in lineage.

4. Virility: A man is expected to have many sons. A woman is considered the field and the man is the seed. Safety and security are dependent on the male children. Virility is considered one of the highest displays of honor.

5. Occupation: Pastoral work of tending camels is respected, but agrarian tasks of tilling soil are not.

6. Bravery: A man is expected to be skillful with the sword and able to defend himself against enemies.

7. Power: Power is ascribed by family name, gender, land, and more. The spirit world is implored to bestow power. Magic is a means to power.

8. Wealth: Wealth may be measured by livestock (including camels), land, water, workers, and family size.

9. Hospitality: Acts of hospitality and generosity, even to strangers, are highly valued. These acts include housing, feeding, entertaining, engaging in commerce, and exchanging stories.

In 1973, Raphael Patai (1910–1986) wrote *The Arab Mind*. Born in Budapest to Jewish parents, Patai did doctoral studies in Semitic languages

---

21. Palmer and Coe, "From Morality to Law."

22. The list is adapted from *The Arab Mind*, 89–102.

and Oriental history. *The Arab Mind*—revised in 1983, reprinted with updates in 2007—has been used as a resource by the US military. Patai devotes the entire first chapter of *The Arab Mind* to clarifying what he means and does not mean by the term *Arab*. Also worth noting are the assumptions of Arabs related to being Arab. Lebanese-Egyptian scholar George Antonius uses three criteria: (a) Arab ancestry, (b) Arabic as a native language, and (c) Arab culture.[23]

In describing the Arab mindset, Patai identifies a number of generalizations that are grounded in Arabic literature. These generalizations, derived from local narratives, describe the differences between the West and Arab cultures. An example from Arabic literature is the *chansons de geste*, sung and told by wandering minstrels in Mitidja, the plains in southern Algeria. These epic poems of heroic deeds personify Western civilization as a ghoul, an evil spirit huge in size and strength, exceedingly ugly, and a master of tricks. It is greedy for wealth. Above all, it is an unbeliever, violating Islamic moral law. In the end, it is subdued and either converted or killed (269).

Table 18 presents several differences in culture noted by Patai:[24]

Table 18: Contrasts Between Western and Arab Cultures

| Western Culture | Arab Culture |
| --- | --- |
| Four percent Muslim | Ninety-nine percent Muslim |
| Religions are interpreted | Religion is revealed |
| Political independence is assumed | Political independence is an ongoing struggle |
| Sees time as linear; orientation is toward the future | Sees time as nonlinear; orientation is toward the past |
| Incessant and insatiable quest for more, especially what is perceived to be better | Undisputed quest for what is perceived to be a purer way of life from the past |
| Focus on progress, change, material benefits, and individual freedoms | Focus on tradition, conformity, religion, and extended family |

23. Antonius, *The Arab Awakening*, 18.

24. Patai, *The Arab Mind*, 268–306.

In summary, identity is collective. An individual in the collective is shamed or honored based on observable behavior that conforms to expectations. Therefore, what emerges as the most important socio-cultural institution is kinship.

## Institutions

American anthropologist George Murdock (1897–1985) is best known for his research about the universals of culture.[25] Cultural forms, like the way we greet each other, change from region to region, but some common categories of culture do not change, regardless of region. Such categories are universal. They have been observed in every culture. For example, every society has a material culture—objects and architecture. Other common categories include kinship, social organization, political organization, economic organization, art and play, and more.[26]

Of all the universal categories, anthropologists agree that one is most important—kinship, the blood relationships between people. [27] Kinship involves family, extended family, and the integrated community. It is culturally defined. In an honor culture, family is central to social organization and has supremacy over the life of an individual. [28] Behavior is predicated upon what the family feels and thinks. Morality is derived from kinship, not written standards. Codes are handed down from ancestors, most often orally. Kinship and descent are keys to determining appropriate observable behavior.[29] Conformity is expected all the time in every circumstance.[30]

25. Murdock compiled a list of "things" anthropologists should look at when observing a society's culture. His list would form the basis of a valid and reliable ethnography and became the basis of his 1938 work *Outline of Cultural Materials*. The categories in the outline are the universals of culture.

26. Cognitive neurologist and philosopher Sam Harris argues that moral universals do not depend on religion. Listen to his TED talk "Science and Morality."

27. Second to kinship are gender and age.

28. See Tatum's *"Why Are all the Black Kids Sitting Together in the Cafeteria?"* Tatum, a professor of psychology and education, analyzes the role of the other in how Black Americans develop racial identity.

29. Palmer and Coe, "From Morality to Law."

30. Kinship is a study in itself, a study that has preoccupied anthropologists for decades. Early notable work belongs to Henry Lewis Morgan (1818–1881), an American anthropologist who observed indigenous people groups in the United States. In 1871, the Smithsonian Institution published his *Systems of Consanguinity and Affinity of the Human Family* (the term *consanguineal* refers to blood relationships; the term *affinal*

## Behavior

In a justice culture, the spotlight is on the individual, so styles of dress and varieties of behaviors abound. My wife and I were recently invited to join her work colleagues for dinner and entertainment at the Motif Jazz Café. I wore pressed blue jeans and an untucked dress shirt. The host, a C-level executive in a national software company, wore a navy-blue blazer. A third

---

refers to marriage relationships). The 600-page work provided foundation for kinship terminology. Other researchers followed, including Radcliffe-Brown, Malinowski, and Gluckman. Table 19 contrasts kinship and descent:

Table 19: Differences Between Kinship and Descent

| Kinship | Descent |
| --- | --- |
| Reference is individual (ego) | Reference is ancestry |
| Almost always significant universally | Significant only in selected societies |
| Reference is relative (I am only the son of one particular person.) | Reference is absolute or permanent (I am either of Arab descent or not and when I die, the descent group endures.) |
| Bilateral | Unilineal, that is, either patrilineage or matrilineage (the source of family identity) |
| The basis for appropriate relating within and outside of the family (includes inheritance) | The basis for land ownership, political representation, and economic cooperation |

Globally, researchers have observed six kinship patterns.

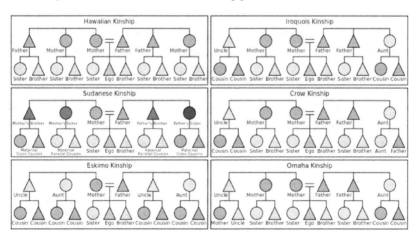

Figure 16: Six Kinship Patterns.

man wore black jeans and a t-shirt. The men and women could have worn most anything. Each of the six people among the three married couples ordered different dinners and drinks. We did not share our dishes with each other. Conversations continued throughout the evening, without any specified order and with no one individual dominating.

In contrast, in an honor culture where conformity to the collective is expected, how one dresses is important. Who arrives when matters. Where one sits is understood and fixed. Who speaks and with whom are understood. In fact, honor may be demonstrated most through silence. What is said is articulated carefully, revealing wisdom. What is said may be said couched in a proverb or parable.[31]

Several years ago, I was invited to speak at a university in Madurai, Tamil Nadu, in southern India. A large and ancient city, Madurai is famous for its elegantly adorned Hindu temples, especially the Meenakshi Temple, dating from the seventh century. Having flown from Bangalore, Karnataka, I was greeted at the airport by my host and was assigned a car and driver for my stay. That evening at the hotel, a small group from the university gathered for dinner, including my host—the administrator of the university extension—and other department heads and professors. As expected, the host ordered food and drinks for everyone at the table. When the dishes came, we shared uniformly, eating only with our right hand. As was customary, the host alone engaged me in conversation. Others listened. There was the customary discussion of esoteric theories of sociology, and at one point, I was asked to share my views on structural functionalism and whether I agreed that structuralism had lost its relevance in academia. Unlike the talk at the Motif Jazz Café, the discussion in Madurai was not casual or informal. My host took time to frame questions properly. The audience displayed patience listening to my formal, even ceremonial answers.

Shortly into this ritual conversation, I noticed that across the table was, of all people, my driver. There he was, seated at the table in this upmarket hotel dining room. I was puzzled. How did this happen? Who approved his presence? What was this Scheduled Caste (SC) man doing among these upper caste university leaders? Did anyone else notice? This was not a problem for me, but I knew it was breaking untold norms.

Suddenly, the driver addressed me directly: "Dr. Strauss, I have a question for you!" The table guests fell silent. The host's mouth dropped open. Everyone knew it was absolutely inappropriate for him to address me, much

31. Muller, *Honor and Shame*, 49.

less even be at the table. Everyone knew he had violated his dharma duty, and that consequences would follow, immediately and even in the karma of his next life. Just as abruptly, my host replied, "Shut up! He does not want to hear from you!" An uncomfortable quiet ensued. And not just at the dinner table. My driver was so shamed that even later, alone with me in the car, he dared not ask me anything.

In southern India, an understood hierarchy is in place. Status is ascribed. People see me as equivalent to a high caste Brahmin. Protocols are clear. Conformity is the norm. My host assumed that the driver had caused me to lose face in such a prestigious setting, so he shamed the driver openly and without mercy. Perhaps some sense of harmony had been restored. Such overarching patterns of culture are not imagined, nor are they the miscalculations of biased instruments of assessment. This incident really did occur in Madurai. The dinner party felt that the driver had violated my honor. What in the West would have been a non-incident and without consequence was, in India, an extraordinary episode. Each of us will never forget it.

Honor cultures the world over require conformity to ceremonious protocols. It's true of India, where I visit and work, and it's true of the American South where I was raised up. Speaking to this focus on externals, Kenneth Greenberg, professor of history at Suffolk University, describes the antebellum days: "Southern gentlemen expected men of honor to wear masks, to display a crafted version of themselves through their voices, faces, noses, and a thousand other projections into the world."[32]

## The Southern Mind

I was born in Augusta, Georgia. My family was Southern. We spoke with a Southern accent. In South Carolina, I attended Dixie High School,[33] where my father taught English grammar and my mother was the librarian. (Less common was my parents' education: both had master's degrees from Clemson University.) At Dixie High, if you insulted someone—which you would not want to do—you would find yourself behind the main building

32. Greenberg, *Honor and Slavery*, 25.

33. The terms *Dixie* and *Dixieland* most often refer to Southern states. The origin of the term is uncertain. In 1767, Charles Mason and Jeremiah Dixon drew a survey or boundary between Pennsylvania and Maryland called the Mason and Dixon Line. The term is used in a minstrel song entitled "Dixie Land," composed by Daniel Decatur Emmett. It was an anthem of the Confederacy during the American Civil War (1861–1864).

during lunch, at the steps of the "Smokers' Club." The smokers would encircle you and the offended party. There was no escape. Even if you accommodated the notion. The insulted would start the interaction—a fistfight for honor.[34] I remember. Once, after the fight was over and I had picked myself up off the ground, several observers passed by and said quietly, "Good job," even though I went down in defeat. It was reckoned honorable to participate, even statesmanlike.[35]

Honor cultures are not monolithic.[36] While Afghanistan, the Arab world, and India are examples of honor cultures, the United States has its own version of an honor culture in the American South. A book of wide critical acclaim is W. J. "Jack" Cash's *The Mind of the South*.[37] Cash explores the mindset of the Old South, digging beneath the surface in search of core assumptions. He starts with what is obvious, known to all of us, that the story we tell is that the Southern man is a gentleman.[38] Cash describes the veneer of aristocracy. From there he looks beneath the surface and observes a culture of honor. Using stories, he describes the outworking of honor in behavior, institutions, values, and assumptions.

---

34. Although not unique to the Old South, dueling was characteristic of it. Originating in Europe and connected with a code of chivalry, a duel was an arranged combat between two individuals, both of whom would regard themselves as respectable gentlemen. The fight could include swords or, later, pistols, but often was hand-to-hand combat. The basis was an insult. The objective was to restore honor. An insult most often was associated with a challenge to the integrity of another, an unmasking of the outward presentation of honor.

35. Greenberg, *Honor and Slavery*, 8.

36. Georges' digital platform honorshame.com highlights five types of honor/shame cultures. See his "Five Types."

37. Cash (1900–1941) was from Gaffney, South Carolina, just outside the larger city of Spartanburg. He attended Wofford College and Wake Forest College (before it became a university). He was a reporter, editor, and author.

38. Cash, *Mind of the South*, 63.

Cash's observation of honor in the Old South is common among historians and sociologists.[39] Ayers, for one, offers a striking contrast between Northern dignity[40] and Southern honor, shown in Table 20.

Table 20: Differences Between the North and South, adapted from Ayers

| North | South |
| --- | --- |
| Dignity | Honor |
| Restraint required | Display celebrated (aristocracy) |
| Abnegation of self (humility) | Assertion of self (individuality) |
| Inward | Outward |
| Opinion of others rebuffed | Respect of others required—key |
| Mastery of autonomous self—key | Lack of self-control |
| Transformation of society | Stratification of society (economically, hierarchically, and locally) |

To underscore the contrast, Ayers offers a pair of metaphors: "Dignity might be likened to an internal skeleton, to a hard structure at the center of self; honor, on the other hand, resembles a cumbersome and vulnerable suit of armor that, once pierced, leaves the self no protection and no alternative

---

39. My wife's distant cousin, Dr. Maxine Appleby, historian at Wofford College, tells stories of honor from her childhood in Moore, South Carolina. She teaches courses about Appalachian women, heroes, music, and medicine. See also Ayers, *Vengeance and Justice*; Berger et al., *The Homeless Mind*; Wyatt-Brown, *Southern Honor*; Elder, *The Sacred Mirror*; Nisbett and Cohen, *Culture of Honor*; Cohen and Nisbett, "Self-Protection," and McWhiney, *Cracker Culture*. A more recent dissertation by Timothy Hayes, *Re-Examining the Subculture of Violence in the South*, is available at http://citeseerx.ist.psu.edu/viewdoc/download?doi=10.1.1.556.275&rep=rep1&type=pdf. Hayes examines the subculture of violence in the South and its relationship to honor. The dissertation's bibliography will be helpful to researchers. Hayes is now a criminal justice professor at the University of North Georgia.

40. Many researchers refer to dignity as a pattern of culture, particularly in the Northern United States. Its characteristics mirror those of justice. See Berger et al., *The Homeless Mind*, 88; Leung and Cohen, "Culture Variation," 507–26; Campbell and Manning, "Macroaggression and Moral Cultures," 692–726 (who argue that a culture of dignity has given way to a culture of victimhood, a return to a sort of honor society, but one in which vengeance is carried out not by individuals but by the state); Kim and Cohen, "Information, Perspective, and Judgments," 537–50; Fosse et al., "When Dignity and Honor Cultures Negotiate," 265–85.

except to strike back in desperation. Honor in the Southern United States cannot be understood without reference to dignity, its antithesis and adversary to the north."[41] Cash, in his turn, argues that the Southern gentleman was not always comfortable in the "vulnerable suit" of aristocracy:

> But there was a flaw in it. In so far as it was aristocratic, it was ultimately not an emanation from the proper substance of the man who wore it, but only a fine garment put on from the outside. If they wrapped themselves in it with seeming ease and assurance, if they could convince themselves for conscious purposes that they were in sober fact aristocrats and wore it by right, they nevertheless could not endow their sub-consciousness with the aristocrat's experience—with calm certainty, bred of that experience, which is the aristocratic manner's essential warrant. In their inmost being they carried nearly always, I think, an uneasy sensation of inadequacy for their role.[42]

Ayers, Cash, and others describe what they sometimes call the "Old South." Perhaps they mean the slave plantation region in the East. They likely are referring to a time before the Civil War. Nevertheless, they compellingly present features of an honor pattern of culture, certainly one different from honor cultures in the Middle East, but an honor culture nonetheless. For three years at Dixie High School, I lived it—and had the bruises to show for it.

The first person to describe the justice-oriented culture of the North as a culture of dignity may have been Peter Berger (1929–2017), a Lutheran theologian and widely regarded sociologist.[43] He contrasts Northern dignity with Southern honor: "The concept of honor implies that identity is essentially, or at least importantly, linked to institutional roles. The modern concept of dignity, by contrast, implies that identity is essentially independent of institutional roles."[44] The term *dignity* has a rich history in philosophical writings, religious canons, and more.[45] As Erin Daly and James May, professors of law at Widener University Delaware Law School, note:

---

41. Ayers, *Vengeance and Justice*, 20.

42. Cash, *The Mind of the South*, 71.

43. Berger et al., *The Homeless Mind*, 88–89.

44. Berger et al., *The Homeless Mind*, 90.

45. Consider these uses of the term *dignity*:

   1. United Nations *Universal Declaration of Human Rights*, Article 1: "All human beings are born free and equal in dignity and rights" (1948).

Human dignity refers to the inherent humanness of each person. It is not an attribute or an interest to be protected or advanced, like liberty or equality or a house or free speech. Rather, human dignity is the essence of our being, without which we would not be human. Human dignity recognizes and reflects the equal worth of each and every member of the human family, regardless of gender, race, social or political status, talents, merit, or any other differentiator.[46]

Dignity is essential to self. By contrast, honor is an ascribed feature, an external attribute. Because these two distinguishable conventions are at the core of cultural patterns, the patterns of justice and honor are therefore profoundly unalike.

## Concluding Comments

An honor pattern of culture dominates the lifestyles of people throughout the Middle East, North Africa, Asia, and Southeast Asia. Versions of honor cultures are also found among ethnic groups in rural America and the Old South. In an honor culture, conformity to a code of honor is the focus, a code derived from the family name and heritage. Kinship is a key socio-cultural institution. Reputation is ascribed to an individual by the family and community.[47]

Two more cultural patterns remain. Next, we describe the overarching pattern of harmony, common in indigenous cultures throughout the world.

---

2. *The Catechism of the Catholic Church*, Part Three, Section One, Chapter One, Article 1: "The dignity of the human person is rooted in his creation in the image of God."

3. Immanuel Kant in *Fundamental Principles of the Metaphysics of Morals* writes that "dignity" is that which has intrinsic worth (4:435).

4. For an inimitable work researching the use of the term *dignity* in post-World War II constitutional writings, see Dupré, *The Age of Dignity: Human Rights and Constitutionalism in Europe*. Catherine Dupré is a law professor at the University of Exeter in South West England and sits on the Advisory Council for the Dignity Rights Project.

46. "Dignity Rights Project"

47. See Appendix F for an additional analysis of honor societies in contrast with others.

Chapter 8

# Harmony

## Opening Remarks

A PROJECT MANAGER FOR a Southern California construction company relates the following story about an oil refinery project in Indonesia. The Indonesian refinery was expanding. To connect the existing refinery's electrical grid to the new expansion required a very large transformer, critical to the expansion's start-up. The first time the transformer was installed, it was wired incorrectly and hence damaged. It was shipped to an outside shop for repair. During the second installation, too, the wiring was done wrong. Again, the transformer went to an outside shop to be fixed.

What was obvious to the contracted Western engineers—faulty wiring causes faulty operation—was not obvious to everyone on the project. After the two failures, the refinery's lead electrical engineer and staff, all from Indonesia, decided the problem lay somewhere else. They made their own arrangements to ensure the third transformer installation attempt would work: they planned a special ceremony to cast demons out of the ground. The hour-long purification ritual at the construction site included dancers, food, even a special shaman. The refinery staff, who were locals and followers of Islam, wholeheartedly agreed with the need for the ceremony. (In fact, they believed this was the problem from the start.) The Western engineers and managers, with their degrees in science and physics, thought it rather amusing, but went along. After the transformer was installed and connected for the third time, it worked fine. In the end, the Indonesians believed it was because of the demon-removing ceremony, but the Western staff believed it was because the wiring was finally correct. Obviously, to the Westerners, it was a technical mistake that when finally corrected allowed the transformer to work just fine. But just as obviously, to the Indonesians, it was an error in ritual—with the demons removed, the transformer worked.

## Harmony Described

All over the world, cultures are dominated by an overarching pattern of harmony. Harmony is generally dominant in indigenous societies where people seek security above all else: haven, safekeeping, and reassurance. People attain the respite they seek by holistic interactions with spiritual and natural forces. In these cultures, people see all life as interconnected. They do not see a difference between the supernatural and natural worlds. For them, the seen and the unseen are not at odds but in tune, equally powerful and inextricable. Table 21 fills out the pattern comparing and contrasting harmony with the other overarching patterns of culture.[1]

Table 21: Four Overarching Patterns of Culture—Harmony

|  | Justice | Honor | Harmony | Reciprocity |
|---|---|---|---|---|
| Worldview | Legality | Community | Security |  |
| Value | Righteousness | Reputation | Respite |  |
| Obligation | To written standards | To an honor code | To holistic interactions |  |
| Identity | Guilty or not guilty | Shameful or honorable | Out of harmony or in harmony |  |
| Spotlight | Individual rights | Family name | Control |  |
| Key Institutions | Codified law, justice system, law enforcement | Kinship, family, extended family, integrated community | The supernatural and natural worlds (not differentiated) |  |
| Outward Observable Behaviors | Truth, individualism, self-efficacy, achieved status, equality | Conformity, collectivism, losing or saving face in others' eyes, ascribed status, hierarchy | Community concord, in-groups, rituals, ceremonies, religious specialists |  |
| Place | The West | The East and Middle East | Global |  |

1. While other chapters describe the overarching patterns in terms of the four layers of culture—worldview, values, institutions, behavior—this chapter describes harmony culture as a whole.

Even though people in harmony cultures see no difference between the supernatural and natural worlds, they do assume that unseen realms and entities are real and powerful. These entities consist of personal spirit beings and impersonal spiritual forces. Examples of these two categories are given in Table 22. Both types of power are a daily concern in harmony cultures.

Table 22: Types of Beings and Forces

| Personal Spirit Beings | Impersonal Spiritual Forces |
|---|---|
| 1. God: in the monotheistic religions: God, Allah, and Jehovah; however, each local mythology likely has its own "Supreme Being" | 1. Blessing: imparted through a spiritual leader's benediction |
| 2. Angels: benevolent spirit beings common to Christianity, Islam, and Judaism | 2. *Baraka*: favor bestowed by Allah on select individuals; gives power and benefit |
| 3. Saints: venerated in Roman Catholicism and Islam | 3. *Yin* and *yang*: opposite but interconnected forces |
| 4. Totem spirits: part of Native American traditions | 4. Karma, fate, and fortune: cause and effect forces |
| 5. Ancestors: the deceased who are still among the living; they bless and curse | 5. *Mana*: a power behind success, often observed in Melanesian cultures |
| 6. Ghosts: usually assumed to be malevolent | 6. Soul substance: an immaterial element of a being that has power and outlives the body |
| 7. Satan: a dominant feature of Islam | 7. Particularistic examples of power to bless and curse |
| 8. Demons: evil spirits | 8. Evil eye (also mouth and touch): often related to envy |
| 9. "Gods": in Hinduism, say, a pantheon of gods with specific functions | 9. Witchcraft: psychic skills |

| Personal Spirit Beings | Impersonal Spiritual Forces |
|---|---|
| 10. Local spirit beings: In Papua New Guinea, the Bisorio people fear the *kowa anage*, little spirits a foot and a half tall, with dreadlocks and red eyes. Each carries a bow and quiver of arrows, which are shot backwards and are the cause of most maladies. The Bisorio believe the *kowa anage* do not exist in Australia. They live only in the Sepik River area of Papua New Guinea. There are similar stories in North India. | 10. Sorcery: black magic |
| 11. Spirit beings in every human, animal, plant, and thing | 11. Magic: supernatural feats |
| 12. Nature: Nature itself is assumed to be a living entity. | 12. Curses and oaths: efficacious invocation of language |
| 13. Metamorphosis: transformation into another physical form through special powers | 13. Objects: imbued with power |
| | 14. Voice: powerful words |
| | 15. Breath and spittle |

## Harmony Differentiated

To people in harmony cultures, these entities are not dormant, influencing life only on rare occasions or in times of catastrophe. No, these unseen spirits and forces are active every day, on the smallest scale. You are walking down the trail, say, and stumble. Why? Was it an arrow of the *kowa anage*? Did someone obtain a bit of your fingernail or hair and utter a curse over it? Is a deceased ancestor unhappy over ritual neglect? In harmony cultures, people strive to understand how these entities influence not some remote afterlife, but day-to-day present existence. Success comes from being able to manage, even manipulate, the influential power of these unseen entities. It's not about developing a personal relationship with these spirit beings; friendship is not at issue. What people seek—the spotlight—is control. It's about avoiding curse and obtaining blessing. Conscious or not, people in harmony cultures continually think, "What must I say and do to maintain harmony?"

In the global West, most people associate the supernatural world and otherworldly activity with religion. We say that our friends who are active in church activities are religious. People in harmony societies, however, though they do believe in supernatural beings and spiritual forces, are not necessarily thinking in religious terms. For Western people, religion usually implies a dichotomy of sacred versus secular, a split between the holy and the worldly. But in harmony cultures, there is no split, no dichotomy. There is no secular. All of life is one whole.

Our usual notion of religion is a bit too rigid. A more flexible and nuanced understanding of religion helps us appreciate how harmony cultures work. The nineteenth-century sociologist Karl Marx claimed, "Man makes religion, religion does not make man. The religious world is but the reflex of the real world . . . the sigh of the oppressed creature, the sentiment of a heartless world, and the soul of soulless conditions."[2] I find his description depressing. No wonder his ideas led to an abolition of religion. In her text *Living Religions*, scholar of world religions Mary Pat Fisher is more generous. She understands religion to be man's attempt "to tie back" to a greater reality that is behind the surface of life. For most cultures, religion-like activity is a basic foundation of life that permeates all aspects of human existence.[3] People do not even think of themselves as religious; they are just living. Religion exists in all human societies, but it is not always easy to distinguish "greater reality" from everyday phenomenon.

Paul Hiebert's seminal work on folk religion helps us analyze religious systems.[4] (Table 23, below, is adapted from Hiebert's writings.) Hiebert makes a helpful distinction between high and low religions. *High religions* are more formal and answer questions about (a) origins, (b) the purpose of life, and (c) ultimate destiny. Logical consistency is important, and so high religions often entail doctrine, catechism, and dogma. Examples include the main world religions: Judaism, Christianity, Islam, Hinduism, and Buddhism. In contrast, *low religions* are more informal and answer questions people face in everyday life, that is, (a) how to assure a productive crop, (b) why a sudden death, and (c) who stole the money. They are less concerned about ultimate realities and more focused on immediate access to power.

2. Marx and Engels, "Religion," 62.

3. Fisher, *Living Religions*, 12.

4. Hiebert et al., *Understanding Folk Religion*, 47–72.

Note that Hiebert uses "low religion" to describe what this chapter simply says is the whole of life.

*High religions* generally have written texts, such as the Bible, the Qur'an, or the Vedas. They are highly institutionalized with formal places of worship, prescribed rituals, and moral codes. However, *low religions* are more informally organized. Rather than through sacred texts, tradition is passed along orally, accompanied by drama and songs. Pragmatism is more important than moral directives or destiny.

Religion rarely appears in a pure form. Many societies practice a *low religion* such as spiritism or tribal animism mixed with certain forms of *high religion* due to proximity and the natural impact of culture diffusion. A high religion like Christianity or Islam often exists in a society as a folk religion, a surface veneer, underneath which are all the practices and underpinnings of tribal animism, sometimes hidden from view. In Christianized societies in the Majority World, for example, devotees may use the pastor for prayer and, at the same time, the shaman for ritual. In some places, the pastor and the shaman may even be the same person. There are examples everywhere of this sort of folk Christianity and folk Islam, where the trappings of high religions are melded to local beliefs and practices.

Here's one example: Several years ago, I facilitated a training in India on the topic of worldview. To attend, many participants had traveled to Bangalore, Karnataka from northeast India, mainly from Nagaland. I used stories from India and elsewhere to illustrate how worldview functions. After one or two days, a participant—he was earning his Master of Arts in Intercultural Studies—asked to share a personal story about worldview with the class. I happily agreed.

He told the class he was a Baptist pastor from Nagaland. (The majority of the population in Nagaland professes to be Christian.) In Nagaland, he said, if you are walking along in your village and are startled by something, your spirit leaves your body and flees to a field outside the village. You know exactly what to do. You go home and lie down to avoid illness, then call the local pastor. He comes to your house and hears your story. He then ventures to the adjacent field. Performing a ritual to call your wayward spirit forth, the pastor mounts it on his own back and carries it to your house. There, he performs another ritual to transfer it back into your body, which, no longer frightened, can once again hold it.

The participant's story was a great example of worldview. It showed many deep worldview assumptions: Human beings are bi-part, consisting of a physical body and an immaterial spirit. Body and spirit can be separated. The spirit is personal, belonging only to that individual. The person continues to be a person, albeit vulnerable, even though the spirit departs. Abrupt fear impacts the human spirit. A normal person does not have the power to retrieve a departed spirit. A shaman—or, in the case of Nagaland syncretism, a pastor—does. The human spirit is subservient to the religious specialist. It can be transported.

His story was also a great example of religious syncretism, that is, the mixing of high and low religions. For some people in Nagaland, Christianity is a veneer. Underneath its formal scriptures and practices and doctrines—indeed, underneath all of life—is tribal animism. Obviously, in the Christian Bible there are no accounts of a religious leader retrieving, transporting, and (re)imparting a separated human spirit. And Western Christians, especially those trained in church doctrine and systematic theology, might find such a practice illogical or contradictory to the teachings of the Church. But in Nagaland folklore, this story is natural and normal. The forms of the low religion are sublimated into the forms of the high religion. The Baptist pastor simply assumes the role of the locally familiar shaman. The function of the practice remains the same. Table 23 goes deeper.

## Table 23: Analysis of Religious Systems

| Personal spirit beings | | Impersonal spiritual forces | |
|---|---|---|---|
| | High religion | | Other worldly: People perceive that these entities reside and activities occur in some other world and during other times |
| Unseen and supernatural: People assume these entities and events are beyond immediate experience and above natural explanation | Cosmic beings: gods, angels, demons, and spirits of other worlds | Cosmic forces: fate, kismet, and karma | |
| | Low religion | | |
| | Low religion: local gods, earthly goddesses, ancestors, ghosts, evil spirits, jinn, fairies, gnomes, animal spirits and totems | Low religion: mana, magic, witchcraft, astrology, charms, amulets, evil eye, evil tongue, feng shui, palmistry, and divination | This worldly: People perceive that these entities exist and events occur in this world |
| | "The excluded middle" | "The excluded middle" | |
| Seen or empirical: People know these entities and events based upon observation and experimentation | Social Sciences: Interaction of living entities such as humans, animals, and plants | Physical Sciences: Interaction of natural objects based upon natural forces | |

Many societies perceive that what Fisher calls "greater reality" consists of personal spirit beings and impersonal spirit forces. Entities and events may be seen or unseen, of this world or other worldly. Western culture knows a great deal about the social and physical sciences. Events and activities in these sciences are observable and measurable. Some in the West also assume that a high god exists but transcends the affairs of this world. Most in the West presuppose that, for the most part, what is seen is what is. In other words, there are no earthly goddesses, evil spirits, mana (soul substance), or a powerful force in an amulet phylactery. However, to people in the Majority World, these low religion entities and events are real. They are of this world and are supernatural at the same time. Because these "middle" entities and events are unknown to the West, Hiebert calls this category as "the excluded middle." It is a category Westerners have ignored far too long.

## Harmony Widespread

Fifty years ago, the British historian Stephen Neill estimated that 40 percent of the world's population follow a harmony pattern of culture.[5] Despite the rise of Western technology and its worldwide appeal, it is likely that this percentage has not diminished. People oriented toward harmony often live in societies where other patterns seemingly dominate.[6] Harmony may hide behind the facade of other patterns. A society may have the elaborate bureaucratic apparatus common in justice cultures, as well as a substructure of clientelistic networks people use to obtain resources, and still, in the deepest parts of people's homes and hearts, be dominated by considerations of harmony.

Take a woman who works as a federal government employee. In her daytime work world, she follows a justice pattern of culture. Then, after work, she returns to a neighborhood influenced by reciprocity, where her security and access to resources hinge on who she knows. But at home she has a sick child, and here harmony takes over. The mother waves a raw egg over her child's chest. She assumes the illness—a malady likely caused by the evil eye—will pass from the child's body into the egg. In the daytime at work, the woman supports enforcing the code of federal regulations. At home, just as strongly, she assumes the efficacy of an animistic ritual called *pasando el huevo*.

Several years ago, I enjoyed an opportunity to do participant observation in Papua New Guinea. My host, from San Diego, California, worked as a missionary in an Iteri village. Late one afternoon, we noticed an Iteri man, new to the village, who apparently had descended from the surrounding

---

5. Neill, *Christian Faith and Other Faiths*, 125.

6. In contrast, societies may appear to be oriented toward harmony, but beneath the surface is another dominant pattern. I recently heard an account of this from Walter Selke, the general director of Northern Canada Evangelical Mission. In a personal conversation on October 2, 2017, Walter shared that among the Cree First Nations people of Saskatchewan, honor trumps harmony and other patterns. The "in-group" loyalty among the Cree (an Algonquian language and the most common aboriginal language of Canada) results in envy and enmity toward other indigenous groups, such as the Dene (The term "dene" is an Athabaskan word for "people.").

mountains down into the river basin where the small village had been assembled. Muscle-bound, he wore his hair long, braided, and pulled back. His only apparel was a jungle gourd tied around his waist with a thin vine. Although the missionary had lived in the region for over five years, he told me he had never seen this man. Yet, he evidently was Iteri. The missionary cautioned me about staring at him. Why, I asked. The missionary said he would think I was using the power of my eyes to influence him. He would perceive my staring as a ritual of control.

## Harmony's Function

In a harmony culture, rituals, ceremonies, and the specialists necessary to enact them are important parts of everyday life. Hiebert argues that the heart of harmony societies is ritual.[7] Often extravagant and expensive, rituals retain tradition, build community, and reinforce social structures. Below the surface of the extravagance and expense are core assumptions and values, that is, the rules and norms of a society. As noted repeatedly in *Overarching Patterns*, people hold these assumptions and values *tacitly*. That is, they are mostly outside of people's awareness. Yet, in ritual, a culture's tacit rules and norms are revealed: "Rituals recreate the social, cultural, personal, and cosmic order necessary for human life by making these rules explicit."[8] Rituals surface deep foundations. They tell stories. Remarkably, rituals so integrate the deep layers of culture that they become what they represent. They are not detached events.[9] Locals perceive that rituals are imbued with power. Rituals incorporate dominant symbols. They not only are narrative in nature, amidst the ceremonial drama acted out, but through the experiential narrative, they also retell the past, emphasizing what is real and right, and instruct the present, highlighting what is expected and appropriate.

To perform these elaborate rituals requires socio-cultural specialists. In the West, these may be labeled as religious specialists. Examples are shamans, palmists, astrologers, healers, diviners, and mystics. These specialists know how to perform the rituals. They have techniques to control the powers of the unseen world for the benefit of daily living.

---

7. Hiebert et al., *Understanding Folk Religion*, 283.

8. Hiebert et al., *Understanding Folk Religion*, 284.

9. Hiebert et al., *Understanding Folk Religion*, 291.

Often in the secular West, the phenomenological reality of a harmony culture's unseen world is misunderstood, doubted, and derided. Westerners always underestimate the power of indigenous people's consciousness and experience. I have seen no greater illustration of this miscalculation than in Christian missionary endeavors. In missionary work—whether Catholic or Protestant—missionaries innocently assume that the priest's work or the evangelist's preaching will spontaneously and easily supplant animistic people's core assumptions, values, and institutions. As if people were an empty cup waiting for the water of life. As if people could convert—totally change their beliefs and habits—in a day. There is little evidence to suggest missionary work works such wonders.

What is clear, though, is that indigenous peoples absorb new things. Almost effortlessly, they integrate what they see as a foreign Western biblical story into their existing metanarrative, their web of stories. Syncretism occurs. Locals may accept that a high god exists, one who at some time and in some way will share benevolence. But their daily animistic practices continue nonstop. They still seek to control personal spirit beings and impersonal spiritual forces.

This phenomenon has been charted. Kenneth Nehrbass, a translation consultant with the Summer Institute of Linguistics and a professor of anthropology at Biola University's School of Intercultural Studies, has worked on religious syncretism in Melanesia.[10] His field work was with the Tannese people among the Vanuatu Islands in the South Pacific. Nehrbass describes four variegated approaches to integrating a story from Scripture with a local culture. Through his mastery of Tannese language and culture, Nehrbass argues not simply that animism is an assumption about fetish power but, more profoundly, that animistic people are interconnected with the physical and supernatural worlds. The ideas people have and emotions they feel are efficacious in all aspects of life.[11] Impact is massive and immeasurable.

What does a sensitivity to harmony cultures look like in a business setting? Perhaps like this. Once along the southwest border of Texas, where I was facilitating a training, a work unit supervisor returned to the regional office. She brought her baby to show off to her colleagues. At the break, I met her and her newborn. As she introduced me to her little girl, I reached out and stroked the baby's shoulder. "Para no darle el mal de ojo," I said.

10. Nehrbass, *Christianity and Animism in Melanesia*.
11. Nehrbass, *Christianity and Animism in Melanesia*, 2.

"So as not to give you the evil of the eye." A non-Hispanic American reader may be caught off guard: Evil eye? Lightly touching the baby? The mother, though, did not noticed anything untoward. My behavior was perfectly normal and, in fact, tacitly expected by this Hispanic woman, a federal government employee, whose family was from Matamoros, Tamaulipas, just south of the border.

Assumptions related to harmony dictate all sorts of things—where one sits, what objects are appropriate or inappropriate, if time and space are fitting, what behavior is proper. In Southeast Asia, one wants to associate with and be close to wise and wealthy people; that way one may acquire their *mana* energy. Training participants in India tell me they sleep with their faces to the east, the direction positive energy comes from. In Eastern cultures, clutter and stagnant air in the office or home restricts the flow of *qi*, a feng shui energy. When training in stratified cultures, if I start an interactive discussion, I am mindful to address the person of the highest social class first. This maintains harmony. In such cultures, training participants or businesspeople almost always defer to those who are male, older, and married, to grandparents or parents. Respecting these and other status markers (wealth and education) preserves harmony.

## Closing Remarks

Thus far, we have covered three overarching patterns: justice, honor, and harmony. Culture experts have long been aware of these three patterns. Using them, culture consultants have designed training courses in cultural competency. These three patterns are powerful tools that explain many cultures around the world. Yet, now and then, a handful of societies have not fit. There are certain contexts where a pattern of justice, honor, or harmony does not capture what is going on. Every so often, culture students realized the three-pattern model did not explain their target culture. Something was missing.

There is a fourth pattern—reciprocity, the back and forth exchange of resources and loyalty. Reciprocity is often interwoven with aspects of the other three patterns. It often emerges in times of crisis. And it's worth considering alongside the other three patterns. The next chapter explains how reciprocity works.

Chapter 9

# Reciprocity

"Clientelism hampers the development of the political institutions necessary for democratic development."[1]

## Opening Remarks

IN OCTOBER OF 2001, in response to the September 11th attacks on New York City and Washington, DC, the US military invaded Afghanistan as part of the campaign Operation Enduring Freedom. A year later, the US government (USG) introduced Provincial Reconstruction Teams (PRTs) into the Afghanistan war theatre.

Because the central government of Afghanistan had lost control to the Taliban and local warlords (or never really had control), the USG speculated that PRTs could empower local governments to be more effective and ultimately conjoin with a central government in Kabul. The long-term goal was to legitimize the central government.[2] The plan was for one PRT per province, though each province was divided into many districts. Each PRT unit included military officers, peacekeeping and security soldiers, civilian police advisors, diplomats, and reconstruction experts. The method of empowering locals was through regional reconstruction projects. The foundational idea of the PRTs was drawn from the discipline of civil/military relations.[3]

The PRT initiative was bold—innovative, but obviously difficult. Needs in the provinces differed. There were language barriers, especially the exceptionally difficult Pashto tongue. The tasks were daunting. The operational environment was dangerous. Providing credible security was practically

1. Hicken, *Clientelism*, 302.
2. Bebber, "Provincial Reconstruction Teams," 3–24.
3. For resources related to CMR, see Footnote 120.

impossible. The USG moved with speed, focusing on quick impact. Failure was common. Vast amounts of money were spent. Lives were lost. It turned out that ordinary project development and accountability proved unmanageable across cultures, at least in this context. Given the ambition of PRTs for democratic rule, how was capacity-building to be done in the provinces? What were the sustainability strategies? How were the USG and coalition partners to overcome centuries of decentralized clan-based loyalties?[4] To what degree did PRT personnel understand local societies?[5]

The roots of local warlordism ran deep. Their role in a given locale was formidable.[6] Warlords were protected by personal local militias. Regionally, they exercised immense power. The clientelism of these environments in Afghanistan thwarted efforts of democracy. And, to date, after years of costly toil, local clientelism has not been surmounted by any invader, not by the Soviet Union, not by the United States.

Not all clientelistic environments are so explosive. However, clientelism endures all over the world. Luis Roniger, professor of Latin American studies at Wake Forest University, characterizes *clientelism* as an old term in the field of human relations, studied predominately in the 1960s and 1970s.[7] The term conjures up memories of feudalism. Despite the dust the word has collected, clientelism still prevails in many geographic areas of the world and among sundry societies. Its impact raises it to the level of an overarching pattern of culture. The book adds it as the fourth overarching pattern of culture.

How do we know if a society is clientelistic? What are the local assumptions and expected behaviors? The chapter provides answers.

## Reciprocity Basics

For several months in 2016, I facilitated cross-cultural trainings for a large government agency whose personnel work along the Southwest border between the United States and Mexico. Among other topics, the curriculum introduced *clientelism*. Few participants had heard the term. But they all lived in places—from San Diego, California to Brownsville, Texas—where

---

4. See the Air Force Culture and Language Center, *Expeditionary Airman Field Guide*.

5. Based on Maley, "Provincial Reconstruction Teams in Afghanistan."

6. Consider Ollapally, "Unfinished Business in Afghanistan."

7. Roniger, "Political Clientelism," 353.

clientelism had shaped local life. Once prompted, many participants told stories about important people in their area who controlled access to resources that others depended on, and how these key relationships worked through informal networks. Though unfamiliar with academic language, most training participants had a sense of clientelism as a way of life—both north and south of the border.

The locals seemed to know instinctively. The training provided words and concepts for what they were already living. At one training in McAllen, Texas, a participant not originally from the area—but who had lived there for fifty years—excitedly supposed, "Wait a minute! This is mafia stuff!" He claimed he had never noticed anything like clientelism in McAllen. Those from McAllen smiled politely. Often, an outsider lives in a community, even for some time, and remains unaware of cultural differences. Here and there things seem strange to him, even stupid. Tasked with accurately analyzing what happens and articulating it, an untrained outsider will have an extremely difficult time.

The academic literature on clientelism describes the relationship between a patron and clients as reciprocal but also asymmetrical. This relationship at times rises to the level of friendship, but more often remains merely an affiliation, aptly described as an "instrumental friendship."[8] In Spanish, the term *lazos*, "ties," captures the link. In clientelism, patron and client are reciprocally bound. It is to these links that people feel an obligation. The exchange between patron and client is reciprocal in that both need resources the other possesses. *Palanca*, "lever," refers to the leverage one needs to get things done amidst the networks one has built. These are "problem-solving networks."[9] Patrons need client loyalty to maintain their prestige and power, while clients need the protection and goods patrons provide.

Resource problems arise when traditional structures like justice and community break down. In a justice culture, an individual is a free participant in the marketplace of life—able to be selfish. In an honor culture, everyone is a dutiful member of a local community—needing to be social or communal.[10] In a reciprocity culture, dyads exchange resources in informal

8. Scott, "Patron-Client Politics," 92. James Scott was a professor of political science and anthropology at the University of Wisconsin and Yale University.

9. Brinkerhoff and Goldsmith's phrase in "Clientelism, Patrimonialism and Democratic Governance," a paper prepared for the US Agency of International Development. Derick Brinkerhoff is associate faculty of public administration and international affairs at Georgetown University.

10. See Shweder et al., "The 'Big Three' of Morality," 139.

networks built over time—people are proactively relational, and have to be. At the core of clientelism is a worldview assumption about reciprocity:[11] Human relationships outside of family exist not so much for individual dignity or for bestowing honor, but mostly for reciprocal exchange of valuable resources. Such exchanges are part and parcel of survival in a society where democratic or other civil institutions often no longer work or are perceived to have broken down.[12]

Table 24 contrasts the features of a democratic society with those of a clientelistic society. When a democratic society erodes and breaks down, the vacuum is filled. Power brokers enter and establish control. In a democracy, power is vested institutionally. But in clientelism, power roles are developed across informal networks. Informed by the work of Brinkerhoff and Goldsmith, Table 24 highlights both positive and negative aspects of the power network that emerges over time. Though clientelism does have some positive aspects, Brinkerhoff and Goldsmith write, "Clientelism is usually seen as lying at the far end of the institutional spectrum from democracy."[13]

Table 24: Contrast Between Democracy and Clientelism

| A Just Democratic Society | Power Network |
| --- | --- |
| Authority derived from societal institutions (official roles and responsibilities) | Authority developed through informal networks (unofficial roles and responsibilities) |
| The rule of law a core value | Loyalty a core value |
| Leaders legally accountable for their actions, which tend to be predictable | Leaders formally unaccountable for their actions and may be unreliable |
| Relationships may or may not be strategic | Relationships are strategic—always |
| Civil society usually integrated | Civil society often fragmented |

11. Allen Hicken, a professor of political science at the University of Michigan, uses the term *contingency* as a synonym for reciprocity: "The element that every definition has in common is the contingent or reciprocal nature of the patron-client exchange" (*Clientelism*, 291).

12. See Roniger, "Political Clientelism" for a more detailed analysis of democracy and clientelism.

13. Brinkerhoff and Goldsmith, "Clientelism," 4.

| A Just Democratic Society | Power Network |
| --- | --- |
| Established policies and procedures | Ad hoc rules and practices |
| Public and private segregated | Public and private are blurred |
| Equal treatment | Preferential treatment |

From immigration patterns, it seems clear that people prefer democratic societies over those that are heavily clientelistic. Specifically, people value how in the former status and wealth are more stable and fair, less subject to the unpredictability of preferential power networks. In Little Rock, Arkansas, not far from the Clinton Presidential Library, I have enjoyed hours of conversation with the owners of an Argentine restaurant who emigrated from Buenos Aires. I once asked what they liked most about Little Rock. Without hesitation, Guillermo replied, "Rule of law!"[14] The cultural contrast observed and lived by Guillermo and his wife Graciela is clear. They prefer the stable structure of a free market in a democratic society to the volatile informality of Argentine clientelism. If an expatriate restaurant owner in the United States still feels such apathy, imagine how much more apathy the less affluent and less powerful back in Argentina feel.

Table 25 analyzes reciprocity using the four-tier model of culture described in chapter 2 (see Figure 9), contrasting an overarching pattern of reciprocity with the other patterns of culture.

---

14. See Thompson et al., *Cultural Theory*, 224, who argue that the political passivity or apathy of the powerless is rooted in frustrated social relationships, especially those with governmental officials: "A fatalistic orientation (the attitude that nothing one can do will influence the government . . .) is thus a learned (and rational) response to a distant, capricious, and unresponsive power imposed from without."

Table 25: Four Overarching Patterns of Culture—Reciprocity

|  | Justice | Honor | Harmony | Reciprocity |
|---|---|---|---|---|
| Worldview | Legality | Community | Security | Clientelism |
| Value | Righteousness | Reputation | Respite | Resources |
| Obligation | To written standards | To an honor code | To holistic interactions | To connections |
| Identity | Guilty or not guilty | Shameful or honorable | Out of harmony or in harmony | Benefited or benefactor |
| Spotlight | Individual rights | Family name | Control | Relationships |
| Key Institutions | Codified law, justice system, law enforcement | Kinship, family, extended family, integrated community | The supernatural and natural worlds (not differentiated) | Exchange, asymmetrical affiliations informal networks |
| Outward Observable Behaviors | Truth, individualism, self-efficacy, achieved status, equality | Conformity, collectivism, losing or saving face in others' eyes, ascribed status, hierarchy | Community concord, in-groups, rituals, ceremonies, religious specialists | Presentation, stratification, interactions |
| Place | The West | The East and Middle East | Global | The South |

# Worldview

In the Global South, where clientelism is a way of life, people naturally tend to focus on relationships in which they are able to exchange resources. Their focus is not necessarily on the rule of law, not on individual rights, though people do respect kinship and gender honor codes and, to a lesser extent, pay attention to harmony.

Asymmetrical affiliations between patrons and clients, clustered in informal networks, develop to form institutions of social organization. The key to the patron-client affiliation is exchange: "There is no tie if there is no exchange."[15] Figure 17 shows the most basic features of reciprocity:

15. Barnes, *Patrons and Power*, 210.

Figure 17: The Exchange is the Function.

## Values

The patron—because of wealth, education, and social or political position—has status. This status yields prestige, influence, honor, and control. The patron is able to provide the client with security, intercession, access, and resources. The patron-client relationship is reciprocal in that the patron makes available needed resources beyond the client's reach, while the client, in return, provides political loyalty and social prestige to the patron. The patron's followers are thus also part of the patron's wealth. Clients broaden the base of the patron's influence and power.[16]

Although the relationship between patron and client may or may not be personal, it is almost always asymmetrical. A hierarchy of power distance exists.[17] Figure 18 more fully illustrates the patron-client relationship, one bound by exchange. The relationship is most effective when the reciprocity is balanced. That is, a patron who demands too much of clients exploits them;[18] a patron who donates too much to clients parents them.

16. See Barnes, *Patrons and Power*; Clark, "Old and New Paradigms for Urban Research"; De Neve, "Patronage and 'Community'"; Eisenstadt and Roniger, *Patrons, Clients, and Friends*; Goodell, "Paternalism, Patronage, and Potlach"; Gordin, *The Political and Partisan Determinants of Patronage*; Kingston, "Patrons, Clients, and Civil Society"; Medard, "The Underdeveloped State in Tropical Africa"; Roniger and Güneş-Ayata, *Democracy, Clientelism, and Civil Society*; Scott, "Patron-Client Politics"; Strickon and Greenfield, *Structure and Process in Latin America*.

17. See Hicken, *Clientelism*, 292; Scott, "Patron-Client Politics," 72; Eisenstadt and Roniger, *Patrons, Clients, and Friends*, 48.

18. See Scott, "Patronage or Exploitation?" 21–40.

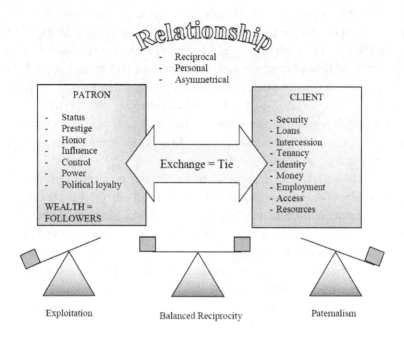

Figure 18: The Reciprocal Relationship of Exchange.

## Institutions

At the institutional level, clientelistic exchanges can be analyzed in several ways—by arena, scope, duration, and tentativeness. First, let's take the *arenas* of an exchange: political, economic, and social.

In the political arena, public resources may be exchanged for political support. These resources involve public funds, jobs, and positions of responsibility.[19] In the political arena, bureaucracy may take the place of a personal relationship, and almost all interactions between patron and client take place through a broker. Political clientelism erodes democratic institutions and fragments the electorate, reducing its collective power.[20] It is a counterforce to democracy.[21]

19. See Fox, "The Difficult Transition from Clientelism to Citizenship," 151–84; Keefer and Vlaicu, "Democracy, Credibility, and Clientelism," 371–406; and Auyero, "The Logic of Clientelism in Argentina," 55–81.

20. Auyero, "Logic of Clientelism," 59–60.

21. Gordin, *The Political and Partisan Determinants of Patronage*, 2.

In the economic arena, a patron or power broker may offer jobs, process paperwork, expedite approvals, or lift restrictions in exchange for money or some other service. Reciprocal exchange is required for an unrestricted flow of commerce.[22] In underdeveloped areas, people focus on immediate consumption: They need money, water, food, and shelter promptly. The situation is a matter of sustenance, even survival. Most likely, stable revenue streams are not to hand, only variable sources of income.[23] In dire circumstances, clientelism is rife. People who need resources turn to those who control them.

In the social arena, a patron's protection may be exchanged for a client's loyalty. If rule of law has broken down—and often this is the cause—the protection of normal state institutions, such as a local police force, may not be available. Residents then turn for security to strategic connections. Along the Southwest border, safety may come from an early morning phone call from a relative or old friend on the other side of the border, giving strategic information long before official channels disseminate the same news. In such areas, safety and security are tied mostly to relationships, not to written standards or procedural protocols.

Second, let's consider the *scope* of an exchange. Scope refers to the patron's and clients' capacity to provide opportunities and reciprocity. Not every patron has the same capacity. Not all benefits are the same. In fact, power brokers compete for scope, a contest that often turns ferocious and deadly. A patron's capacity is always observed and measured.

Third, take the *duration* of an exchange. Informal reciprocal networks are not permanent. Networks are often specific to time and place, changing from location to location. Promising connections are often made and maintained long before any resources are requested. In new locales one must develop new networks.[24]

Finally, we can analyze the *tentativeness* of an exchange. In clientelism, a patron's power is not fixed. Control of resources changes hands. Patrons and would-be patrons struggle for power. Conflict is common. Violence is often inevitable. There are usually imbalances. Negotiation and renegotiation are ongoing. Distrust is ordinary. Even a cursory look at current events along the

22. For the impact of clientelism vs. state capacity on economic development, see Bustikova and Corduneanu-Huci's "Clientelism, State Capacity and Economic Development: A Cross-National Study." Lenka Bustikova is a professor in the School of Politics and Global Studies at Arizona State University.

23. Brinkerhoff and Goldsmith, *Clientelism*, 2.

24. Hicken, *Clientelism*, 291.

Southwest border of the United States and Mexico, particularly in northern Mexico, provides boundless examples of such tentativeness.

The previous paragraphs analyze the exchange at a moment in time. But we can also analyze the exchange across time. At what stages in a society's development is clientelism a real possibility? One view—indebted to Max Weber—is that clientelistic political systems are a transitional stage, more likely in societies moving from a traditional government organized by kinship to a more impersonally-organized or bureaucratic government.[25] In a traditional society, the reciprocal relationship may be between a landlord and workers. In a more modern urban setting, the reciprocal relationship is between a patron and client. In the former case, the workers likely have direct contact with the landlord. In the latter, the patron is more distant, the exchange network being public and mediated by a political system.

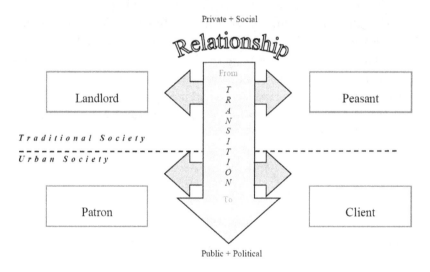

Figure 19: Transition from Patrimonial to Political.

Weber's view may be true, but equally evident is a reemergence of clientelism when democracies fail and in the midst of a fledgling republic.

## The Good and the Ugly

Patron behavior falls on a moral spectrum. As an example of a benevolent patron, let's take a case from the New Testament. Early in John's Gospel

25. Barnes, *Patrons and Power*, 10.

is the story of Jesus's encounter with a Samaritan woman at Jacob's well, located at the small village of Sychar near Shechem, beneath nearby Mt. Gerizim. In this well-known story, Jesus assumes the role of a patron and invites the woman to be a client. Table 26 analyzes the text of John 4:4–42, using South African theologian Abiola Mbamalu's insights into how reciprocity works in the passage.[26] The table identifies the roles and responsibilities of each party, showing their reciprocal exchange.

In the narrative, Jesus journeys into Samaria and stops around noon in Sychar, at Jacob's well. Thirsty, he asks an approaching Samaritan woman for a drink. But a woman should not be speaking with a man; and a Samaritan should not be speaking with a Jew. So the unnamed woman does not trust him. Jesus knows he has something of greater value the woman unknowingly needs. As a benevolent patron, he initiates a reciprocal relationship.

The reciprocal exchange is water for water, that is, physical water that quenches thirst for "living" water that leads to eternal life. The relationship is asymmetrical. The biblical Messiah is conversing and relating with a Samaritan of mixed race, a woman, and an outcast in her community. And the benefits are mutual: Jesus' thirst is satisfied and his message about the Messianic Kingdom is spread locally and made available to everyone. The woman's life is changed, she gains honor, and she assumes a new role as a broker for her patron.

Table 26: Jesus and the Samaritan Woman

| Feature of Patronage and Clientelism | Patron | Client |
|---|---|---|
| Position | Jesus the Messiah | An unnamed Samaritan woman (likely an outcast, as she comes to the well alone) |
| Power distance | Male, a Jew | Female, of mixed race |
| Resource | Living water (eternal life) | Water to quench thirst with means to retrieve it from Jacob's well, which was deep |
| Initiation | He asks her for water. | She responds reluctantly at first due to mistrust: Jesus appears as a stranger with no connection to the land and ancestry. |

26. Mbamalu, "Patronage and Clientelism in the Fourth Gospel," 1–8.

| Feature of Patronage and Clientelism | Patron | Client |
| --- | --- | --- |
| Immediate outcome (benefit) | Thirst quenched | Life-changing encounter with the Messiah |
| Long-term outcome (balanced reciprocity) | Mission fulfilled | In a new role as a broker with ascribed status, she successfully spreads the word about the Messiah in her local community. |
| Scope | Living water for everyone | Racial and geographic limits: Jacob, his sons, his flocks, our fathers, this mountain, and this water |

But patrons are not always so benevolent. When I was a small boy, my family lived in the Dominican Republic. We first arrived in the capital city of Ciudad Trujillo (now Santo Domingo) in 1960, when I was only five years old. Rafael Leonidas Trujillo (1891–1961) was still dictator. In 1930, the Dominican people had revolted against President Horacio Vasquez. Trujillo—a member of a criminal gang in his youth and having risen rapidly through the military ranks—seized the moment and amassed power. After ruling tyrannically for thirty years, Trujillo was assassinated on May 31, 1961. He was only one of many Latin American *caudillos*, "strongmen," usually military leaders.

During his three-decade reign, "The Era of Trujillo," he maintained public order and practiced fiscal prudence. He freed the Dominican Republic from foreign supervision. He improved sanitation and constructed roads, built schools and enhanced nationalism. At the same time, Trujillo expected complete obedience, total control. His thirst for power and money was insatiable. He seized land. His family expropriated businesses— cattle, sugar, tobacco, and lumber companies. (At his death in 1961, he owned over a hundred of them.) His personal display was extraordinary— elaborate uniforms, neckties, perfect grooming, and perfume. His sexual appetite, never quenched, always included young girls. Trujillo kept an execution list. Whoever opposed him felt his inevitable cruelty. They were found out, imprisoned, tortured, murdered. Trujillo ordered the Parsley Massacre, during which the Dominican army slaughtered Haitians, an estimated 10,000 to 35,000 people.

Although at times reprimanded by the United States for these human rights abuses, Trujillo enjoyed remarkable American support.

Representative Hamilton Fish III, for example, a New York Republican and ranking member of the House Foreign Affairs Committee, strongly advocated for Trujillo. Fish opposed Franklin D. Roosevelt's New Deal and was anti-Communist, so supporting authoritarian regimes like Trujillo's was an easy step.[27] Once when Trujillo visited the United States, Fish spoke at a dinner in Trujillo's honor: "General, you have created a golden age for your country. You will go down in history as a builder greater than all the Spanish Conquistadores together."[28]

But great builders are often great destroyers. Robert D. Crassweller, a lawyer for the Department of State, in his full-length biography of Trujillo, rounds out the picture: "He was egotistic, eventually to the point of megalomania. He was greedy. His sensuality and sexual drive were extraordinary. He was not merely amoral but profoundly immoral. He loved display and drama in every act of life. He loved to build, to create large and striking effects, and to transform the landscape."[29] His image was indeed everywhere. Like every Dominican living room or kitchen, ours displayed Trujillo's portrait. Sometimes in the evenings, we would see men on our property. Conscious of our status as foreigners, we did not confront them, assuming they were Trujillo's observers. I still remember the day in May 1961 when our cook Teresita entered my father's home office to share the frightening news: on a road outside the capital Trujillo had been assassinated. Her voice quivering, she said, "Se mató al Jefe!" Trujillo was dead.[30]

Like Trujillo, the caudillo—"El Jefe"—personifies the worst in clientelism. My father writes: "There was no place in the island where his power did not reach. Anything and anyone were his, at his request—or they were no more! Those who resisted his power disappeared. No one, including us from America, dared to speak against him. All of us were, to one degree or another, mesmerized."[31]

---

27. Fish, "The Menace of Communism."

28. Crassweller, *Trujillo*, 324.

29. Crassweller, *Trujillo*, 5.

30. Just after the assassination of Trujillo, my father wrote a five-page essay chronicling his experience that began with Teresita's terrifying announcement. See the complete essay in Appendix H.

31. Sam Strauss, Jr., "The Day They Killed Trujillo," 3.

# Behavior

In a reciprocity society, what everyday behaviors are common? People are relational, always connecting and reconnecting. They enjoy their interactions, acquaintances, and friendships. Time slows down. Informal networks pervade all of life. People maintain contacts. Their greetings are more formal and elaborate, their conversations more intense. Who you know matters more than what you know. Relationships provide access. A patron and client work together to get things done.

In northern Guatemala, for example, when I visit the city of Quetzaltenango, I am hosted by a local friend who owns a large coffee plantation. He has numerous employees. Everyone there knows him. His coffee is exported widely, even to a distributer in Little Rock, Arkansas. Everyone there knows his wealth and power. Our reciprocal exchange goes something like this: In a potentially dangerous area, my association with the plantation owner gives me protection. At the same time, my visit gives him another level of status. As my patron during my visit, he provides access to what I am completely unable to furnish on my own—safety and security. How does he behave? And how do I respond? He takes the lead. He introduces me to people. He is the consummate host. I understand my local status and assume the lesser role.

Likewise, in Argentina, I enjoy a professional relationship with the Society of Intercultural Education Training and Research. Based in Buenos Aires, the society's impact is felt throughout the Southern Cone. Marcelo, Shirley, Natalia, and others host me, introduce me, and provide access to opportunities otherwise unavailable. We are bound by friendship—and an exchange of resources. Often, such reciprocity is not immediate. Months after connecting with someone, I may get a telephone call with a request. These calls no longer surprise me. In fact, I expect them from my contacts in reciprocity cultures.

When I work in a reciprocity culture, I stay alert to networks, relationships, and important people. To get things done, I do not appeal to laws, rules, or written contracts. In Argentina, I do not tell stories of my prestigious grandfather, one of the vice-presidents of the Georgia Power Company. Instead, I understand that to move my agenda forward, I need to spend time with the right people. This activity is not one-sided. As I benefit, so do others. So I spend time with families, eating dinners together and staying up late talking. In Argentina, we enjoy Malbec and discuss the Boca Juniors. My goal—and theirs—is to build our informal network.

A business agreement—perhaps my true aim—is a secondary outcome. The agreement is sealed in high-context friendship, not by low-context writing on a piece of paper.

## Concluding Remarks

In societies where reciprocity is the overarching pattern of culture, other patterns of culture—justice, say—are admittedly visible. In any clientelistic society one will likely find federal and local governments, a capital city, government buildings with government offices with government employees sitting at desks, laws based on a written constitution, and law enforcement. However, if the public perceives that these traditional institutions of culture are corrupt, that is, not functioning according to the rule of law, clientelism begins to emerge and spread. It becomes the dominant pattern in local settings and beyond.

Clientelism is a way of life in the Global South. Reciprocal relationships of exchange are developed in informal networks. Access to power and resources is available to everyone in the network. The same is emerging as a norm in the United States. See more in Appendix I.

# Part Three: Functioning in the Structures

Chapter 10

# Business Practices
# Across Cultures

## Opening Remarks

A SOCIETY'S OVERARCHING PATTERN of culture displays its core worldview assumptions, values, socio-cultural institutions, and outward observable behaviors (see Figure 9). The identified pattern denotes generalizations about the system of culture as a whole. No aspect of life is unaffected. Whether we realize it or not, whether we want to admit it or not, everything we say and do is culturally derived and similarly patterned to people around us. Values are manifested over time and particularly in times of crisis, values such as rights, roles, relationships, and rituals.

Those of us who work in intercultural environments must recognize how an overarching pattern of culture impacts professional behavior. Let's consider one aspect of professional behavior: style of leadership. The experienced leader already knows the style she prefers, and has likely worked years to hone it. But is it effective across cultures? What will locals in a different cultural environment expect of us? In which situations should we lead collaboratively, in which authoritatively? The same types of questions can be asked about other business processes: communication, conflict management, project management, and so on.[1]

---

1. The cultural tendency across business processes may not always be the same. Just because an honor culture may be collaborative in a conflict situation does not mean it will be collaborative in another business process, for example, negotiation. See Aslani et al., "Dignity, Face, and Honor," 1178–1201.

## Business Processes

Using the lens of overarching patterns of culture, Table 27 analyzes critical business behaviors. Note the different ways people from different patterns perceive business processes. Based on how they see the world, they will form tacit expectations. As a cross-cultural worker, if I meet those expectations, no one will notice anything. Everything will appear normal. (Culture is outside of our awareness.) But if I do not meet expectations, I will appear strange, which will likely impede my effectiveness. Before the reader descends into the details of Table 27, several brief illustrations about leadership may help establish the ways overarching patterns work.

In a justice culture, most people see themselves as individuals with personal rights, potential roles, and corresponding responsibilities. People have a strong sense of egalitarianism, at least as an ideal. Everyone is equal and must be treated equally. In employment, everyone has equal opportunities. In the United States, federal laws prohibit discrimination on the basis of race, color, nation of origin, language, gender, religion, age, disability, and more. These are protected categories in a quest toward leveraging diversity and leading inclusivity.

In a justice culture, then, people in the workplace expect at least a consultative role in decisions that are made, especially when those decisions impact their work unit. People want a voice, if not a vote. Further, work teams commonly practice a participative approach to leadership. If a supervisor is autocratic in style, the work unit notices it, and notes it to each other. Likewise, in much political activism in the United States, the goal is decreasing power distance. Activists fight for equity in power and a resulting mutuality.

In other patterns of culture, however, leadership takes different forms. In honor cultures, people are much more comfortable with authoritative leaders and a top down management style. Here, power is typically not shared, or evenly distributed. It is derived from ascribed identity that does not change. Relationships are unequal. In Bangalore, India, for example, at the India Institute of Intercultural Studies, my doctoral students do not choose research topics for their class projects. I do. I am expected to choose them, and to choose them wisely. This is perfectly normal for them. But to me it is strange—and challenging.

Similarly, in reciprocity cultures, an authoritarian style is common. People expect the individual or group that controls access to resources to attain and maintain power. This role may change as resources are depleted or supplied elsewhere, but people expect a clear distinction between the powerful and the less powerful.

Finally, in harmony cultures, those who garner power—family patriarchs, religious specialists, and community leaders—do so through sharing and cooperating. However, this cooperation differs from a participative approach where power distance is low. On not a few occasions, as I have led and trained across cultures, I have been politely criticized for not acknowledging and relying upon the ever-present power of the spirit world.

Table 27 describes other professional behaviors per the patterns of culture.

Table 27: Seeing Professional Behavior through the Lens of Overarching Patterns

Professional Behavior

| Overarching pattern | Leadership | Communication | Conflict management[2] | Project management[3] |
|---|---|---|---|---|
| Justice | Based upon strong individualism and its resulting egalitarianism, a participative or consultative style of leadership works best. | Based upon the emphasis on right and wrong, communication needs to be clear, precise, and direct. There is a tendency to summarize or present the "bottom line up front." | A tendency toward:<br><br>• Avoidance<br><br>• *Competitive*<br><br>• Compromise<br><br>• Collaborative<br><br>Conflict may be viewed as positive, leading to the emergence of the best ideas. | What is in focus?<br><br>• Topic<br><br>• Relationships<br><br>• Identity<br><br>• Process<br><br>People prefer to "stay on topic" and follow a prescribed process, often organized in a logic model. |

2. The major tendencies in the conflict management column come from the Thomas-Kilmann Conflict Mode Instrument (TKI), a tool used globally to measure a person's tendencies in man*aging conflict.* See Kilmann Diagnostics, "Overview."

3. Used here, the TRIP model for managing conflict also applies more broadly to project management. TRIP refers to goals. See Hocker and Wilmot, Interpersonal Conflict, 91–106.

Professional Behavior

| Overarching pattern | Leadership | Communication | Conflict management[2] | Project management[3] |
|---|---|---|---|---|
| Honor | High power distance is characteristic of honor societies. *Power* in this context is ascribed by identity markers such as land, lineage, language, family name, gender, age, wealth, and more. The person of the leader is the source of authority. | Amidst high power distance and an orientation toward honor and shame, communication tends to be ordered hierarchically, more formal, and indirect. What is said will meet the expectations of others. Silence speaks volumes. A third party may be employed. | A tendency toward:<br>• *Avoidance*<br>• Competitive<br>• Compromise<br>• *Collaborative*<br>Conflict may be avoided to save face. Collectivists may tend to collaborate rather than compete. | What is in focus?<br>• Topic<br>• Relationships<br>• Identity<br>• Process<br>Who says and does what is as critical as what is said and done. The stakeholders are more critical than the actual process. With identity always in view, people expect respect. |
| Harmony | Harmony societies may or may not be high power distance.[4] A family patriarch or matriarch may hold a position of honor, but a religious specialist will have access to the spirit world. A patriarch will garner honor through sharing and cooperating. | Verbal restraint through self-discipline is important and communicates respect. A message may be understated to maintain respite and security. A "stop-pause" style of speech is common. The pause of silence bespeaks respect. Contrast with the overlapping style in clientelism. | A tendency toward:<br>• *Avoidance*<br>• Competitive<br>• Compromise<br>• *Collaborative* | What is in focus?<br>• Topic<br>• Relationships<br>• Identity<br>• Process<br>Harmonious relationships are the context for effectiveness and success. |

4. See "Group-Grid Theory" in Mary Douglas's Natural Symbols.

Professional Behavior

| Overarching pattern | Leadership | Communication | Conflict management[2] | Project management[3] |
|---|---|---|---|---|
| Reciprocity | High power distance is common in clientelistic societies. *Power in this context is understood as the control of access to resources.*[5] Leadership style tends to be autocratic. | In this relational society, communication is key. It is vibrant, articulate, and may be characterized by a style of "overlapping speech", in which what is said may be secondary to the experience of simply saying it. Amidst the energy, there is skillful tact and diplomacy. | A tendency toward:<br>• Avoidance<br>• Competitive<br>• Compromise<br>• *Collaborative* | What is in focus?<br>• Topic<br>• Relationships<br>• Identity<br>• Process<br>Establishing relationships, even if brief or "on the surface" at the beginning, is more important than topics and processes. Relationships in networks create opportunity. |

## Contrasts Illustrated in Mid-South Law Enforcement

One of the key socio-cultural institutions in a justice culture is law enforcement. It may be the most important institution. Police officers across the United States communicate factually. As they perceive the circumstances, based upon a trail of evidence, they state the truth. Arrests are made only on the basis of probable cause. Detentions are carried out because of reasonable suspicion. If an officer has no probable cause or reasonable suspicion, a citizen must feel the freedom to walk away from an officer in a consensual encounter. If the citizen does not feel that freedom, the officer is violating the citizen's Fourth Amendment rights. When communicating, officers'

5. See Adams, Energy and Structure: A Theory of Social Power. Adams taught anthropology at the University of Texas in Austin. He writes, "Power is that aspect of social relations that marks the relative equality of the actors or operating units; it is derived from the relative control by each actor or unit over elements of the environment of concern to the participants" (9–10). Adams is informed by his scholarly research but may also be influenced through his field experiences in Guatemala and Argentina, societies where clientelism dominates.

style is bottom line up front. In conflict, officers are competitive. When performing their duties, officers usually focus only on topic (the facts of the case) and process (police procedures).

The overarching patterns of culture significantly impact law enforcement in the United States, particularly in urban settings. The following example is taken from Little Rock, Arkansas and is used by permission from Chief Kenton Buckner. In Little Rock, officers in the field represent a justice pattern of culture. They are out in communities to serve and protect. They do not create the municipal, state, or federal laws, but they enforce them. Officers and detectives think in terms of right and wrong based upon the rule of law. They are justice oriented, being themselves a representation of a justice culture's most important institution. During the 2018 training sessions, officer self-assessments showed that in conflict mitigation 35 percent of respondents said *topic* was the most important goal and 65 percent selected *process*. This is in marked contrast to the Black American communities they serve.[6]

While Little Rock police officers represent a justice culture, local Black American neighborhoods are more oriented to the honor pattern common to much of the South. Dan McAdams, professor of psychology and director of the Foley Center for the Study of Lives at Northwestern University, traces the honor and solidarity of Black culture to the slave narratives. Written by freed slaves with the encouragement of abolitionists, these stories chronicle the lived experiences of men, women, and children on the plantations and elsewhere.[7]

In 2018 self-assessments, most officers stated that they understood the Black American communities of Little Rock were honor oriented. As to conflict mitigation, 60 percent of the officers stated they understood that Black Americans would likely choose *identity* as the goal of conflict mitigation. What does this mean concretely in a real world setting? When responding to a call, an officer will communicate factually and follow a scripted

6. Little Rock—the capital and largest city in Arkansas—has close to 200,000 inhabitants. It is the seat of Pulaski County. The metropolitan area has over 700,000 people. In the city, whites make up 53 percent of the population, and Black Americans 42 percent. The rest of the population is made up of Asian Americans, American Indians, and other ethnicities.

7. See McAdams, *Redemptive Self*, 148–81. One example of the Black American slave narratives is *Twelve Years a Slave*, written by Solomon Northup before the Civil War. A free black man from New York, he was kidnapped and sold into slavery in the South. In 2013, director Steve McQueen turned the narrative into an award-winning film.

procedure. Detention of an individual will be based upon reasonable suspicion, a legal phrase defined by the law. With Lady Justice blindfolded, regard will not be given to race, gender, family name, wealth, or any other marker of ascribed or achieved status. Family history of the detained is not a factor in the scripted procedure. Factual information is the basis for the encounter. All the while, a young Black American man who may be the subject in the detention or encounter will at his core be expecting respect regardless of the facts. For him, identity will always be the focus.

In southwest Little Rock, the growing Hispanic community is evidently power oriented. These differences in overarching patterns of culture have profound implications for law enforcement and the judicial system overall. In Little Rock, both honor and power patterns tend to conflict with the justice pattern. Without an understanding of the patterns, people will misunderstand, misjudge, take offense, inappropriately describe or accuse, and much more. Solutions rest in cultural competencies.

## More Examples from Business Experiences

Recently, Global Perspectives Consulting was hired by a well-known organization based in Colorado to provide executive coaching during the launch of a new division in Singapore. After several initial semi-structured interviews with organizational leaders in Colorado, GPC was unexpectedly asked to observe and evaluate a live video conference between the Colorado executive team and the new Singapore team. The meeting lasted two hours. The Singapore team members were all Asian, except for one man from Great Britain. The meeting facilitator, who was from Colorado, asked that team members introduce themselves one-by-one and identify what they did. The Colorado team went first. There was little consistency in their content. Their style was extremely informal: they mostly gave only their first names; they made miscellaneous comments about where they were from, their likes and dislikes, sports. The order of introduction was simply one after the other, from right to left. As for physical posture, almost everyone sat leisurely, leaning back with legs crossed. It was after 5 PM in Colorado. People were tired, ready to go home.

The informality and casual approach belied the stature of all the US participants. Out of seven people in the Colorado conference room, four had PhDs in their field. Two were published authors. All had traveled and worked internationally. The organization they work for is elite.

The project manager in Colorado, whom the organization had tasked to lead the opening of the Singapore offices, assumed everyone knew who he was and what he did. Slouched back in his chair, his arms crossed behind his head, he merely said, "Hi, my name is John." That was it. He was wearing a golf shirt with blue jeans.

After the US team had introduced themselves, the facilitator asked the Singapore team to follow suit, but did not designate who should go first. An awkward silence ensued. Breaking the silence, the gentleman from Great Britain said, "I will go first!" He was sitting on the far left. When he finished, the person next to him, a young Muslim woman from Malaysia, did not go next. She waited. An older Asian man followed. He sat upright and presented himself formally and professionally, as did everyone else on that side of the world. He took time to explain his education and work experience that preceded this "great opportunity" to co-lead the opening of the Singapore branch. He was wearing a dark business suit. When finished, he asked if there were any questions or comments. There were none. The US participants gave no comments. No welcomes. No congratulations. No expressions of honor and expectation.

After another brief moment of silence, also awkward, he glanced to his right, though not saying anything, to an associate. She responded immediately with a similar introduction—proper, formal, detailed. Others followed suit. Last of the Singapore team, the woman from Malaysia introduced herself. Her style was similar. As she spoke, the gentleman from Great Britain reached over, several times, to squeeze her shoulder, interrupting her with sincere expressions of enthusiasm about her role on the Singapore team. (Later, while debriefing, GPC asked the US team if they noticed the physical contact between the man from Great Britain and the Muslim woman. None had. To them, there was nothing strange about it. But the US team did say, "This is going to be interesting—they're different!"

GPC's executive coaching to the leadership team regarding behaviors across cultures came after the fact. The abrupt meeting exposed real differences. What would you have said and done during the video conference? Here are several considerations GPC offered among many:

1. Assume there are real cultural differences that may impact effectiveness. People in their essence are the same, but culturally they are not. Essential sameness does not negate cultural difference. *Action step*: Be on the lookout for differences, both verbal and nonverbal.

2. We are all on autopilot, doing what is normal to us and not recognizing explicitly what it is. Cultural competency means turning off the autopilot. *Action step:* Slow down (put on the brakes) and be aware of one's own speech and behavior.

3. Note the egalitarian individualism implicit in the US team's behavior, in contrast to the Singapore team's hierarchical collectivism. The US participants were informal and casual in what they said, how they appeared, how they sat, who sat where, and what they did. The order of who spoke did not matter. Everyone was the same. There were not really any protocols. Almost anything was fine. But why was the facilitator facilitating? Who had appointed her? What was her status that warranted such a role? The Singapore participants were formal in speech and proper in their ritual. What was said represented identity and revealed status. Resumes were key. Who sat where was critical and who spoke first was important to maintain respect. How one appeared was significant. *Action steps:* Consider sitting upright, dress in business casual, identify who is in the meeting and their expected roles, communicate in more detail, and be mindful of terminology, idiomatic expressions, cultural events, and illustrations that may or may not translate across cultures. It is entirely possible that the Singapore participants did not know where Parker, Colorado, was or had never heard of the Denver Broncos.

4. A laissez-faire approach likely will miscommunicate disrespect. *Action step:* Consider managing the meeting with more formality.

5. Interrupting and physical contact have deeper implications. *Action step:* Permit a coworker to communicate fully and do not display physical affection unless it is clear that it is warranted and welcomed.

Further examples abound. On the outskirts of Hyderabad, Andhra Pradesh, in India, a business colleague from the United States scolded a group of Indian participants who had excitedly digressed, reflecting out loud in Telegu (their local language) about the topic on the table. He cautioned them angrily in English, "Be quiet! We must stay on topic!" At the immediate break, in a sidebar conversation, I defended their high context style of communication rather than a time-conscious, bottom-line-up-front approach.

Facilitating a business lunch in Bangalore, India, another business colleague took time in the initial introduction to identify the title of my upcoming sixty-minute talk and thank the general manager of the Ramada Bangalore for hosting the event. He acknowledged several important local business owners from the metropolis who had honored us by attending. Finally, he introduced the man who would introduce me. He was the eldest participant at the event, a retired professor of chemistry who lived in the upscale suburb of Koramangala. While a professor, he had traveled often to Iraq to advise Saddam Hussain in the development of chemicals for business use. Also, he was a personal friend of mine. The elderly man took his time walking to the podium. Then, eloquently, he introduced me with detail and exaltation. In this context of honor and reciprocity, my impact was already established and certain even before I uttered my first word. What I said in that training environment was less significant than who I knew from within the local informal networks.

Often in the application of training across cultures, tendencies and expectations are revealed that apply broadly to other business processes. What is important in training across cultures? What applications can be made to other behaviors?

## Training Variations across the Overarching Patterns of Culture

The overarching patterns of culture largely determine how a society does formal and informal training. In my work with the Little Rock Police Department in 2017, I provided training in cultural diversity and cultural competency. From the officers themselves, I soon heard about the differences between how whites, blacks, and Hispanics facilitate training. To what degree are these differences derived from the overarching patterns of culture—justice, honor, and reciprocity? Below are some preliminary comments based on observations made broadly in the field.

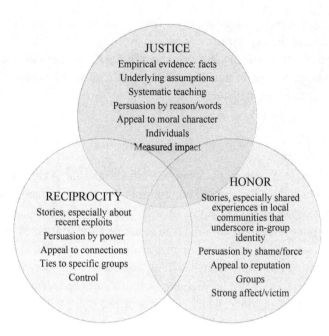

Figure 20: Training across Cultures.

In Little Rock, black facilitators of cultural diversity have tended to shame white officers for past historical and collective grievances. From an honor pattern of culture, these facilitators see the world through the eyes of in-group identity with storied shared experiences. They may not be aware that others do not see the world similarly simply by virtue of cultural patterns. These trainers are utterly frustrated with how white officers commonly respond to such shaming: they feel insulted and deny culpability. Generally, their assumptions are based on individualism. They are not part of any group, they say. They are not guilty of wrongdoing. They may not even believe in corporate guilt. And so, typically, the cultural diversity trainings have failed.

Both white and black facilitators of in-service trainings who are justice oriented communicate factually, summarily, and focus on what is and is not truth. Resources are cited. Studies in criminology form the foundation for theory and practice.

Hispanic detectives and beat officers emphasize to me the importance of complying, even in impossible scenarios, with Chief Kenton Buckner's directives. They see Buckner as the jefe. He is the ultimate patron, controlling access to resources, commendations, promotions, and all the good graces of the department.

Drawing from the insights presented in Figure 20, the skilled culture trainer adapts content design and delivery based upon the expectations of the cross-cultural participants.

## Concluding Comments

This book explains several basic but powerful truths about culture. Everything we say and do comes from our culture—our learned, shared patterns of perception and behavior. Even though it feels so natural and normal, no one is born with their culture set in stone, or fixed in their blood. Culture is a social construct, built up over centuries by a particular group of people. Culture is far more than just how people look, what they say and do, or their outward observable behavior. Culture has deep layers. It includes socio-cultural institutions, which promote or prohibit people's actions. At its center, culture is shaped by values about what should be, and by core worldview assumptions about what is real.

A local does not notice the same things as an outsider. Both have different perceptions. Locals rarely notices variations in speech and behavior. But often an outsider easily notices them. For locals, behavioral variations are not meaningful, but an outsider has to learn which variations change the meaning and significance of a word, a gesture, or a response.

All over the world, people's speech and behavior display patterns. Their language has patterns. Their culture does, too. Just as all languages have rules and norms, so do cultures. And just as some languages have similar patterns, so do some cultures. This book argues that there are overarching patterns of culture. It presents four: justice, honor, harmony, and reciprocity.

Justice dominates life in the Global West. Rule of law is the underlying assumption. And, best if law is codified and written. In the Global West, the individual is in the spotlight.

Not so, in an honor culture. In such, likely in the Middle East and East, the community is paramount. Family name and reputation are foremost. What is said and done brings honor and shame to the extended family and community. And it is the community that decides what is honorable and shameful.

Throughout the world, mostly in indigenous societies, the dominant pattern of culture is harmony. People seek harmony not only in human relationships but also in otherworldly interactions.

In the Global South, finally, reciprocity or clientelism dominates. Informal networks are important—in many locations, they are the means of survival. Powerful men and women control access to resources. Others need that access and in turn reciprocate with loyalty and service.

These patterns are real and easily observed as one travels or interacts with others. While we can't predict what any one person will do in every circumstance, we can estimate what most people will tend to do. If one travels to Denver, Colorado, English will be the prevailing language. Dress will be business casual. Talk will be informal, mostly about sports, the weather, and a recent trek into the mountains. As across much of the United States, people's behavior will be individualistic and egalitarian. The patterns are there.

Effective intercultural communication requires cultural competency. To deny differences is to take away story and identity. To rigidly generalize is to commit the error of essentialism. However, sophisticated stereotyping helps one live and work successfully in a cross-cultural setting.

Without these intercultural insights and cultural competencies, we cannot manage deprivation of norm and adapt our speech and behavior to our intercultural environment. However, with understanding and skills, our CQ drive, knowledge, strategy, and action are sharpened and we experience the joy of human exchange across cultures.

Appendix A

# Timeline of Definitions
# of *Culture*

THROUGHOUT THE EIGHTEENTH AND nineteenth centuries in France and
England, the term *culture* meant "refinement." One wanted be "cultured,"
that is, educated and socially elegant. While this meaning is still exists,
cultural anthropologists define culture differently, as seen in the descriptions below. There are several ways to examine the definitions of culture.
Appendix A lists several influential definitions chronologically. However, in
*Redefining Culture: Perspectives Across the Disciplines*, editors John Baldwin,
Sandra Faulkner, Michel Hecht, and Sheryl Lindsley analyze hundreds of
definitions of culture thematically,[1] finding seven prominent themes: (a)
structure, (b) function, (c) process, (d) product, (e) refinement, (f) power,
and (g) group-membership.[2] Additionally, two helpful resources that trace
the history of anthropological theory and consequently the meaning of the
term *culture* are Alan Barnard's *History and Theory in Anthropology* and
Jon R. McGee and Richard Warms' *Anthropological Theory*. Here, we offer
a timeline of definitions of culture:

1871—Sir Edward Tylor: "That complex whole which includes knowledge,
  beliefs, art, law, morals, custom, and any other capabilities and habits acquired by man as a member of society."[3] [The British Tylor was
  a cultural evolutionist. He believed people's culture evolved through

1. 27–52. Each editor is a professor of communication, not cultural anthropology.

2. Gustav Jahoda (1920–2016), an Austrian-born psychologist who taught for over
four decades at the University of Strathclyde, examines several current and seemingly
conflicting definitions of culture and concludes that while we may never agree what
culture is, we should still continue using the term. See "Critical Reflections," 289–303.

3. Tylor, *Primitive Cultures*, 1. For more about shifts in defining *culture* anthropologi-
cally, see Jahoda, "Critical Reflections," 289–303.

stages: from savagery to barbarian to civilized. Few researchers now subscribe to cultural evolution.]

1911—Franz Boas: "The totality of the mental and physical reactions and activities that characterize the behavior of the individuals composing a social group."[4] [Professor of anthropology at Columbia University, Boas was less drawn cultural evolution, preferring "historical particularism." By this, he and his students understood the cultural relativity of each social group and saw each group distinctly.]

1912—Emile Durkheim: "The totality of beliefs and sentiments common to the average members of a society forms a determinate system with its own life."[5] [Durkheim, a French sociologist, saw culture as a "conscience collective" influenced by factors he called volume, intensity, rigidity, and content.[6]]

1934—Ruth Benedict: "A more or less consistent pattern of thought and action" tied to the "emotional and intellectual mainsprings of that society."[7] [Boas' student, Benedict emphasized the articulated whole configuration of culture. She saw repeated patterns prevalent in particular societies.]

1936—Ralph Linton: "The total social heredity of mankind."[8] [He distinguished the form, function, use, and meaning of culture, an analysis that has endured.]

1950s—A. Radcliffe-Brown: "The process by which a person acquires . . . knowledge, skill, ideas, beliefs, tastes, sentiments."[9] [He was impressed with the structure and function of social life and saw culture as the processes carried out in social functions.]

4. *Mind of Primitive Man*, 159.

5. *Division of Labor in Society*, 79.

6. For an analysis of Durkheim's four characteristics of the "conscience collective" see chapter 5.

7. *Patterns of Culture*, 46.

8. *Study of Man*, 78, 402–4.

9. *Structure and Function in Primitive Society*, 4–5.

1944—Bronislaw Malinowski: "The integral whole consisting of implements and consumers' goods, of constitutional charters for the various social groupings, of human ideas and crafts, beliefs and customs."[10]

1949—Clyde Kluckhohn: "A way of thinking, feeling, [and] believing."[11]

1952—Alfred Kroeber and Clyde Kluckhohn: "Patterns, explicit and implicit, of and for behavior acquired and transmitted by symbols, constituting the distinctive achievement of human groups."[12] [They say a culture's core consists of historically derived traditional ideas with corresponding values. Cultural differences are historical phenomena found in the Bible, ancient Greek writings, and venerable Chinese scholarship.

1953—Robert Redfield: "[A people's] total equipment of ideas and institutions and conventionalized activities."[13] [Redfield distinguished between *culture* and *worldview*.]

1954—Kenneth Pike: Etic and emic distinctions[14]

1963—Louis Luzbetak: "A design for living."[15] [Father Luzbetak did field work in New Guinea in the 1950s and taught at Divine Word Seminary in Techny, IL. He earned his doctorate in cultural anthropology from the University of Fribourg, Switzerland. In 1988, he submitted a copy of his book *The Church and Cultures* to Pope John Paul II during a papal audience at the Vatican.]

1973—G. Linwood Barney: "Acquired [and shared] knowledge which one uses to interpret experience and generate behavior."[16] [Barney's four layers of culture—*worldview*, *values*, *institutions*, and *observable behavior*—were long lost in the literature but reintroduced by Hesselgrave,[17] and later became the model of culture used by Worldview Resource Group and Global Perspectives Consulting. After

---

10. *A Scientific Theory of Culture*, 36.
11. *Mirror for Man*, 23.
12. *Culture*, 357.
13. *Primitive World*, 85.
14. *Language*.
15. *Church and Cultures*, 60–61.
16. "Supracultural and Cultural," 48–55.
17. 1991, 102–3.

doing field work in Laos and Vietnam with the Hmong people, Barney earned his PhD in anthropology from the University of Minnesota and taught for twenty-five years at the Jaffray School of Missions in Nyack, New York.]

1973—Clifford Geertz: Members of each society share webs of symbolic meaning that are acted out publicly.[18]

1979—Marvin Harris: "The learned repertory of thoughts and actions exhibited by the members of social groups."[19] [A cultural materialist, Harris sees culture as more a response to environment and human needs than an ideology. Culture is not a mental construct.]

1979—James Spradley: "The acquired knowledge that people use to interpret experience and generate social behavior."[20]

1999—Paul Hiebert: "The more or less integrated systems of ideas, feelings, and values and their associated patterns of behavior and products shared by a group of people who organize and regulate what they think, feel, and do."[21]

2014—Judith Martin and Tom Nakayama: "Learned patterns of perception, values, and behaviors, shared by a group of people, that are dynamic and heterogeneous."[22] [Martin and Nakayama, fellows in the *International Academy for Intercultural Research*, have written popular and widely used textbooks about intercultural communication.]

2016—Worldview Resource Group: "Learned, shared patterns of perception and behavior." [WRG emphases these five key terms and suggest *culture* is a broader term while *worldview* is a core element within culture. A distinction between the two terms is critical. Students may know a culture's outward observable features but know nothing about a culture's core worldview assumptions hidden beneath the surface. The less known about a culture's worldview, the less predictable its participants' behavior.]

18. *Interpretation of Cultures*, 5–12, 453.

19. *Cultural Materialism*, 47.

20. *Ethnographic Interview*, 5.

21. *Anthropological Insights*, 30. Also see Hiebert's seminal *Cultural Anthropology*.

22. *Experiencing Intercultural Communication*, 32.

# Cultural Intelligence (CQ)

CULTURAL INTELLIGENCE (CQ) IS the capability to function effectively across cultures. The Cultural Intelligence Center in Holt, Michigan has identified four sets of capabilities that consistently predict adjustment and performance in intercultural settings. They are CQ Drive, CQ Knowledge, CQ Strategy, and CQ Action.

1. The CQ Drive capability is your natural interest, enjoyment, confidence, and perseverance in cross-cultural situations. To some degree these are intrinsic, deeply rooted in personality, identity, and values. However, CQ Drive may be improved.

Table B.1: CQ Drive

| What is CQ Drive? | What are its sub-dimensions? | What does high CQ Drive look like? | Personal development tips |
|---|---|---|---|
| A person's motivation to engage others from different backgrounds, behaviors, and worldviews. | • Intrinsic interest<br>• Extrinsic interest<br>• Self-efficacy | High CQ Drive means a willingness to learn and adapt to cultural differences, while low CQ Drive indicates a preference for the familiar. | • Leave the hotel room in Buenos Aires, Argentina and walk about the block<br><br>• Take the nearby subway to the next stop and back<br><br>• Go to an adjacent store and buy something you need |

2. CQ Knowledge is your acquired understanding of culture general and specific. How do people behave? What socio-cultural institutions promote and prevent such behavior? What are people's values? Identity markers? What are the core worldview assumptions from which all else is derived? Interestingly, some intercultural training is limited to simply knowledge, without incorporating the remaining 75 percent of CQ capabilities.

Table B.2: CQ Knowledge

| What is CQ Knowledge? | What are its sub-dimensions? | What does high CQ Knowledge look like? | Personal development tips |
|---|---|---|---|
| CQ Knowledge refers to your understanding of culture itself and how it works, that is, how it impacts the way people think and behave. CQ Knowledge starts with understanding your own culture. | • Business<br>• Values and norms<br>• Socio-linguistic<br>• Leadership | High CQ Knowledge is displayed by both culture general and culture specific insights. | • Read about the history of the region<br>• Buy and use a Lonely Planet travel guide<br>• Learn ten (10) practical expressions in the local language<br>• Understand a common leadership approach and why |

3. CQ Strategy is the extent to which you are aware of yourself and others in an intercultural setting plus your ability to plan how to manage those situations effectively. How does the process of negotiation change in a hierarchical, shame/honor, and high context culture? Applied to cross-cultural ministry, a weighty degree of responsibility in culture adjustment and culture competency lies with the newcomers to any region. They must learn *how* to learn about culture, what questions to ask (internally and to others), what observations to make, what adjustments are necessary, and how to manage personal expectations. The answers are found in CQ Strategy. Planning, awareness, and checking are three integral components of CQ Strategy that are grounded in empirical data from CQ research.

Table B.3: CQ Strategy

| What is CQ Strategy? | What are its sub-dimensions? | What does high CQ Strategy look like? | Personal development tips |
|---|---|---|---|
| CQ Strategy refers to a person's awareness and ability to plan appropriately given cultural dynamics. Going further, CQ Strategy bespeaks of one's ability to understand how to adapt behavior across cultures. Finally, this capability also includes monitoring whether or not a person behaves appropriately in a cross-cultural setting. | • Planning<br>• Awareness<br>• Checking | High CQ Strategy anticipates and predicts cultural events relying on alertness rather than simply moving forward on the basis of semi-automated assumptions and behaviors. | • Do not operate on cruise control<br>• Plan where to go, what to do, and how to relate<br>• Rather than being absorbed in self-consciousness, look up and around at what is happening |

4. CQ Action is what you actually do in a cross-cultural situation to relate and work. How do you adapt behavior to different cultural norms? To what degree are you able to be flexible?

Table B.4: CQ Action

| What is CQ Action? | What are its sub-dimensions? | What does high CQ Action look like? | Personal development tips |
|---|---|---|---|
| CQ Action, refers to the actual behavioral changes a person makes in the cross-cultural setting. It has to do with what we do, whether in Rome, Italy, or at the office in Denver as we work with colleagues who originate from Mumbai, India. | • Speech acts<br>• Verbal<br>• Nonverbal | High CQ Action means a person is comfortable in the cross-cultural context and is able to turn off "auto-pilot" and make adaptations. | • Practice your practical expressions<br>• Make a friend in the host society<br>• Adapt how you speak and behave |

The four sets of CQ capabilities are integrated. You may have confidence that you can be effective across cultures, but lack culture general and specific knowledge. In fact, you may not be effective. Or, you might have culture knowledge, but not know how to adapt your behavior accordingly. Although CQ Drive may be mostly intrinsic, CQ is not a fixed capability. You are able to develop your cross-cultural understanding and skills. A key in this development is reflection. Who are you? What are you doing? Who are others? To what degree are they the same or different?

# Cross-Cultural Awareness
# of Self and Others

High

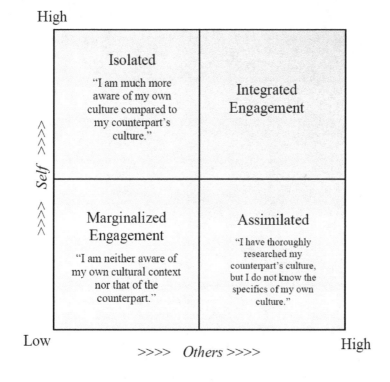

Figure C-1: Cross-Cultural Awareness of Self and Others.

ROBERT STRAUSS, ANGELA EDWARDS, and Elena Steiner have created an assessment to measure a person's awareness of self and others in the cross-cultural environment.[1] In programs of instruction for intercultural training, it may be common to focus on the similarities and differences of others. However, the starting point for cultural competence is knowing oneself. The assessment measures to what extent and how well a person is awareness of his or her own core assumptions, values, and behaviors. Given that baseline, one can see the delta or differences between self and other. The assessment asks sixty questions that are informed by the model of culture designed by GPC (see Figure 9).[2]

More broadly, two assessments measure broad worldview tendencies. See the Worldview Assessment created by Worldview Resource Group in 2013.[3] Also, see the Worldview Analysis Scale created by Dr. Ezemenari Obasi, researcher at the University of Houston, and colleagues in 2009.[4]

1. Angela Edwards, PhD, is an Executive Coach at the Center for Creative Leadership in Colorado Springs. She has researched the impact of Cultural Intelligence (CQ) on the dyad relationship between a "C" level leader and the executive coach. Elena Steiner is the Founder of Global Perspectives Consulting and a PhD candidate in the Hugh Downs School of Human Communication at Arizona State University. She is researching how a critical analysis of story helps one understand worldview.

2. The terms *isolated* and *assimilated* in CCASO are borrowed from the research of John Berry. In his *Model of Acculturation*, the term "assimilation" means that an individual excludes his own culture and seeks to become part of the dominant society with its majority culture. "Isolated" means that an individual retains his own culture but does not seek to become part of the dominant society.

3. An analytical tool for the WRG Worldview Assessment is available at http://www.wrg3.org/21/resources/Worldview%20Assessment%20Analysis_April%202013.pdf.

4. Obasi, "Worldview Analysis Scale."

# A Robert Strauss Book Review
# of *Milestones* by Sayyid Qutb

FIRST PUBLISHED IN 1964, this manifesto by an imprisoned religious theorist lays out guiding markers for a reconstructed religious civilization.[1]

## Preface

With unequaled frankness and far-reaching generalizations, Qutb describes a whole world given over to ignorance and rebellion. In what ways? By following man-made false laws/customs that unquestionably result in failure.

In the manifesto *Milestones*, Qutb identifies landmarks and road signs on the path toward vital values and a healthy way of life. He describes an ideal religious community—a vanguard.

## Chapter 1: A unique generation

He says that today we must look to the past—to a unique generation of people wholly submitted to God. They lived during the seventh century in a desert region known to the ancients as Aravia. Amidst them a Prophet was chosen, through whom God revealed himself and a way of life for all mankind. There were three striking characteristics of this unique generation:

---

1. Sayyid Qutb (1906–1966) was an Egyptian activist (Sunni Muslim), author (24 books), and educator. For two years, he was educated in Greeley, Colorado. A member of the Muslim Brotherhood, he was arrested and executed by hanging in 1966 for conspiracy to assassinate Egyptian President Gamal Nasser. He is regarded as the architect of Islamism.

1. They committed themselves unwaveringly to the revelation from God. Qutb says the revelation was "purified from the influence of all other sources" (p. 17).

2. They adopted its content and the lifestyle of the Prophet as a total way of life. These resources guided every moment of their lives (p. 19).

3. They completely rejected and separated themselves from others who lived in a state of ignorance.

## Chapter 2: The nature of the way of life

Those in this unique generation submitted by faith to the creed "there is no deity but God." They subjugated themselves to God's revelation, including his universal law. They rejected all other laws in any shape or form (p. 36). The earth belongs to God. Man is servant to God alone. All other tyranny is wicked. What is being described is not a theory but a way of life—a system that extends into all aspects of life (pp. 32–33).

## Chapter 3: Characteristics of the vanguard society

The central characteristics are these:

1. They believe and affirm there is only one God.
2. They devote their entire lives in submission to him alone (p. 47).
3. They know the Prophet is the Messenger of God.
4. They strive to abolish existing systems.
5. They endeavor to construct a new civilization (pp. 50–51).

## Chapter 4: The Struggle

Without doubt, there will be a great struggle to establish this reconstructed religious civilization. Throughout the whole earth (p. 72) there will be striving against ignorance. Such striving may take the form of proclamation or provocation. Human antagonists include nonbelievers, hypocrites, friends of Satan, and treacherous orientalists. Structural obstacles will be contemporary organizations, authorities, political systems, man-made laws, and socio-economic systems (pp. 55–63).

The struggle is not a temporary phase in the way of life but an eternal state wherein the earth is cleansed of corruption and God's Lordship is established over the entire earth (pp. 64–65).

## Chapter 5: A way of life

The distinctive feature of the way of life is that it is all or nothing. It is simple, practical, and clear (p. 77).

## Chapter 6: The universal law

The will of God is evident in his universal law, derived from God's revelation and from the Messenger of God's practice (p. 87). God's law governs the entire universe, including all the physical and biological aspects of human beings.

## Chapter 7: The real civilization

According to this way of life, there are only two kinds of societies, the reconstructed religious civilization and the society of ignorance (p. 93). In the former, human beings submit to the authority of God alone and enter into his service (p. 95). Family is the basic construct of the society, defined by husband, wife, and children. The rearing of children is the most important function of the family (p. 97).

## Chapter 8: Relationship to culture

In this way of life there are not hypotheses of "God and culture" or "God in culture," as if an authorized and acceptable culture of man exists apart from God. The law of God *is* the culture of mankind.

## Chapter 9: Nationality

The real civilization is not bound by nationality or geographic region. The revelation of God differentiates all of mankind into two categories: the home of submission and the home of hostility (p. 118). All mankind resides in one or the other. The essential question is between submission and rebellion (p. 137).

## Chapter 10: Changes

The differences between believers and nonbelievers are immense. The vanguard community does not compromise (p. 129). There is no mixing (p. 130). Truth and falsehood do not co-exist. Here is a description of the chasm (p. 140):

Table D.1: The Chasm Between Believers and Nonbelievers

| The Way of Submission | The Way of Ignorance |
| --- | --- |
| Worship of God alone | Worship of people, earthly things, gods, and unseen spirits |
| Submission to the authority of God only | Accommodation of human traditions, socio-cultural institutions, and man-made laws |
| Good and pure | Evil and corrupt, whether an ancient or modern variety |
| Full and valuable | Hollow and worthless |
| Comprehensive | Fragmented |

## Chapter 11: Triumphant

The vanguard community is strong, steadfast, and superior (p. 141). It has permanent truth—the most perfect form of understanding (p. 142). The outlook is bright and beautiful (p. 143). The law of God and its system of life are perfect.

Qutb writes, "The believer holds on to his religion like the holder of a precious stone in the society devoid of religion, of character, of high values, of noble manners and of whatever is clean, pure and beautiful" (p. 146). He will prevail, be it through "striving, hard work, fighting and martyrdom" (p. 147).

## Chapter 12: The way

The story of the people who believe in God is one where they encounter tyrannical and oppressive enemies who deny the right of human beings to believe in the All Mighty. The righteous and honorable are pitted against the arrogant, mischievous, criminal and degraded.

Qutb concludes, "The struggle between the believers and their enemies is in essence a struggle of belief, and not in any way of anything else" (p. 159). The conflict is not political or economic or racial. It is faith versus unbelief. The enemies are angered—no, enraged, only because of the faith of the vanguard community.

The enemies of the believers make every attempt to divert attention to man-made structures of governance, material possessions, and wealth. The intent is to confuse and to extinguish the flame of belief. It is a trick (p. 159). Believers must not be deceived by the enemy.

# Appendix E

# Parallels Between Language and Culture

CHAPTER 3 DISCUSSES THE emic/etic distinction developed by linguist Kenneth Pike. Table E.1 in this appendix charts his application of linguistic terms, concepts, and functions to cultural behaviors. The parallels are remarkable. Culture and language acquisition is a prerequisite fundamental to effectiveness across cultures. In the same way that one would learn language, one would also learn culture. In the table, look at the parallel from the smallest units of distinct sounds to the largest units of discourse and story.

Table E.1: Parallels Between Language and Culture

| Language | Unit | Culture |
|---|---|---|
| Phonological sound (phoneme): for example, the consonant "t" versus the vowel "i"—emic units considered distinct by the native speaker | Smallest uniquely purposeful form, distinct from all others[1] | Ideal thoughts, feelings, and purposive behaviors (including nonverbal gestures)—what should be said and done, and often what one thinks he or she has said and done |

1. Kenneth and Evelyn Pike refer to this as a "unit with contrastive-identificational features" in *Grammatical Analysis* (1977, 1–2). For example, "p" and "b" have different identities. Though they both are bilabial stops, "p" is aspirated and voiceless, whereas "b" is unaspirated and voiced. The features in the differences create the separate identities. Beyond their structure, Eugene Nida adds that no morphemes are identical in meaning (Morphology, 151). There are no real synonyms. "Peace" and "tranquility" are not synonymous. One may attend a "peace conference" but would not refer to it as a "tranquility conference."

| Language | Unit | Culture |
| --- | --- | --- |
| Aspirated "t" at the beginning of a word but unreleased at the end of a word—etic differences mostly outside the native speaker's awareness | Variations in form[2] | Actual thoughts, feelings, and behaviors—what one actually said and did, slightly varied depending on cultural context |
| Distinct morphological meaning unit (morpheme): like "-ish" as a non-root suffix or "self" as a root word—a minimum lexical unit or the lowest grammatical filler (it has no grammatical parts within it) | Clustered forms[3] | A piece of wooden ash crafted into the shape of a baseball bat in the gloved hands of the designated hitter who is standing in the batter's box on a baseball playing field facing the pitcher constitutes a cluster of forms denoting a specific meaning.[4] |
| "In-" and "Im-" as prefixes with the same meaning, but impacted phonetically by the consonant that follows. Consider "intolerable" and "impossible" where the prefix denotes the same meaning. | Variations in clustered forms | The next batter may use an aluminum bat, a different brand of batter's glove, and a different batting stance—but is still understood as a hitter up to bat. The baseball fan is not confused by the variations. |
| Syntactical utterance: "The content of Table 25 is adapted from the work of Ward Goodenough." This sample sentence illustrates an arrangement of clustered forms. | Intelligible arrangement of clustered forms | If a batter hits the pitched ball beyond the infielders into the outfield, all participants and spectators understand that the batter just "hit a single," is now on first base, and represents a run that can be scored if other batters are equally successful. Scoring more runs than the opponent is the object of the game of baseball. |

2. An English speaker may say the word "pack" faster or slower, loudly or softly. Regardless of these etic differences, an English hearer will recognize it as the same word (from an emic perspective).

3. "Distribution" in tagmemics, that is, the existence and function of a unit in relationship to other units.

4. Note that just as suffixes like "ish" or "-less," a kind of "class," fill the same "slot" in the clustered or distributed forms, so in the same way items in the culture clusters fill slots. Gloves are worn on the hands. Hands hold the bat. Feet are arranged in an effective stance in the batter's box. All together, they represent a hitter up to bat.

| Language | Unit | Culture |
|---|---|---|
| Description, statement, explanation, command, proposition, and more | Types of arrangements of clustered forms | Football is also a team sport with a similar objective to baseball.[5] But it looks quite different from baseball. Likewise, a business team works together on a project with a stated goal and identifiable resources. |
| Prose versus poetry along with other genres of speech | Style of arrangements | One baseball team may rely more on speed, that is, beating out ground balls for hits, stealing bases, taking an extra base, and always scoring from second base on a single. They run the risk of being thrown out. Another baseball team may rely on power for home runs and extra-base hits. They run the risk of striking out. |
| "Goooooaal" shouted at a *futbol* match differs from the term "goal" used in a management meeting. | The place in which the arrangement is used | The baseball diamond differs from the football gridiron. |
| Per the Babylon Bee—Pastor Joel Osteen saying, "Be happy!" to stranded rooftop flood victims in Houston, Texas during Hurricane Harvey as he drives past them in his yacht, *SS Blessing*. | The time wherein the arrangement is used | At the business luncheon, the guest speaker will not "sing" her speech. A particular style of communicating is expected depending on time and place. |
| "What is the problem, sweetheart?" said to my daughter versus "What is the problem, officer?"—the "what is the problem" takes on different meanings based upon the context. | The context of the arrangements | The same gesture has different meanings depending on the sport. Take, in baseball, the umpire's sign that a runner is safe at a base versus, in football, the referee's designation that a forward pass is incomplete. |

5. The references are to American football not soccer (futbol).

| Language | Unit | Culture |
|---|---|---|
| A story—discourse | A purposeful collection of arrangements | As a baseball fan, I may buy tickets to see my favorite team play a home game. I drive and park. I watch and understand the game. I will bring a baseball glove given the outside chance I may be able to catch a foul ball hit into the stands. I may or may not buy a hotdog, peanuts, and drink. At the seventh inning stretch, I will stand with everyone else and sing the chorus to the 1908 song "Take Me Out to the Ball Game." I cheer for my team and yell at the umpires. This is the storied experience of being a baseball fan.[6] |
| The characters, plot, time, and place in the story as a whole create the intended overall meaning. | Semantic meaning | A good hitter and fast runner will likely be the leadoff hitter. The strongest baseball player who more frequently than others hits a home run will bat cleanup, that is, number four in the lineup. A great defenseman at second base who is not a great hitter will bat later in the lineup. The pitcher will bat last. This plot or strategy is part of the game of baseball and understood by all. |

6. The time and place for yelling at the umpire is understood. I can do so without consequences. I may yell but not throw anything. Also, I may not climb out of the stands and approach the umpire on the field of play. In other settings, I am not able to yell at a person of authority without consequences. I will suffer some penalty if I were to yell at the judge in a court of law or my supervisor at Regis University. In those circumstances, society provides other appropriate avenues for expressing displeasure.

| Language | Unit | Culture |
| --- | --- | --- |
| In writing, an exclamation mark, or in speaking, a change in intonation, marks meaning. In discourse, words and phrases like "so" or "to sum up," among many others, mark a change in direction and meaning. | Special meaning markers | The catcher, by somewhat hidden hand signs, signals to the pitcher what to throw—one finger for a fast ball, two for a curve ball. When the outfield catches a popup fly ball for out number two, he signals to his adjacent outfielder "two outs" with his fingers to remind him. In that setting, the sign of two fingers means two outs, not a curve ball. |
| All initial voiceless consonants are aspirated. Vowels contiguous to "m" and "n" are nasalized. Intonation rises at the end of a question. In speaking and writing, parallelism is preferred. A powerful opening in a discourse may include a striking statistic or commanding quote. | Tendency toward symmetry | Almost all batters take a practice swing before stepping into the batter's box. Many shortstops will banter with the hitter by yelling something like, "Batter, batter!!" All first basemen mitts are the same but differ from catchers' mitts. The fielder catching a popup will yell, "I've got it!" Few players will slide into first base. |
| In the word "selfless," the core meaning comes from "self," the root, rather than "-less," the suffix. In a speech, the central message is elaborated in the body of the talk, not the introductory greeting (Good morning everyone! Thank you for inviting me to speak to you.). | Likelihood that core meaning is at the nucleus rather than the margins | The essence of the baseball game occurs on the playing field and involves the players themselves. The most important aspect of the baseball game is not who the man is who is vending the hot dogs, yelling out, "Hot dogs, get your hot dogs here!" |

Table F.1 shows 15 units of correspondence between language and culture. Indeed, there are more. It is clear that an equivalent parallel exists between language and culture. Related to language, rules and patterns are in place from the smallest unit of sound to larger, more complex systems of grammar. Language provides the means to communication. If rules and patterns were not followed, speaking is possible but would be unintelligible.

Related to culture, rules and patterns are also in place. Culture is not fabricated in the moment. From ideal concepts of what to say and do, to complicated purposeful collected arrangements, culture is ordered and predictable, especially by those with an emic perspective. The rules and patterns provide the meaning people need to explain the past, make sense of the present, and give trajectory to the future.

Appendix F

# Combinations of Patterns

## J+R = Justice and Reciprocity

IN PROTESTANT CHRISTIAN WRITINGS, many consider a doctrinal high-point to be Paul's Epistle to the Romans. In Romans, commentators say that Paul argues for justification by faith in Jesus Christ.[1] In salvation, what is efficacious is the gift of faith exercised rather than the merit of works performed. The whole of the book lays a foundation for an overarching pattern of justice. The treatise itself is not a culture, but describes one of the four patterns displayed in the Kingdom of God as revealed in the Bible.

However, a sociological curiosity is described in Romans 5. In verse 12, Paul pivots to present a theological foundation for the justification he has been describing in the two previous chapters. He begins with, "Therefore, just as . . .". In the ten verses that follow, Paul then parallels two representatives, two bases, and two lifestyles. The pivot is from justice to reciprocity. It is from rule of law to clientelistic representation. One representative is Adam and the other is Christ.

The text reads as follows (verses are distinguished through the superscript):

> [12] Therefore, just as sin entered the world through one man, and death through sin, and in this way death came to all people, be-cause all sinned—[13] To be sure, sin was in the world before the law was given, but sin is not charged against anyone's account where there is no law. [14] Nevertheless, death reigned from the time of Adam to the time of Moses, even over those who did not sin by breaking a command, as did Adam, who is a pattern of the one to come. [15] But the gift is not like the trespass. For if the many died

---

1. See Cranfield, *Romans*. Cranfield (1915–2015) was Professor of Theology for thirty years at the University of Durham in northeast England.

by the trespass of the one man, how much more did God's grace and the gift that came by the grace of the one man, Jesus Christ, overflow to the many! [16] Nor can the gift of God be compared with the result of one man's sin: The judgment followed one sin and brought condemnation, but the gift followed many trespasses and brought justification. [17] For if, by the trespass of the one man, death reigned through that one man, how much more will those who receive God's abundant provision of grace and of the gift of righteousness reign in life through the one man, Jesus Christ! [18] Consequently, just as one trespass resulted in condemnation for all people, so also one righteous act resulted in justification and life for all people. [19] For just as through the disobedience of the one man the many were made sinners, so also through the obedience of the one man the many will be made righteous. [20] The law was brought in so that the trespass might increase. But where sin increased, grace increased all the more, [21] so that, just as sin reigned in death, so also grace might reign through righteousness to bring eternal life through Jesus Christ our Lord.[2]

The parallelism is both contrastive and comparative. On one side is the lifestyle of those who do not follow Christ contrasted on the other side with the lifestyle of those who do follow Christ. The first category is said to be "in Adam" and the second "in Christ." These are positional phrases that bespeak representation or federal headship rather than organic unity. In the text, the focus is on the parallel between the one Adam and the one Christ. Twelve times the word "one" is used in these brief verses to convey seminal identification.

Table F.1 analyzes the text and shows the similarities ("as . . . so") and differences ("not as" and "much more") between the two federal heads, representing two groups of people. Interestingly, the contrast is presented as dystopia versus utopia.

---

2. Holy Bible, New International Version®, NIV® Copyright ©1973, 1978, 1984, 2011 by Biblica, Inc.® Used by permission. All rights reserved worldwide.

Table F.1: Parallels Between Federal Heads
(verses from text shown in parentheses)

|  | In Adam | In Christ |
| --- | --- | --- |
| Human group | Those who do not follow Christ | Those who do follow Christ |
| Background text | Romans 1:18—3:20 | Romans 3:21—5:11 |
| One historical action | Adam's sinful disobedience in the Garden of Eden, historically some 4,000 years before the time of Christ (12, 14, 15, 19) | Christ's godly obedience to death of the cross, about 2,000 years ago (18, 19) |
| Divine responses | Judgment (16, 18) | The gift of grace (15–18) |
| Divine verdicts | Condemnation (16, 18) | Justification |
| Consequences | Death (12, 14, 21) | Eternal life (17, 18, 21) |
| Who is impacted? | All people (12, 18) | All people (18), who believe (17) |
| Monarchs | Sin and death reign (14, 17, 21) | Grace reigns (21) |

The doctrine presented in Romans 5:12–21 is remarkable theologically and illustrative sociologically. It is astonishing in that the text says God sees every person in the world in one of only two ways, either in Adam or in Christ. Regarding the first way of life, as the representative of all humans, Adam's act of sin was considered by God to be the act of all people and God's penalty of death was judicially applied to everybody. Similarly, yet differently, Christ is the federal head of all who follow him, the representative before God of those who exercise the gift of faith in him, and the divine patron providing access to God's resources of grace and forgiveness. In the midst of a treatise about justice, the writer introduces this clientelistic reciprocity between God and man. The representative is Jesus Christ. Access to justification is through him. Combined patterns of culture are illustrated in this biblical text.

This theological accounting is inimitable. The text is illustrative sociologically. It perfectly shows the structure and function of clientelism. Clients are beholden to patrons. Related to Adam, Romans 5 says that in the eyes of God, all mankind is bound to Adam. They suffer consequences per his act. Related to Christ, the text says all who follow him receive benefits, not per their merits but by gracious gifts from a federal head, a patron, who is benevolent.

## H+H = Honor and Harmony

The combination of honor and harmony is common, especially throughout the Middle East and Asia. Social relationships are ordered by a code of honor and interactions are impacted by harmony. These patterns are inextricable. In some of these regions, there is an overlay of the monotheistic religion of Islam, but underneath, at a level where day-to-day life takes place, the combination of honor and harmony are a way of life. This combination is also prevalent among First Nations peoples of North America.

Author Anne Fadiman poignantly illustrates this combination of honor and harmony in her book *The Spirit Catches You and You Fall Down* (1997). Her true story focuses on Lia Lee (1982–2012), a Hmong child diagnosed with severe epilepsy, whose refugee family made a long trek from Laos to the United States, settling in central California in the small community of Merced. At first, Lia's parents spoke little English. The doctors at Merced Community Medical Center did not speak Hmong and, until later, were without interpreters. Lia experienced her first seizure at three months and a grand mal seizure at four. Fadiman details the long, sad saga of her physical struggles.

From the beginning of Lia's medical challenges, misunderstandings between her parents and doctors led to friction. Her parents were skeptical of Western medical institutions. This bias came from family experiences in Laos. At a more fundamental level, the parents assumed that Lia's physical challenges were due to the spirit world. They naturally made these assumptions. They were not conflicted in their worldview. Reality was clear to them. Early, they understood that Lia's soul had departed her body due to a frightful experience.[3] They knew that her physical illness was caused by disharmony in the spirit world and also that Lia now had unique spiritual perspectives and abilities that others did not. Her parents knew she was destined for a role of honor in her community. At the same time, health care professionals understood her problems physiologically. Treatment was required, including medicine and therapy.

3. This phenomenological understanding is common in other parts of the world as well. For example, in India, I have been told stories about strikingly similar experiences.

The conflict between her parents and the medical team is an example of other distinct patterns of culture entering into the West, where a justice pattern is overarching. However, the purpose for including Lea's story in Appendix F is to show the combination of honor and harmony in the Hmong family. In her book, Fadiman shares a detailed firsthand account of a pig sacrifice carried out on Lea's behalf by a shaman. Chapter 19 recounts the story. Extended family members gather early in the morning. Honor is shown in every relationship. Roles and responsibilities are understood. There are no distinctions made between this world and the unseen world. Everyone present is aware that what is said and done is rooted in the tradition of ancestors. No one doubts the role of the spirit world in Lea's life and future. Harmony is maintained with impersonal spiritual forces and anticipated with ancestors. Honor and harmony are inextricably linked together in a normal way of life.

# Appendix G

# Pattern Assessment

Appendix G offers two tools for evaluating pattern tendencies. The first is simple and swift. It identifies two common chronic characteristics of each pattern. If the two characteristics are commonly observed, then the overarching pattern of culture may be assumed, at least as a starting point of evaluation.

Table G.1: Quick Assessment of Overarching Pattern

| Pattern | Justice | Honor | Harmony | Reciprocity |
|---------|---------|-------|---------|-------------|
| Traits | Individualism | Collectivism | | |
| | Rules | Reputation | Rituals | Roles |

The following four short stories illustrate the overarching patterns and show the two common chronic characteristics of each. The stories are real but anonymity is attained by changing the names and places.

## Justice

"Only two months ago, Megan, a single lady from Bonners Ferry, Idaho, moved away from her family to Denver, Colorado. She had been hired by a prominent software company as an Accounts Receivable Specialist. Early on a Friday afternoon, she confronted a coworker about what she perceived to be repeated mistakes in the software uploads. Megan felt everyone understood the protocols and there was no reason to deviate from them. She spoke clearly and directly so that there would be no mistake in what she said."

Note in the short story that Megan, a single lady, moved across country to take a job. She was not bound to family per geography. In an office setting, long-term relationships may not be necessary in following clearly stated rules. Rules are in focus, not identity markers, relationships, or, to a lesser extent, roles. She did not go through a chain-of-command, but in her specialist position assumed a right to speak up about unnecessary mistakes.

## Honor

"We have worked together on projects for the United States Government. The projects are challenging. The team of experts are without parallel. Born in Taiwan, Jia Ting earned a PhD in Social Psychology. We work together more closely than anyone else. One day she told me she really was not interested in Social Psychology, but her father had suggested she go into the field. She did so to honor him and maintain the reputation of his name. Recently, Jia Ting told me that her parents were moving from China to Canada to live with her until their passing."

Jia Ting lives and works with others based upon a group orientation. She is not an individualist. Any personal aspirations are folded into those of family, especially its patriarch.

## Reciprocity

"Fabien is a chiropractor in Uruguay, one of only a few. It seems everyone in Montevideo knows him and many come frequently for activator treatments. I always notice that there are no fifteen-minute appointments managed assiduously throughout the workday. People linger. Conversations are protracted, at least from my perspective. Almost always, the topics are broader than chiropractic medicine. Fabien frequently makes follow-up calls on behalf of his clients to powerful people he knows throughout the capital city."

In the setting of Montevideo, a group orientation is ever present. In a position of power, because of his wealth, fame, and informal network of friends, Fabian assumes the role of patron for his clients.

# Harmony

"I was in northern Saskatchewan, Canada, having breakfast with a friend from a Cree background, who is the pastor of a local First Nations church. As we ate, he described an event from the previous night. He was driving past the local cemetery where his grandfather is buried when he felt his grandfather's spirit communicating with him. My friend stopped the car and stood on the side of the road. He knew what his grandfather wanted. He sang a song to his grandfather that had been sung at his wake. 'Wake up! The sun is rising. Already, the birds are singing. It is beautiful throughout our land.'—the Cree sunrise song."

The Cree are group oriented. Family is extremely important. Ancestors are venerated. Doing the right thing at the right time is imperative. The ritual of singing is part of Cree tradition.

Appendix G also provides a second, more detailed assessment through sets of statements. This assessment is not scientific but may be useful for discussion. Generally, it indicates the tendencies a person has in speech and behavior per an overarching pattern of culture. The assessment begins with nine statements and four possible answers each to make the statement a complete sentence. The strongest answer of the four is awarded 3 points. A second strongest answer is awarded 2 points. The remaining two answers are awarded zero points. Here are the nine statements with their possible answers. It is important to think of a non-work context while completing the statements. Consider how you would think and behave if you were with family and friends.

# Assessment

1. When I don't know what to do, I at least try to do what . . .
   a. is right versus what is wrong.
   b. guards the reputation of my family or community.
   c. brings peace into my life.
   d. provides for family needs.
2. For me, the worst thing is to . . .
   a. be guilty of breaking the law.
   b. be dishonored in the eyes of my family or community.
   c. be at odds with others.

    d. not have to access needed resources.

3. What I value the most is . . .

    a. my individual rights.

    b. the goodness of my family name.

    c. control over my circumstances.

    d. key relationships with important people.

4. What holds a society of people together is . . .

    a. a fair and impartial system of justice.

    b. clearly defined tight knit communities.

    c. healthy relationships with others.

    d. networks of useful people.

5. If _____ broke down, society would crumble.

    a. the legal system.

    b. my local community.

    c. people's relationships to the spiritual world.

    d. back and forth ties with influential people.

6. I feel most loyal to . . .

    a. written standards of law.

    b. the example of honorable superiors.

    c. activities that please my own relatives, especially if they are visiting or live nearby.

    d. the wishes of important people.

7. I feel I am important because . . .

    a. of my accomplishments.

    b. of my family status.

    c. I faithfully follow established traditions.

    d. I have access to needed resources.

8. I value people based on . . .

    a. their built-in worth.

    b. how well they do what the community expects of them.

    c. how faithful they are to timeless traditions.

    d. the good things they can provide to others.

9. When I say something, I need to . . .

    a. tell the truth rather than a lie.

    b. show honor to those who deserve it.

    c. not anger others.

    d. make sure I remember who has power.

## Answer Sheet

Complete each statement by choosing only two of the answers provided. Place an "X" in the appropriate box for an answer that most strongly describes how you would think and behave with family and friends. Place an "X" in the appropriate box for your second most strong answer.

Table G.2: Answer Sheet

| Answers | Strongest | | | | Second strongest | | | |
|---|---|---|---|---|---|---|---|---|
| | A | B | C | D | A | B | C | D |
| Statement 1 | | | | | | | | |
| 2 | | | | | | | | |
| 3 | | | | | | | | |
| 4 | | | | | | | | |
| 5 | | | | | | | | |
| 6 | | | | | | | | |
| 7 | | | | | | | | |
| 8 | | | | | | | | |
| 9 | | | | | | | | |
| | Number of choices x "3" | | | | | | | |
| | | | | | Number of choices x "2" | | | |
| | Total tally of points | | | | | | | |

After completing all nine statements (two answers each), multiply the number of "strongest" choices by "3" per each column (A–D). In the same way, multiply the number of "second strongest" choices by "2" per each column (A–D). Tally the total number of points per column. Column A represents Justice. Column B, Honor. Column C, Harmony. Column D, Reciprocity.

Likely, one of the patterns will display as overarching (the greatest number of points). Other patterns will be indicated by a distribution of scores. Do you feel your scores accurately describe your cultural tendencies as described in *Overarching Patterns*?

Appendix H

# The Day Trujillo was Killed
## by Sam Strauss, Jr. [1]

"SE MATO AL JEFE," she said, her voice quivering like I had never heard—
Teresita, our dark-skinned Dominican cook. Having only about a year of
Spanish language study behind me, I asked her to repeat the words several
times. Suddenly, what had never occurred to me as possible was clear, although the full weight of it would take weeks and months to realize. "They
have killed the Chief." Trujillo was dead! He had been killed! But how? And
by whom? She did not know. She gave only the fact, no details. The dictator
of the Dominican Republic for over thirty years was dead.

It was May, 1961. All of the other North American missionaries in
our small Bible school were home on leave. The bulk of the responsibilities
of running a forty-acre training school for young, Dominican preachers
was upon this inexperienced, struggling teacher. At the time most of the
students were home on vacation, too. But five or six were still around the
campus, along with a few national cooks and workers. Besides Teresita, I
was the first on the grounds to know that he was dead.

Within several minutes, however, everyone knew. Their reaction was
much like mine: shock, unbelief, questions. Who had done it? What of
the army and the police? What of the threats made by the priests that
when Trujillo was dead, we would follow! And the great question: "What
will be next—for the country, for the Dominicans, and for us, evangelical
missionaries?"

Only two months before, I had braved a cheering crowd of 10,000
to approach within thirty feet of the podium on which sat the Jefe, Rafael
Leonidas Trujillo, Benefactor, Chief, and only "legal" thief in the Dominican

---

1. Adapted for clarity by Christopher Strauss, the grandson of Sam Strauss, Jr.

Republic. It was a parade given in his honor (by himself). Thousands of *campesinos* had been brought into the city in recognition of their leader. He was flanked by machine-gun carrying guards and well-armed members of his cabinet. In spite of the weaponry and stern looks on the faces of the guards, I experienced no fear as I pressed my way through the crowd toward the podium. Two secret service men followed my every step, their hands grasping Colt .45 caliber automatic pistols inside their coats. They were making sure that this "Yankee" would make no sudden move toward their leader. Their own lives depended upon their protection of the Chief. Having gotten within shooting distance of the president, I lifted my Argus 35mm camera above my head and, without aiming, snapped two color slides of him. The guards did not ask and I did not tell them that all I was interested in was a picture of Trujillo for my slide collection. I made no incorrect moves but slowly slipped out of the crowd, feeling rather brave and proud that I had a candid photograph of one of the most ruthless men who had ever lived on the earth. It was as if I had taken a picture of Hitler, close in, without saluting him!

And now he was dead! Impossible, I thought. Like many, I had been caught up in thinking there was something immortal about this man, Trujillo. He had escaped so many plots! He had maintained absolute control on this small island country of three million people for so long. Whatever he wanted, he obtained. But now the life he had struggled for so long to keep was gone.

Trujillo was maneuvered into power around 1930 by the departing U. S. Marines. Step by step, he moved up in power by the vacuum left by the United States' withdrawal from the country. Year by year, he seized more and more power, property, and prestige, until by 1960 he was attempting to order the Catholic Church around. His pictures were everywhere. In every Dominican home, they hung on the walls beside pictures of the Virgin Mary and wooden crosses. (Hitler had used the same strategy in Germany in the 1930s. He replaced the stars on Christmas trees with swastikas.) Trujillo's statues covered the land. Half of the streets' names had something to do with the Trujillo family. There was no place in the island where his power did not reach. Anything and anyone were his, at his request—or they were no more! Those who resisted his power disappeared. No one, including us Americans, dared to speak against him. All of us were, to one degree or another, mesmerized. True, those in leadership in our school knew that he was a killer, but we had an unwritten rule to keep quiet about him.

In the days to follow, the details of his demise become known. Two cars, filled with assassins, meet Trujillo's car on an unguarded stretch of a wide highway just out of Ciudad Trujillo (later renamed Santo Domingo). Trujillo is alone, except for his chauffeur. One car comes up from the rear. Men well known to the Jefe open fire with light machine guns and pistols. A second car blocks the way ahead. Trujillo's chauffer is forced to pull to the side of the road. Grabbing a Thompson .45 caliber sub-machine gun, the chauffer opens fire on the assailants. But realizing the hopelessness of the situation, he soon drops his weapon and flees into the nearby underbrush. Trujillo is left alone with his pearl-handled Colt .38 revolver. Leaning on the front fender of the car, he exchanges shots with those in the blocking car. The chaser car's occupants empty out and approach the Jefe from the rear. In five seconds it is over. Almost eighty shots perforate his body. Trujillo lies dead on the edge of the highway. The Dominicans later wrote a song to celebrate the event: "Mataron el chivo en el camino," "They killed the goat on the highway."

The assassins dumped the bullet-riddled corpse into the trunk of a car and quickly departed the scene to execute the next step in the "golpe de estado." Returning to the capital, they rode around all night looking for the rest of the members of the plot. But something went wrong with the communications and the plot began to fall apart. The army leaders that were to give the order to kill the rest of the clan and take over the government could not be found. The body was left in the trunk of the car while the killers tried to sleep and then make their next move. But it was too late for them. The next morning a milkman discovered a pool of blood under the rear of the car and notified the authorities. The loyal police quickly moved in. One by one, the killers were caught and summarily executed. The government did not fall. Oppression, graft, and murder continued under the auspices of Trujillo's son Radames. Finally, after over a year of struggle and American pressure, the Trujillo family was ousted and replaced by men of a gentler temperament.

But who will forget those first days of surprise, amazement, fear, and doubt. Was he really dead? Was it just a guise to see who was loyal to him and who really hated him? My first reaction, that he was not dead and soon would reappear, continued with me for several weeks. The funeral was elaborate. Heads of states came to pay their respects.

Thousands of women dressed in black wept profusely. The radio was full of solemn, stately music. Flags flew at half-mast. His casket was placed in an almost royal crypt in a large Dominican cathedral. But there was no body in the casket! After the final overthrow of the Trujillo family, the press reported that the casket never contained the remains of the Chief. His body had been placed in a freezer and kept until Radames left the island with it. In exile, he buried his father in France.

That's what the papers reported. But did they tell the truth? Did they really kill him? All who were connected with the plot are now dead. The chauffeur was never heard from again. There were no photographs. Was he really dead? Could the so often used expression "Viva Trujillo" be true? Was Teresita right when she came in my office and gasped the words "Se mato al Jefe?"

## Appendix I

# Further Research Needed

MUCH MORE SHOULD BE researched related to the four overarching patterns of culture and others. This book provides a mere summary to alert the cross-cultural worker to expectations, one's own and those of others in the cross-cultural setting.

I suggest six possible areas of further research. Research has already begun. Others as well are seeing the emerging trends.

## Current Trends in the United State of America

In what ways is the USA drifting away from justice toward a unique form of clientelism? What evidence shows this transition has already begun? To what degree have institutions broken down and corruption intruded? What are the ramifications? Are there two types of clientelism emerging, one as a sequel to income inequality but the other tactical? Related to tactical strategies, what are the tactics of neoreactionaries?[1]

How is an emerging culture of victimization explained?[2] How does the management of microaggressions fit into the emerging clientelism? Or, is

1. See https://rationalwiki.org/wiki/Neoreactionary_movement Mencius Moldbug, blogger but by day is a software engineer named Curtis Yarvin, is said to be a founder of neoreaction (NRx). The Neoreactionary Movement is mostly based on the ideas of Yarvin. It supplants democracy with a monarch-style governance of elitists.

2. Microaggressions were first examined by Bradley Campbell and Jason Manning, both Professors of Sociology, in 2014 through an article entitled "Microaggressions and Moral Culture", *Comparative Sociology* 13, 692–726. In February 2018, they published an expanded and updated analysis in *The Rise of Victimhood Culture: Microaggressions, Safe Spaces, and the New Culture Wars*, Palgrave Macmillan. Also, see Jonathan Haidt's keen analysis at: http://righteousmind.com/where-microaggressions-really-come-from/ Haidt is a Social Psychologist at the New York University Stern School of Business.

this phenomenon also an outcome of an overdependence upon law? In what ways is this trend similar and dissimilar to honor in the Old South?

Also, how pervasive is the emerging culture of dystopia?[3] Why does it seem tradition, foundations, and hope are lost? Has integral dignity been lost? In what ways is apocalypse related to dystopia? If true, is this an unintended consequence of a departure from justice without functional substitutes?

## Social Media

How is the "fame-based" culture of social media[4] similar to the honor pattern of culture? What are the differences? Conversely, how do people use social media platforms to shame oppressors and influence authorities to take action against the oppressors?

## Secret Shame

Thomas Scheff, Professor Emeritus from the Department of Sociology at the University of California in Santa Barbara, expands the research of Charles Horton Cooley (1922), Norbert Elias, (1939), and others. These earlier works explore the assumption that secret or hidden shame is the source of violence.[5] Scheff adds to the research. In addition, see *Violence: Reflections on a National Epidemic* by prison psychiatrist James Gilligan. Gilligan identifies the role of shame in the etiology of murder. Is there a correlation between shame and violence in societies where honor is the overarching pattern of culture? If yes, why? To what extent? What may be other causes? What is a way of mitigation?

---

3. See *The Age of Dystopia: Our Genre, Our Fears, and Our Future* edited by Louisa MacKay Demerjian. Also, a Jackson Wu blog entitled "Is Western Culture Dystopian? at http://www.patheos.com/blogs/jacksonwu/2017/06/20/western-culture-dystopian/.

4. For example: likes, friends, followers, connections, looks, clicks, and more

5. See also *The Banality of Suicide Terrorism: The Naked Truth About the Psychology of Islamic Suicide Bombing* (2010) by Nancy Hartevelt Kobrin, Fellow at the American Center for Democracy.

## Honor and Violence

Honor and violence—correlation or causation?[6] Is there valid and reliable evidence of violent responses to a perceived affront? Was this true in southern culture of the USA in the past? Is this true in the urban ghetto today? See the gang research compiled by Steve Nawojczyk, primarily related to Little Rock, Arkansas. Also see Lindsey L. Osterman and Ryan P. Brown (2011). "Culture of Honor and Violence Against the Self." What is the relationship between southern culture and the urban ghetto? Is the link valid? See Thomas Sowell (2006), *Black Rednecks and White Liberals.*

## Honor versus Face

*Shame* in an Arab context in contrast to loss of "face" in an Asian context – Both contexts are said to be honor cultures.[7] But, evident differences exist. In what ways is shame different from loss of "face"? Stella Ting-Toomey, Professor of Human Communication Studies at California State University in Fullerton, California, has written extensively about "face negotiation theory." She contrasts face-saving and face-giving styles. See *Understanding Intercultural Communication* (Oxford University Press, 2012, 195–203) by Stella Ting-Toomey and Leeva C. Chung. Chung is at the University of San Diego.[8]

## Assessments

What assessments are available to determine which pattern is overarching in what context? Currently, assessments for determining overarching patterns are scarce. KnowledgeWorkx provides one that measures three patterns. Appendix G takes a stab at providing an assessment to measure four patterns, but will need to be fine-tuned in its verifiability and reliability. Such assessments are not foolproof, but they do provide a good starting point for further study and reflection.

---

6. Nisbett and Cohen, *Culture of Honor.*

7. In Arabic, it is said that one "whitens" or "blackens" one's face.

8. See    http://www.familysecuritymatters.org/publications/id.9077/pub_detail.asp for a blog post that contrasts Japanese and Arab cultures.

# References

Abou-Zeid, Ahmed A. "Honour and Shame Among the Bedouin of Egypt." In *Honour and Shame: The Values of Mediterranean Society*, edited by Jean G. Peristiany, 235–59. Chicago: University of Chicago Press, 1966.

Adams, Richard N. *Energy and Structure: A Theory of Social Power*. Austin: University of Texas Press, 1975.

Addelston, H. K. "Child Patient Training." *Chicago Dental Society Review* 38 (1959) 27–29.

Air Force Culture and Language Center. *Expeditionary Airman Field Guide*. Montgomery: Air University Culture Center, 2017.

Al-Saleh, Yasmine. "Amulets and Talismans from the Islamic World." http://www.metmuseum.org/toah/hd/tali/hd_tali.htm.

Antonius, George. *The Arab Awakening: The Story of the Arab National Movement*. London: Hamish Hamilton, 1938.

Aristotle. *Politics*. Translated by Ernest Barker. New York: Oxford University Press, 2009.

Aslani, Soroush, et al. "Dignity, Face, and Honor Cultures: A Study of Negotiation Strategy and Outcomes in Three Cultures." *Journal of Organizational Behavior* 37 (2016) 1178–1201.

Auyero, Javier. "The Logic of Clientelism in Argentina." *Latin American Research Review* 35 (2000) 55–81.

Ayers, Edward L. *Vengeance and Justice*. New York: Oxford University Press, 1984.

Bahnsen, Greg L. *Van Til's Apologetic: Readings and Analysis*. Phillipsburg, NJ: Presbyterian and Reformed, 1998.

Baldwin, John R., et al. *Redefining Culture: Perspectives Across the Disciplines*. Mahwah, NJ: Lawrence Erlbaum Associates, 2006.

Bandura, Albert. "Self-Efficacy: Toward a Theory of Behavioral Change." *Psychological Review* 84 (1977) 191–215.

Barnard, Alan. *History and Theory in Anthropology*. Cambridge: Cambridge University Press, 2003.

Barnes, Sandra T. *Patrons and Power: Creating a Political Community in Metropolitan Lagos*. Bloomington: Indiana University Press, 1986.

Barney, G. Linwood. "The Supracultural and the Cultural." In *The Gospel and Frontier Peoples*, edited by R. Pierce Beaver, 48–55. Pasadena, CA: William Carey Library, 1973.

Bebber, Robert J. "The Role of Provincial Reconstruction Teams (PRTs) in Counterinsurgency Operations: Khost Province, Afghanistan." *Small Wars Journal* (2008) 3–24.

Benedict, Ruth. *The Chrysanthemum and the Sword: Patterns of Japanese Culture*. 1946. Reprint, Boston: Houghton Mifflin, 2005.

———. *Patterns of Culture*. 1934. Reprint, Boston: Houghton Mifflin, 2006.

Berger, Peter, et al. *The Homeless Mind: Modernization and Consciousness*. New York: Random, 1973.

Berreman, Gerald D. "Anemic and Emetic Analyses in Social Anthropology." *American Anthropologist* 68 (1966) 346–54.

Berry, John. "Acculturation: Living Successfully in Two Cultures." *International Journal of Intercultural Relations* 29 (2005) 697–712.

———. "Psychology of Acculturation: Understanding Individuals Moving between Cultures." In *Applied Cross-Cultural Psychology*, edited by Richard Brislin, 232–53. Newbury Park, CA: Sage, 1990.

Bodding, P. O. *A Chapter of Santal Folklore*. Kristiania, Norway: A. W. Brogger, 1924.

Boettner, Loraine. *Roman Catholicism*. Phillipsburg, NJ: Presbyterian and Reformed, 2000.

Bormann, Ernest G. "Fantasy and Rhetorical Vision: The Rhetorical Criticism of Social Reality." *Quarterly Journal of Speech* 58 (1972) 398.

Bowman, James. *Honor: A History*. New York: Encounter, 2006.

———. "Whatever Happened to Honor?" http://www.jamesbowman.net/articleDetail.asp?pubID=1169.

Bradt, Kevin. *Story as a Way of Knowing*. Kansas City: Sheed & Ward, 1997.

Brinkerhoff, Derick W., and Arthur A. Goldsmith. "Clientelism, Patrimonialism, and Democratic Governance: An Overview and Framework for Assessment and Programming." *U. S. Agency for International Development*. Bethesda, MD: Abt Associates, 2002.

Brown, Brené. "Listening to Shame." https://www.ted.com/talks/brene_brown_listening_to_shame.

Bruce, Joshua R. "Uniting Theories of Morality, Religion, and Social Interaction: Grid-Group Cultural Theory, the 'Big Three' Ethics, and Moral Foundations Theory." *Psychology & Society* 5 (2013) 37–50.

Bruneau, Thomas, and Florina Christiana Matei. "Towards a New Conceptualization of Democratization and Civil-Military Relations." *Democratization* 15 (2008) 909–29.

Bruner, Jerome. *The Culture of Education*. Cambridge, MA: Harvard University Press, 1996.

Bustikova, Lenka, and Cristina Corduneanu-Huci. "Clientelism, State Capacity and Economic Development: A Cross-National Study." https://papers.ssrn.com/sol3/papers.cfm?abstract_id=1449000##.

Campbell, Bradley, and Jason Manning. "Macroaggression and Moral Cultures." *Comparative Sociology* 13 (2014) 692–726.

———. *The Rise of Victimhood Culture: Microaggressions, Safe Spaces, and the New Culture Wars*. Basingstoke, England: Palgrave Macmillan, 2018.

Cash, W. J. *The Mind of the South*. New York: Vintage, 1941.

Chao, Xia, et al. "Culture and Personality." https://anthropology.ua.edu/cultures/cultures.php?culture=Culture%20and%20Personality.

Clark, Terry Nichols. "Old and New Paradigms for Urban Research." *Urban Affairs Review* 36 (2000) 3–46.

Cohen, Dov, and Angela Leung. "A CuPS (Culture x Person x Situation) Perspective on Violence and Character." In *Human Aggression and Violence: Causes, Manifestations, and Consequences*, edited by Phillip Shaver and Mario Mikulincer, 187–200. Washington, DC: American Psychological Association, 2010.

Cohen, Dov, and Richard E. Nisbett. "Self-Protection and the Culture of Honor: Explaining Southern Culture of Honor." *Personality and Social Psychology Bulletin* 20 (1994) 551–67.

Confucius. *Analects*. Translated by Raymond Dawson. Oxford: Oxford University Press, 2008.

Cooley, Charles Horton. "The Social Self: The Meaning of 'I.'" In *Human Nature and the Social Order*, revised ed., edited by Charles Horton Cooley, 168–210. New York: Charles Scribner's Sons, 1922.

Cranfield, Charles. *Romans: A Shorter Commentary*. Grand Rapids, MI: Eerdmans, 1988.

Crassweller, Robert D. *Trujillo: The Life and Times of a Caribbean Dictator*. New York: Macmillan, 1966.

Dale, Edgar. *Building a Learning Environment*. 1940. Reprint, Bloomington: Phi Delta Kappa, 1972.

Daly, Erin, and James R. May. "Dignity Rights Project" https://delawarelaw.widener.edu/prospective-students/jd-program/jd-academics/signature-programs/dignity-rights-project/.

Daniel, Pete. "Bayonets and Bibles: The 1957 Little Rock Crisis." Paper presented at the 1998 inauguration of the Women's Emergency Committee.

Deacon, Terrence W. "The Symbol Concept." In *The Oxford Handbook of Language Evolution*, edited by Kathleen Gibson and Maggie Tallerman, 393–405. New York: Oxford University Press, 2011.

———. *The Symbolic Species: The Co-Evolution of Language and the Brain*. New York: Norton, 1997.

Demerjian, Louisa MacKay. *The Age of Dystopia: Our Genre, Our Fears, and Our Future*. Newcastle, United Kingdom: Cambridge Scholars, 2016.

De Neve, Geert. "Patronage and 'Community': The Role of a Tamil 'Village' Festival in the Integration of a Town." *Journal of the Royal Anthropological Institute* 6 (2000) 501–20.

Dewey, John. *Experience and Education*. New York: Touchstone, 1938.

Dhonau, Jerry. "Negro Girl Turned Back, Ignores Hooting Crowd." *The Arkansas Gazette*, September 5, 1957, 1–2.

Dodds, E. R. *The Greeks and the Irrational*. Berkeley: University of California Press, 1951.

———. "From Shame-Culture to Guilt-Culture." In *Honour and Shame: The Values of Mediterranean Society*, edited by Jean G. Peristiany, 28–63. Chicago: University of Chicago Press, 1966.

Douglas, Mary. *Natural Symbols: Explorations in Cosmology*. New York: Pantheon, 1982.

———. *Purity and Danger: An Analysis of the Concepts of Pollution and Taboo*. 1966. Reprint, London: Routledge, 1984.

Douthit, George. "CHS Emptied by Bomb Scare Shortly After U.S. Troops Force Integration." *The Arkansas Democrat*. September 25, 1957, 1.

Du Bois, Cora. *The People of Alor: A Social-Psychological Study of an East Indian Island*. Minneapolis, MN: University of Minnesota Press, 1944.

Dumézil, Georges. *Servius et la Fortune – Essai sur la fonction sociale de louange et de blâme et sur les éléments indo-européens du cens romain*. Paris: Gallimard, 1943.

Dupré, Catherine. *The Age of Dignity: Human Rights and Constitutionalism in Europe*. Portland, OR: Hart, 2015.

Durkheim, Emile. *The Division of Labor in Society*. Translated by W. D. Halls. New York: The Free Press, 1984.

———. *The Elementary Forms of the Religious Life*. Translated by Joseph Ward Swain. New York: The Free Press, 1965.

———. *Selected Writings*. Translated by Anthony Giddens. Cambridge: Cambridge University Press, 1972.

Earley, P. Christopher. *Face, Harmony, and Social Structure: An Analysis of Organizational Behavior Across Cultures*. New York: Oxford University Press, 1997.

Edwards, Angela, unpublished research.

Eisenstadt, S. N., and Luis Roniger. *Patrons, Clients, and Friends: Interpersonal Relations and the Structure of Trust in Society*. Cambridge: Cambridge University Press, 1984.

Ekman, Paul. *Emotions Revealed: Recognizing Faces and Feelings to Improve Communication and Emotional Life*. 2nd ed. New York: St. Martin's, 2003.

Elder, Robert. *The Sacred Mirror: Evangelicalism, Honor, and Identity in the Deep South: 1790–1860*. Chapel Hill, NC: University of North Carolina Press, 2016.

Elias, Norbert. *The Civilizing Process: Sociogenetic and Psychogenetic Investigations*. Translated by Edmund Jephcott. 1939. Reprint, Oxford: Blackwell, 2000.

Erikson, Erik. *Childhood and Society*. New York: Norton, 1950.

Erler, Edward J. "Who We Are as a People—The Syrian Refugee Question." *Imprimis* 45 (2016) 1–5.

"Face." In *The Oxford English Dictionary*. http://www.oed.com.

Fadiman, Anne. *The Spirit Catches You and You Fall Down*. New York: Farrar, Strauss and Giroux, 1997.

Feaver, Peter D. "The Civil-Military Problematique: Huntington, Janowitz, and the Question of Civilian Control." *Armed Forces & Society* 23 (1996) 149–178.

Finley, M. I. *The World of Odysseus*. New York: Meridian, 1959.

Fischer, Craig. *Legitimacy and Procedural Justice: A New Element of Police Leadership*. Washington, DC: U.S. Department of Justice, 2014.

Fish, Hamilton. "The Menace of Communism." *Annals of the American Academy of Political and Social Science* 156 (1931) 54–61.

Fisher, Mary Pat. *Living Religions*. 8th ed. Upper Saddle River, NJ: Prentice Hall, 2010.

Fosse, Sébastien M., et al. "When Dignity and Honor Cultures Negotiate: Finding Common Ground." *Negotiation Conflict Management Resolution* 10 (2017) 265–85.

Fox, Jonathan. "The Difficult Transition from Clientelism to Citizenship." *World Politics* 46 (1994) 151–84.

Fried, Morton. "Anthropology and the Study of Politics." In *Horizons of Anthropology*, edited by Sol Tax, 181–90. Chicago: University of Chicago Press, 1964.

Geertz, Clifford. *The Interpretation of Cultures*. New York: Basic, 1973.

Georges, Jayson. "Five Types of Honor-Shame Culture." http://honorshame.com/types-honor-shame-cultures/.

———. "Resources." https://www.zotero.org/groups/honorshame/items/.

Giddens, Anthony. "Introduction." *Emile Durkheim: Selected Writings*. Cambridge, MA: Cambridge University Press, 1997.

Gilligan, James. *Violence: Reflections on a National Epidemic*. New York: Random, 1997.

Goldingay, John. *An Introduction to the Old Testament: Exploring Text, Approaches & Issues*. Downers Grove, IL: InterVarsity, 2015.

González-Wippler, Migene. *Complete Book of Amulets and Talismans*. St. Paul, MN: Llewellyn, 1991.

Goodell, Grace E. "Paternalism, Patronage, and Potlach." *Current Anthropology* 26 (1985) 247–57.

Goodenough, Ward. *Culture, Language, and Society*. 2nd ed. Menlo Park, CA: Benjamin/Cummings, 1981.

Gordin, Jorge P. "The Political and Partisan Determinants of Patronage in Latin America: 1960-1994: A Comparative Perspective." *European Journal of Political Research* 41 (2002) 513–49.

Green, Thad B., et al. "The Practice of Management: Knowledge vs. Skills." *Training & Development Journal* 39 (1985) 56–58.

Greenberg, Kenneth S. *Honor and Slavery*. Princeton, NJ: Princeton University Press, 1997.

Haidt, Jonathan. *The Righteous Mind: Why Good People are Divided by Politics and Religion*. New York: Pantheon, 2012.

Hall, Edward. *Beyond Culture*. New York: Anchor, 1976.

———. *The Dance of Life: The Other Dimension of Time*. New York: Anchor, 1983.

———. *The Hidden Dimension*. New York: Anchor, 1966.

———. *The Silent Language*. New York: Anchor, 1959.

Halverson, Jeffry R., et al. *Master Narratives of Islamist Extremism*. New York: Palgrave Macmillan, 2011.

Harris, Marvin. *Cultural Materialism: The Struggle for a Science of Culture*. New York: Vintage, 1979.

———. "History and Significance of the Emic/Etic Distinction." *Annual Review of Anthropology* 5 (1976) 329–50.

———. *The Rise of Anthropological Theory: A History of Theories of Culture*. Updated edition. Walnut Creek, CA: Altamira, 2001.

Harris, Sam. "Science and Morality." https://www.ted.com/talks/sam_harris_science_can_show_what_s_right.

Hayes, Timothy. *Re-examining the Subculture of Violence in the South*. Dissertation presented in 2006 retrieved at http://citeseerx.ist.psu.edu/viewdoc/download?doi=10.1.1.556.275&rep=rep1&type=pdf

Heine, Steven J. "Self as a Cultural Product: An Examination of East Asian and North American Selves." *Journal of Personality* 69 (2001) 881–905.

Herskovits, Melville J. *Man and His Works: The Science of Cultural Anthropology*. New York: Alfred Knopf, 1948.

Hesselgrave, David. *Communicating Christ Cross-Culturally: An Introduction to Missionary Communication*. 2nd ed. Grand Rapids, MI: Zondervan, 1991.

Hicken, Allan. "Clientelism." *Annual Review of Political Science* 14 (2011) 289–310.

Hiebert, Paul. *Anthropological Insights for Missionaries*. Grand Rapids, MI: Baker, 1999.

———. *Cultural Anthropology*. Grand Rapids, MI: Baker, 1976.

———. *Transforming Worldviews: An Anthropological Understanding of How People Change*. Grand Rapids: Baker Academic, 2008.

Hiebert, Paul, et al. *Understanding Folk Religion: A Christian Response to Popular Beliefs and Practices*. Grand Rapids: Baker, 1999.

Ho, David Yau-fai. "On the Concept of Face." *American Journal of Sociology* 81 (1976) 867–84.

Hocker, Joyce L., and William W. Wilmot. *Interpersonal Conflict.* 2nd ed. Dubuque, Iowa: Brown, 1985.

Hofstadter, Richard. *Anti-Intellectualism in American Life.* Toronto: Random, 1963.

Hofstede, Geert. *Cultural Consequences: Comparing Values, Behaviors, Institutions, and Organizations Across Nations.* 2nd ed. Thousand Oaks, CA: Sage, 2001.

———. *Culture's Consequences: International Differences in Work-Related Values.* Newbury Park, CA: Sage, 1980.

———. *Cultures and Organizations: Software of the Mind.* New York: McGraw-Hill, 1997.

———. "The 6-D Model of National Culture." https://geerthofstede.com/culture-geert-hofstede-gert-jan-hofstede/6d-model-of-national-culture/.

———. *Uncommon Sense about Organizations: Cases, Studies, and Field Observations.* Newbury Park, CA: Sage, 1994.

House, Robert, et al., eds. *Culture, Leadership, and Organizations: The GLOBE Study of 62 Societies.* Thousand Oaks, CA: Sage, 2004.

Ibsen, Charles A., and Patricia Klobus. "Fictive Kin Term Use and Social Relationships: Alternative Interpretations." *Journal of Marriage and Family* 34 (1972) 615–20.

Illich, Ivan. *Shadow Work.* New York: Marion Boyars, 1981.

Jahoda, Gustav. "Critical Reflections on Some Recent Definitions of 'Culture.'" *Culture & Psychology* 18 (2012) 289–303.

Johnson, Thomas H. "The Taliban Insurgency and an Analysis of *Shabnamah* (Night Letters)." *Small Wars and Insurgencies* 18 (2007) 317–44.

Kant, Immanuel. *Fundamental Principles of the Metaphysics of Morals.* Translated by Thomas Kingsmill Abbott. Retrieved October 10, 2018 at https://ebooks.adelaide. edu.au/k/kant/immanuel/k16prm/index.html.

Kearney, Michael. "A World View Explanation of the Evil Eye." In *The Evil Eye*, edited by Clarence Maloney, 175–92. New York: Columbia University Press, 1974.

———. *World View.* Novato, CA: Chandler & Sharp, 1984.

Keefer, Philip, and Razvan Vlaicu. "Democracy, Credibility, and Clientelism." *The Journal of Law, Economics, and Organization* 24 (2008) 371–406.

Kilmann Diagnostics. "An Overview of the Thomas-Kilmann Conflict Mode Instrument (TKI)." http://www.kilmanndiagnostics.com/overview-thomas-kilmann-conflict-mode-instrument-tki.

Kim, Young Hoon, and Dov Cohen. "Information, Perspective, and Judgments about the Self in Face and Dignity Cultures." *Personality and Social Psychology Bulletin* 36 (2010) 537–50.

Kingston, Paul. "Patrons, Clients, and Civil Society." *Arab Studies Quarterly* 22 (2000) 1–18.

Kirk, Russell. *Roots of American Order.* 1974. Reprint, Wilmington, DE: Intercollegiate Studies Institute, 2003.

Kluckhohn, Clyde, and Dorothea Leighton. *The Navajo.* Revised Edition. New York: Anchor, 1962.

Kluckhohn, Florence Rockwood, and Fred L. Strodtbeck. *Variations in Value Orientations.* Evanston, IL: Row, Peterson, 1961.

Kobrin, Nancy Hartevelt. *The Banality of Suicide Terrorism: The Naked Truth About the Psychology of Islamic Suicide Bombing.* Dulles, VA: Potomac, 2010.

Kohls, Robert L., and John M. Knight. *Developing Intercultural Awareness: A Cross-Cultural Training Handbook.* 2nd ed. Yarmouth, ME: Intercultural, 1981.

Kottak, Conrad Phillip. *Mirror for Humanity: A Concise Introduction to Cultural Anthropology.* 9th ed. Boston: McGraw-Hill, 2013.

Kraft, Charles. *Christianity in Culture: A Study in the Dynamic Biblical Theologizing in Cross-Cultural Perspective.* Maryknoll, NY: Orbis, 1979.

Kroeber, Alfred and Clyde Kluckhohn. "Culture: A Critical Review of Concepts and Definition." *Philosophy and Phenomenological Research* 14 (1953) 270–271.

Lee, Joseph J. "The Native Speaker: An Achievable Model?" *Asian EFL Journal* 7 (2005) 152–63.

Leung, Angela K. Y., and Dov Cohen. "Within- and Between-Culture Variation: Individual Differences and the Cultural Logics of Honor, Face, and Dignity Cultures." *Journal of Personality and Social Psychology* 100 (2011) 507–26.

Lewis, Bill. "Governor Gets Plea of Mothers League." *The Arkansas Gazette.* September 29, 1957, 1–2.

Lewis, C. S. *The Discarded Image: An Introduction to Medieval and Renaissance Literature.* Cambridge, MA. Cambridge University Press, 2004.

Linton, Ralph. *The Study of Man: An Introduction.* New York: D. Appleton-Century, 1936.

Luzbetak, Louis J. *The Church and Cultures.* Maryknoll, NY: Orbis, 1988.

Maley, William. "Provincial Reconstruction Teams in Afghanistan—How They Arrived and Where They are Going." *NATO Review* Autumn (2007) https://www.nato.int/docu/review/2007/issue3/english/art2.html.

Malinowski, Bronislaw. *A Scientific Theory of Culture and Other Essays.* Chapel Hill, NC: University of North Carolina Press, 1944.

Margolis, Frederic, and Chip Bell. *Understanding Training: Perspectives and Practices.* San Diego, CA: University Associates, 1989.

Martin, Judith, and Tom Nakayama. *Experiencing Intercultural Communication: An Introduction.* 5th ed. New York: McGraw-Hill, 2014.

Marx, Karl. "Contribution to the Critique of Hegel's Philosophy of Right." Translated by unknown. In *On Religion,* edited by Karl Marx and Friedrich Engels (41–58). Moscow: Foreign Language Publishing House, 1955.

Mbamalu, Abiola. "Patronage and Clientelism in the Fourth Gospel." *Luce Verbi* 47 (2013) 1–8.

McAdams, Dan P. *The Redemptive Self: Stories Americans Live By.* Revised and Expanded Edition. New York: Oxford University Press, 2013.

McGee, R. Jon, and Richard L. Warms. *Anthropological Theory: An Introductory History.* 6th ed. Lanham, MD: Rowman and Littlefield, 2016.

McWhiney, Grady. *Cracker Culture: Celtic Ways in the Old South.* Tuscaloosa, AL: University of Alabama Press, 1988.

Mead, Margaret. *Cooperation and Competition Among Primitive Peoples.* New York: McGraw-Hill, 1937.

Medard, Jean-Francois. "The Underdeveloped State in Tropical Africa: Political Clientelism or Neo-Patrimonialism?" In *Private Patronage and Public Power: Political Clientelism in the Modern State,* edited by Christopher Clapham, 162–92. New York: St. Martin's, 1982.

Miller, William Ian. *Bloodtaking and Peacemaking: Feud, Law, and Society in Saga Iceland.* Chicago: University of Chicago Press, 1990.

————. *Humiliation: And Other Essays on Honor, Social Discomfort, and Violence*. Ithaca, NY: Cornell University Press, 1995.

Minkov, Michael. *Cross-Cultural Analysis: The Science and Art of Comparing the World's Modern Societies and Their Cultures*. Los Angeles: Sage, 2013.

Morgan, Henry Lewis. *Systems of Consanguinity and Affinity of the Human Family*. Washington City: Smithsonian Institution, 1871.

Muller, Roland. *Honor and Shame: Unlocking the Door*. Bloomington, IL: Xlibris, 2001.

Murdock, George, et al. *Outline of Cultural* Materials. New Haven, CT: Institute of Human Relations, 1938.

Musil, Alois. *The Manners and Customs of the Rwala Bedouins*. New York: American Geographical Society, 1928.

Naugle, David. *Worldview: The History of a Concept*. Grand Rapids, MI: Eerdmans, 2002.

Nehrbass, Kenneth. *Christianity and Animism in Melanesia: Four Approaches to Gospel and Culture*. Pasadena, CA: William Carey Library, 2012.

Neill, Stephen. *Christian Faith and Other Faiths: The Christian Dialogue with Other Religions*. New York: Oxford University Press, 1970.

Neyrey, Jerome. "Toward of Bibliography on 'Honor and Shame.'" http://www3.nd.edu/~jneyrey1/honor.htm.

Nida, Eugene. *Customs and Cultures: Anthropology for Christian Missions*. 1954. Reprint, Pasadena, CA: William Carey Library, 1975.

————. *Morphology: The Descriptive Analysis of Words*. 2nd ed. Ann Arbor, MI: University of Michigan Press, 1974.

Nisbett, Richard E., and Dov Cohen. *Culture of Honor: The Psychology of Violence in the South*. Boulder, CO: Westview, 1996.

Northrop, F. S. C. *The Meeting of East and West*. New York: Collier, 1946.

Obasi, Ezemenari M., et al. "Construction and Initial Validation of the Worldview Analysis Scale (WAS)." *Journal of Black Studies* 39 (2009) 937–61.

Ollapally, Deepa. "Unfinished Business in Afghanistan: Warlordism, Reconstruction, and Ethnic Harmony." *Special Report Number 105* by the United States Institute of Peace, April 2003.

O'Neill, Barry. *Honor, Symbols, and War*. Ann Arbor, MI: University of Michigan Press, 1999.

Opler, Morris Edward. "Themes as Dynamic Forces in Culture." *American Journal of Sociology* 51 (1945) 198–206.

Osterman, Lindsey L., and Ryan P. Brown. "Culture of Honor and Violence Against the Self." *Personality and Social Psychology Bulletin* 37 (2011) 1611–23.

Palmer, Craig T., and Kathryn Coe. "From Morality to Law: The Role of Kinship, Tradition and Politics." https://politicsandculture.org/2010/04/29/from-morality-to-law-the-role-of-kinship-tradition-and-politics/.

Patai, Raphael. *The Arab Mind*. 1973. Reprint, Tucson, AZ: Recovery Resources, 2007.

Pease, Arthur Stanley. "Things Without Honor" *Classical Philology* 21 (1926) 27–42.

Pennell, T. L. *Among the Wild Tribes of the Afghan Frontier: A Record of Sixteen Years Close Intercourse with the Natives of the Indian Marches*. London: Seeley, 1913.

Pike, Kenneth. *Language in Relation to a Unified Theory of the Structure of Human Behavior*. Glendale, CA: Summer Institute of Linguistics, 1954.

————. *Phonemics: A Technique for Reducing Languages to Writing*. Ann Arbor, MI: University of Michigan Press, 1976.

Pike, Kenneth, and Evelyn Pike. *Grammatical Analysis*. Arlington, TX: University of Texas and Summer Institute of Linguistics, 1977.

Pitt-Rivers, Julian. "Honor." In *International Encyclopedia of the Social Sciences*, edited by David Sills, 509–10. New York: Macmillan, 1968.

———. "Honour and Social Status." In *Honour and Shame: The Values of Mediterranean Society*, edited by Jean G. Peristiany, 17–77. Chicago: University of Chicago Press, 1966.

Priest, Robert J., et al. "Missiological Syncretism: The New Animistic Paradigm." In *Spiritual Power and Missions: Raising the Issues*, edited by Edward Rommen, 9–87. Pasadena, CA: William Carey Library, 1995.

Pryce-Jones, David. *The Closed Circle: An Interpretation of the Arabs*. 1989. Reprint, Chicago: Ivan R. Dee, 2009.

Quinonez, Natasha. "3 Domains of Learning." https://blog.udemy.com/domains-of-learning/.

Qutb, Sayyid. *Milestones*. 1964. Translated by Abdul Naeem. New Delhi: Islamic Book Service, 2001.

Radcliffe-Brown, A. *Structure and Function in Primitive Society: Essays and Addresses*. New York: Macmillan, 1965.

Redfield, Robert. *The Primitive World and Its Transformations*. Ithaca, NY: Cornell University Press, 1953.

Renteln, Alison Dundes. "Relativism and the Search for Human Rights." *American Anthropologist* 90 (1988) 56–72.

Rieff, Phillip. *My Life Among the Deathworks: Illustrations of the Aesthetics of Authority*. Charlottesville, VA: University of Virginia Press, 2006.

Rodriguez Mosquera, Patricia M., et al. "Attack, Disapproval, or Withdrawal? The Role of Honour in Anger and Shame Responses to Being Insulted." *Cognition and Emotion* 22 (2008) 1471–98.

Roniger, Luis. "Political Clientelism, Democracy, and Market Economy." *Comparative Politics* 36 (2004) 353–75.

Roniger, Luis, and Ayşe Güneş-Ayata, eds. *Democracy, Clientelism, and Civil Society*. Boulder, CO: Lynne Rienner, 1994.

Rousseau, Jean-Jacques. *Social Contract*. 1762. Translated by Charles Frankel. New York: Hafner, 1947.

Rusbult, Craig. "What Is a Worldview?—Definition and Introduction." http://asa3.org/ASA/education/views/index.html.

Sapir, Edward. *Selected Writings in Language, Culture, and Personality*, edited by David Mandelbaum. Berkley, CA: University of California Press, 1949.

Scheff, Thomas J. "Shame and Conformity: The Deference-Emotion System." *American Sociological Review* 53 (1988) 395–406.

Scheff, Thomas J., and Suzanne M. Retzinger. *Emotion and Violence: Shame and Rage in Destructive Conflicts*. 1991. Reprint, Lincoln, NB: iUniverse, 2001.

Schwartz, Shalom H. "Are There Universal Aspects in the Structure and Contents of Values?" *Journal of Social Issues* 50 (1994) 19–45.

Scott, James C. "Patron-Client Politics and Political Change in Southeast Asia." *American Political Science Review* 66 (1972) 91–113.

———. "Patronage or Exploitation?" In *Patrons and Clients in Mediterranean Societies*, edited by Ernest Gellner and John Waterbury, 21–40. London: Duckworth, 1977.

Shweder, Richard A. *Thinking Through Cultures: Expeditions in Cultural Psychology.* Cambridge, MA: Harvard University Press, 1991.

Shweder, Richard, et al. "The 'Big Three' of Morality (Autonomy, Community, and Divinity) and the 'Big Three' Explanations of Suffering." In *Morality and Health*, edited by Allan M. Brandt and Paul Rozin, 119–72. New York: Routledge, 1997.

Siegel, Larry J. *Criminology: Theories, Patterns, and Typologies.* 11th ed. Belmont, CA: Wadsworth, 2012.

Simmel, Georg, "The Stranger." Retrieved at https://www.infoamerica.org/documentos_pdf/simmel01.pdf.

Smith, Lee. "Inside the Arab Mind: What's Wrong with the White House's Book on Arab Nationalism." http://www.slate.com/articles/news_and_politics/foreigners/2004/05/inside_the_arab_mind.html.

Solomon, Jerry. "Worldviews." https://probe.org/worldviews/.

Sowell, Thomas. *Black Rednecks and White Liberals.* New York: Encounter, 2006.

Spradley, James. *The Ethnographic Interview.* Orlando, FL: Harcourt Brace Jovanovich, 1979.

Stephanson, Anders. *Manifest Destiny: American Expansion and the Empire of Right.* New York: Hill and Wang, 1995.

Stewart, Edward C., and Milton J. Bennett. *American Cultural Patterns: A Cross-Cultural Perspective.* Revised edition. Boston: Intercultural, 1991.

Strauss, Robert. "Civil-Military Relations." http://www.gpccolorado.com/civil-military-relations/.

———. "Culture: The Rules of the Game." http://www.gpccolorado.com/culture-rules-game.

———. "Developmental Model of Intercultural Sensitivity." http://www.gpccolorado.com/developmental-model-of-intercultural-sensitivity/.

———. "Essentialism and Universalism." In *The International Encyclopedia of Intercultural Communication*, edited by Young Yun Kim. Somerset, NJ: Wiley, 2017.

———. *Introducing Story-Strategic Methods: Twelve Steps toward Effective Engagement.* Eugene, OR: Wipf & Stock, 2017.

———. "Worldview Assessment." Available at http://www.wrg3.org/21/resources/Worldview%20Assessment%20Analysis_April%202013.pdf.

Strauss, Sam. "The Day They Killed Trujillo." Unpublished manuscript.

Strickon, Arnold, and Sidney M. Greenfield, eds. *Structure and Process in Latin America: Patronage, Clientage, and Power Systems.* Albuquerque, NM: University of New Mexico Press, 1972.

Tadmor, Carmit T., et al. "Not Just for Stereotyping Anymore: Racial Essentialism Reduces Domain-General Creativity." *Psychological Science* 24 (2013) 99–105.

Tatum, Beverly Daniel. *"Why are all the Black Kids Sitting Together in the Cafeteria?": And Other Conversations About Race.* New York: Basic, 2003.

Tennent, Timothy. *Theology in the Context of World Christianity: How the Global Church is Influencing the Way We Think about and Discuss Theology.* Grand Rapids, MI: Zondervan, 2007.

Thomas, Ted A., and Seth George. "The Impact of Worldviews on Training and Education in Iraq and Afghanistan." *InterAgency Journal* 7 (2016) 24–33.

Thompson, Michael, et al. *Cultural Theory.* Boulder: Westview, 1990.

Thompson, William E., and Joseph V. Hickey. *Society in Focus: An Introduction to Sociology.* 5th ed. Boston: Pearson, 2005.

Tibi, Bassam. *Arab Nationalism: A Critical Inquiry.* New York: St. Martin's, 1971.

Ting-Toomey, Stella, and Leeva C. Chung. *Understanding Intercultural Communication.* 2nd ed. New York: Oxford University Press, 2012.

Toews, John, ed. *The Communist Manifesto by Karl Marx and Frederick Engels with Related Documents.* Boston: Bedford/St. Martin's, 1999.

Trompenaars, Fons, and Charles Hampden-Turner. *Riding the Waves of Culture: Understanding Diversity in Global Business.* 2nd ed. New York, McGraw-Hill, 1998.

Trout, Robert. "Crowed Jeers as Negro Students Attempt to Enter Central High." *The Arkansas Democrat,* September 4, 1957, 1–2.

———. "Growing Violence Forces Withdrawal of 8 Negro Students at Central High." *The Arkansas Democrat,* September 23, 1957, 1.

———. "High School Off Limits to All Negros." *The Arkansas Democrat,* September 10, 1957, 1.

Tylor, Sir Edward. *Primitive Cultures: Research in the Development of Mythology, Philosophy, Religion, Art, and Custom.* London: Bradbury Evans, 1871.

United Nations. "Universal Declaration of Human Rights." http://www.un.org/en/universal-declaration-human-rights/.

Van Rheenen, Gailyn. *Communicating Christ in Animistic Contexts.* Pasadena, CA: William Carey Library, 1991.

Volf, Miroslav. *Exclusion and Embrace: A Theological Exploration of Identity, Otherness, and Reconciliation.* Nashville, TN: Abingdon, 1996.

Walsh, Brian J., and J. Richard Middleton. *The Transforming Vision: Shaping a Christian World View.* Grand Rapids, MI: Intervarsity Academic, 1984.

Watt, Jonathan M. "Religion as a Domain of Intercultural Discourse." In *The Handbook of Intercultural Discourse and Communication,* edited by Christina Bratt Paulston, et al., 482–95. Chichester, UK: Wiley-Blackwell, 2012.

Weber, Max. *From Max Weber: Essays in Sociology.* Translated by H. H. Gerth and C. Wright Mills. Abingdon, UK: Routledge, 1948.

———. *The Protestant Ethic and the Spirit of Capitalism.* Translated by Talcott Parsons. 1904. Reprint, New York: Routledge, 2001.

Weil, Simone. *The Need for Roots.* Boston: Beacon, 1960.

Wexley, Kenneth N., and Gary P. Latham. *Developing and Training Human Resources in Organizations.* 3rd ed. 1981. Reprint, Upper Saddle River, NJ: Prentice Hall, 2002.

Wimmer, Andreas. *Nation Building: Why Some Countries Come Together While Others Fall Apart.* Princeton, NJ: Princeton University Press, 2018.

World Bank. "Worldwide Governance Indicators." http://info.worldbank.org/governance/wgi/index.aspx#home.

Wu, Jackson. "Is Western Culture Dystopian? Retrieved at http://www.patheos.com/blogs/jacksonwu/2017/06/20/western-culture-dystopian/.

Wyatt-Brown, Bertram. *Southern Honor: Ethics and Behavior in the Old South.* Oxford: Oxford University Press, 1982.

Yarvin, Curtis (Mencius Moldbug). "Neoreactionary Movement." See https://rationalwiki.org/wiki/Neoreactionary_movement.

# Index

207

CPSIA information can be obtained
at www.ICGtesting.com
Printed in the USA
LVHW030024180919
631433LV00007B/148/P